The Genes of Culture

Lance Strate
General Editor

Vol. 6

The Understanding Media Ecology series is part
of the Peter Lang Media and Communication list.
Every volume is peer reviewed and meets
the highest quality standards for content and production.

PETER LANG
New York • Bern • Berlin
Brussels • Vienna • Oxford • Warsaw

Christine L. Nystrom

The Genes of Culture

Towards a Theory of Symbols, Meaning, and Media, Volume 1

Edited by
Carolyn Wiebe and Susan Maushart

PETER LANG
New York • Bern • Berlin
Brussels • Vienna • Oxford • Warsaw

Library of Congress Cataloging-in-Publication Data

Names: Names: Nystrom, Christine L., author. | Wiebe, Carolyn, editor. |
Maushart, Susan, editor.
Title: The genes of culture: towards a theory of symbols, meaning,
and media. Volume 1/Christine L. Nystrom;
edited by Carolyn Wiebe and Susan Maushart.
Description: New York: Peter Lang, [2021].
Series: Understanding media ecology; vol. 6
ISSN 2374-7676 (print) | ISSN 2374-7684 (online)
Includes bibliographical references.
Contents: v. 1.
Identifiers: LCCN 2020005899 | ISBN 978-1-4331-7660-9 (v. 1; hardback)
ISBN 978-1-4331-7664-7 (v. 1; paperback) | ISBN 978-1-4331-7661-6 (v. 1; ebook pdf)
ISBN 978-1-4331-7662-3 (v. 1; epub) | ISBN 978-1-4331-7663-0 (v. 1; mobi)
Subjects: Culture. | Signs and symbols. | Technology—Social aspects.
Classification: LCC HM621 .N97 2021 | DDC 302.2—dc23
LC record available at https://lccn.loc.gov/2020005899
DOI 10.3726/b16789

Bibliographic information published by **Die Deutsche Nationalbibliothek**.
Die Deutsche Nationalbibliothek lists this publication in the "Deutsche
Nationalbibliografie"; detailed bibliographic data are available
on the Internet at http://dnb.d-nb.de/.

Unless otherwise indicated, the contents of the Prologue, Part I and II are
© 2020 by the estate of Christine L. Nystrom and reprinted by permission.

© 2021 Peter Lang Publishing, Inc., New York
29 Broadway, 18th floor, New York, NY 10006
www.peterlang.com

All rights reserved.
Reprint or reproduction, even partially, in all forms such as microfilm,
xerography, microfiche, microcard, and offset strictly prohibited.

"Thinking again?" the Duchess asked, with another dig of her sharp little chin.

"I've a right to think," said Alice sharply, for she was beginning to feel a little worried.

"Just about as much right," said the Duchess, "as pigs have to fly ..."
—*Alice's Adventures in Wonderland*, Chapter 9

Table of Contents

Acknowledgments ix
Foreword xi

Introduction 1
Prologue 7
    Narrative: The Ecology of Tales, Tools, and Social Change 7
    On Science and Truth: An Antic Dialogue 14

PART I —Meaning
Language and Symbol Systems 23
    Media, Self, and Society: Notes on George Herbert Mead 23
    From Cry to Speech: The Shift from Signalic to Symbolic Functions of
        Signs in Human Evolution 31
    Information Theory 36
        Information Theory: Terms and Definitions 36
        Supplementary Notes on Norbert Wiener, Information, and Relativism 37
        The Shannon-Weaver Model of Communication, Information,
            Predictability and Knowledge 44
        Ideas I Find Particularly Useful from Information Theory/Cybernetics 46

Media, Meaning, and Behavior 49
    Chapter 1: Environments, Ecology, and Evolution 49
    Chapter 2: The Structure of Situations 59
    Chapter 3: Exploring Space 76
    Epilogue: The Semanticist's Joke 93
The Genes of Culture 95
    Attention Universe! 95
    Steps to an Ecology of Learning 96
    What We Say, and What We Do: A Case of Bad Form 102
    Symbols, Thought, and Reality: The Contributions of Benjamin Lee
        Whorf and Susanne K. Langer to Media Ecology 105
    You Are Who You Eat: Monsters and Meanings 130

PART II Media Ecology
From Symbol to Medium 139
    Some Characteristics of Media 139
    Some Generalizations about the Biases of Media 140
    Nystrom's Laws of Media Change 140
    Some New Generalizations 141
Media Environments 143
    Immediate Man: The Symbolic Environment of Fanaticism 143
    Television and Truth 157
    What Television Teaches about Sex 167
    Literacy as Deviance 175
    The Crisis of Narrative 180

Acknowledgments

Many people made this long-overdue volume possible. First, we'd like to thank Peter Nystrom, Chris's brother, for giving us permission to publish her work. From the starting line of this project—nearly a decade ago!—he has been supportive and helpful.

Anne Garfinkel, Chris's good friend and neighbor, had to foresight to save the wonderful prologue to this volume from Chris's trashbin. Her close friend and colleague, Henry Perkinson, put us on to *The Gadfly*, an old NYU newspaper. JoEllen Fisherkeller, her successor in the Media Ecology PhD program, generously shared the files Chris had given her at handover. Martin Levinson and Ben Hauck shared zip files of the many pieces Chris wrote for *ETC*, and freely gave permission to reprint.

The remaining contributors were all, at different times, Chris's students. Margaret Cassidy and Sue Barnes sent boxes containing vintage Nystrom handouts and notes. Bob Blechman emailed copies of her early Media Ecology Conference presentations. Eva Berger even had a piece from an Israeli news interview translated for us.

Other students who helped move things along were Brian Cogan, Peter Fallon, David Linton, Robert Albrecht, M.J. Robinson, Casey Lum, Josh Meyrowitz, Paul Levinson, Stephanie Gibson, and Ed Wachtel—providing publishing advice, missing bibliographic information and ideas, and help securing permissions. Lance

Strate accepted with alacrity our proposal for publication in the Media Ecology Series he edits for Peter Lang. And our editor Erika Hendrix has been the epitome of publishing patience and fortitude.

Finally, our profound gratitude to Sal Fallica who, early on—he's probably forgotten this by now—offered perhaps the most encouraging words of all, "Do you need money?"

Foreword

In the Age of the Internet, where screen-time increasingly mediates all that we see and do and think, the task of interrogating our symbolic environment has never been more relevant, or more urgent. And Christine Nystrom, as these pages will indisputably attest, was a sublime and ruthless interrogator.

"All that we know," observed theoretical physicist Werner Heisenberg, "is a result of the questions we ask." He was one of Nystrom's intellectual heroes—students will remember her office door at NYU bore what is surely the world's nerdiest bumper sticker: "Heisenberg may have slept here"—and like him she had a genius for formulating questions.

For Nystrom, many of those questions were about change. She was fascinated with the implacable churn of human experience across time and space—from the dawning of consciousness to the twilight of the Gutenberg Galaxy, and the deep, unnavigable darkness beyond. And the questions she returned to again and again sought to crack the code of human symbolic evolution—whether by examining how new technologies arise, or why babies babble, or the respects in which literacy is a form of deviance.

At once philosophical and refreshingly pragmatic, Nystrom's work in communication studies brings together ideas about the self, symbols and culture in strikingly clear and original ways. Alongside her internationally acclaimed colleague, friend and collaborator Neil Postman, Nystrom was one of the founders of the discipline of media ecology—in important respects, *the* founder, for it was she who first articulated a coherent theoretical framework for the discipline she defined simply as the study of "the complex relationships between communication environments and human values, perceptions, feelings, and behavior."

Unlike Postman, whose hugely influential works layered story, anecdote and example to build memorable social commentary and cultural criticism, Nystrom's thought is unerringly systematic and scrupulously logical. Her scientific background—including, perhaps surprisingly, an undergraduate degree in chemistry—informed this approach. And her acuity in discerning patterns and articulating organizing principles is perhaps her greatest contributions to the field—see, for example, her "Laws" of media change (p. 26). (I once accused Nystrom of suffering from "physics envy." She snorted with a mixture of derision and delight ... but did not deny it.) At the same time, she was acutely aware of the limitations of a strictly scientific approach to human affairs—as evidenced in one of her most powerful essays, "An Antic Dialogue" in which two thoughtful ants debate the origins of the many unexplained phenomena of their world.

As with Nystrom's admired colleagues—luminaries ranging Marshall McLuhan and Lewis Mumford to Eric Havelock and Elizabeth Eisenstein—her work has had a resounding influence on the modern field of media studies, and informs many of its contemporary sub-fields and adjacent disciplines. Her impact, so disproportional to her published output, is palpable in the pages of today's media scholars, many of whom were her students. For Postman, with whom she taught at NYU for over 30 years, she was a collaborator, critic, and crap-detector. They were, intellectually, a single unit. In important respects his work was also *their* work, as he was always the first to acknowledge. He admired and deferred to her as to no other. In some ways, Nystrom was the Socrates to Postman's Plato, shunning the limelight of publication and publicity, content, mostly, to make her intellectual mark as a brilliant teacher, adviser and conversationalist.

As a result, her published work—until now—was scattered in obscure journals, and her very best writing stayed in the proverbial desk drawer. In this she was like another of her intellectual heroes, the social psychologist George Herbert Mead, whose stature was the direct result of his students publishing his work, much of it from classroom notes, posthumously. Fortunately (for you)—unlike Mead—Nystrom was an extravagantly gifted writer. Her prose is always lively, accessible and succinct. She abhorred jargon. And her sense of humor, her irrepressibility as a thinker, fairly leaps off the page.

As an aphorist, Nystrom at times rivals Thoreau, Wilde and Shaw, with axioms like "NOW is the byword of our age, and the present its only tense" or "Problems that history is powerless to inform, philosophy is powerless to solve" or "The more we talk, the farther we get from what we wanted to say," or, more playfully, "Cannibalism is the sincerest form of flattery."

I said earlier that Nystrom had a genius for asking questions. As any of her former graduate students could tell you, her favorite one—of which we all lived in dread—consisted of just two simple words: "So" and "what?" Roughly translated as "why should I, or anybody else, *care* about your research question, dissertation topic or 'problem in the field'?"—the "So what?" question was fired at generations of students with a cool and steely gaze that was vintage bad-cop Nystrom. (The good-cop was the Nystrom who routinely spent every vacation, weekend and sabbatical tirelessly annotating and editing those same students' theses.)

As it applies to her own corpus, however, the "So what?" question is a no-brainer. Nystrom's best work is indispensable for the student of media today because of the framework it offers for understanding symbolic activity across the entire sweep of human history, a framework that has never been equaled for breadth, elegance or tensile strength. She aimed to produce a Grand Unified Theory of human communication—one that placed symbolic activity at the core, within an ecological perspective informed by insights from particle physics, systems theory, and evolutionary biology. And if that sounds downright quixotic—well, it was in some ways. "Sorry to say," she observed of her own work, with characteristic acerbity, "there is a price to be paid for a vision so broad. It is not given to mortals to see widely and intimately at the same time." But that audacity of mind also yielded remarkable insights, many of them even more resonant today than during her own lifetime.

"The ultimate irony," she wrote some 30-odd years ago, "is that we now stand at a point where the literate, digitalizing mind presents us with knowledge of the universe that our senses cannot fathom. We know more than we can understand." And "How are we to prepare the young, whom we already scarcely know, for a future we cannot imagine, from a past that has been swept away?" (1987). "Like the Sorcerer's Apprentice," she noted elsewhere, employing an image later shared by Postman in *Technopoly* (1987) "we are awash in a flood of information. And all the sorcerer has left us is a broom." Nystrom's work offers a prophetic analysis of the challenge of evidentiary, "scientific" thinking in the information age—where almost nothing is directly experienced by our senses—prefiguring the specter of the Age of Fake News with chilling accuracy.

> But if we come to use "eternal truth," "subjective truth," and "objective truth" all as synonyms, let "truth" slide into "authenticity," "authenticity" into "consistency," "consistency" into "credibility," "credibility" into "effectiveness," "effectiveness" into "popularity"—or worse, bury them all under an amorphous jelly called "entertainment" and "appeal"—we shall have battered our language to the bluntness of a shovel. And such an instrument can serve only to blunt our sensibilities and responses—to life and to art.

Above all symbolic gifts, Nystrom prized language—for its poetry as much as its precision—and she looked with horror on the looming crisis of its fate in the digital age. "For what makes us human, in the end," she wrote, "is the 'words whirling around in our heads,' and the price for ignoring them—or at least certain ones of them—is exile from the human community." At the same time, she understood history well enough to apprehend that "peak literacy," as she and her generation knew it, was a vestigial enterprise. "We are anomalies ourselves, transitional creatures, neither here nor there," she wrote, "—cartoon figures trapped on a frail limb far from the main trunk of cultural evolution with the saw in our hands, looking back in the moment of realization that we have just hacked it through, before the limb falls."

Along with another NYU colleague and friend, education philosopher Henry Perkinson, Nystrom was a fallibilist first and foremost. Indeed, the very idea of the inevitability of imperfection was at the core of both her scholarly thought (eventually encapsulated in her "Principle of Progressive Inadequacy") and her private and deeply felt spirituality. Despite the boldness of her ideas, and the confidence with which they found expression, she saw "the courage to be wrong" to be among the greatest of intellectual gifts.

For Nystrom, thinking—whether about the psychology of cannibalism or *Charlie's Angels*, the syntactic structure of Hopi or the etiquette of beachgoing—was more than an occupation. It was an artform, an extreme sport, and her favorite form of play. As she wrote in the introduction to a student text,

> This is a book about media ecology. It is not the map of communications environments that future generations of explorers may one day produce. Think of it, instead, as a set of rough notes from the field …. Think of it too as an invitation. If the territory interests you and the prospect of an adventure without visible end sounds like fun, pack up your curiosity, your powers of observation, and your courage to be wrong. And come along.

Standing at the threshold of this sprawling, subversive, and utterly original work, it's an invitation that's impossible to resist.

Dr. Susan Maushart
Perth, Western Australia

Introduction

For Christine Nystrom, exploring ideas—a.k.a. thinking—was what education was all about. Invariably, with her, that exploration was creative, challenging, provocative—and rewarding. The pieces included here offer readers a generous glimpse of that. They've been selected not because they are flawless—something Nystrom would have scoffed at—but because they enrich our capacity to understand our present and thus, perhaps, better contribute to our future. Nystrom's work remains significant because of its potential to inspire new questions and suggest novel points of departure in the quest to make sense of our symbolic systems and media environments.

Much of the material in this volume—the conference papers, class handouts, or chapters from never-completed books—is published here for the first time. Yet in all her work, what we see is a considerate and experienced writer—one who wrote with the reader in mind. Nystrom's prose is pleasantly, clearly, jargon-free. Whether summarizing a complex theory or synthesizing many ideas into an orderly train of thought, she has a knack for making the convoluted straightforward, and for making the overlooked apparent. While extending an invitation to explore the odd perspective or entertain a provocative slant, almost without exception, these pieces suggest the impetus to conversation.

The first piece, "Narrative: The Ecology of Tales, Tools, and Social Change," was found separately from her other work, unpublished and, as far as we know, uncirculated. We have no idea when she wrote it, but it certainly seems she intended, at least at one point, for it to frame and organize what we've come to call her "magnum opus," *Human Symbolic Evolution: A Study of Tales, Tool, and Social Change* (Volume 2 of this series). What we do know for certain is that it provides a wonderful introduction to Nystrom's attitude and approach to scholarship—one of "inclusiveness and connectedness" that introduces the range and scope of her interests and ideas. More importantly, it is an invitation to engage in what is perhaps today's largest and most central conversation: "to assess where we stand just now in the living tale of our species and our tools, and the problems we must solve if we do not wish to end it."

Although "On Science and Truth: An Antic Dialogue" is not a groundbreaking work, it has proven an enduringly useful piece, both in the classroom and for keeping my own biases in check. I first used it to help introduce Plato's Cave to undergraduates and, as frequently happens when using Nystrom's work, students remembered and referred back to it throughout the term. Where the allegory of the cave addresses *how* humans construe reality and, subsequently, the limits of what we can know, the Antic Dialogue emphasizes the inherent limitations of any single perspective and the inevitability of human (or insect, as the case may be) fallibility—with a light, appropriately antic touch.

Part I, "Meaning," introduces Nystrom's approach to and fascination with how symbols work—about how and why we are so inexorably driven to make meaning, and how that relates to our humanity. "Meaning-making is the core of human communication, the center from which any adequate model of communication must proceed." The first two conference papers (we have been unable to determine when the first was delivered) deal with the shift from the signalic mode to symbol-using in human development. The last—an edited compilation of course notes—deals with knowledge and its relationship to information.

I've used "Media, Self and Society" in classes not only when I want students to get a sense of what it means to learn language, but also when I want them to think about the assumptions we carry with us and take for granted—whether about identity, education, morality, or values. This short essay provides an extremely readable way to approach seminal ideas (especially how language gives rise to notions of self, self-consciousness and mind), and to open up the conceptual baggage that comes with learning language and internalizing culture. Students like it because it is challenging, but they can "get it"—and because it matters.

"From Cry to Speech" deals with the shift from signalic to symbolic language—how it relates to meaning, how it occurs in childhood and how it might have arisen in the course of human evolution. Here Nystrom provides a clear and coherent description of the underestimated capacity of the signalic paradigm—that is, the use of signs as signals—in animal communication and human evolution; the creative explosion that occurs in human development—both for the human baby and the species—with the shift to symbolic language; and the tentative and tenacious overlap between the two.

The excerpt from Nystrom's course notes regarding Information Theory—ideas synthesized from Shannon-Weaver, Jeremy Campbell, Noam Chomsky and especially Norbert Wiener concerning feedback and entropy, redundancy, structure, differentiation, and chaos—illustrate why any study of *what* we know is necessarily a study of *how* we know. While every student of communication has suffered through the transactional model of communication, with its accompanying Shannon-Weaver diagram—"sender" and "receiver" at its two endpoints, with message and noise in between—most of us have, with relief and perhaps a bit of joy, moved on to the more colorful vistas provided by communication, culture, and media studies. Nystrom of course recognized the inadequacies of the sender/receiver model, but she also grasped its profound implications: that information is best conceptualized as an activity (rather than a thing); and best defined as simply that which we don't know. In this context, she explores the relationships between predictability and knowledge, information and relativism—which inform her tidy list of "Ideas I Find Particularly Useful from Information Theory/Cybernetics."

Nystrom also recognized how firmly embedded the Shannon-Weaver model is in our thinking about communication. The *Media, Meaning and Behavior* manuscript—excerpts from an unpublished student text—opens with a brief critique of that model: an observation regarding the way it orients our thinking about communication toward questions of "effectiveness." Instead, Nystrom poses a model of communication grounded in the notion of "situation" and questions of meaning and context, examining meaning-making relative to space and time (undoubtedly taking her cue from Harold Innis' *The Bias of Communication*, 1951).

We close the manuscript with a brief epilogue, "The Semanticist's Joke"—an excerpt from an article that explored the notion of "transitional space"—and a reflection on our failure to see the obvious, that is: "the container" (the form of a medium) for "the thing contained" (its content). The article was probably, initially, an idea for a subsequent chapter.

The "Genes of Culture" section begins with a brief piece, "Attention Universe!" (initially written as a Foreword for a volume of *ETC*), which highlights concerns regarding the relation between symbol systems and the things we know, and how the things we know from direct experience are dwindling, relative to knowledge acquired from mediated experiences. Nystrom poses the question of how, given this media environment, General Semantics might broaden its scope—and explores the challenges faced by individuals seeking to recognize "truth." These concerns are further elaborated in "Steps to an Ecology of Learning," a book review of *Education for Adaptation and Survival*, where she draws incisive distinctions between veracity and values, between science and belief, and offers a "reality" check on what science can tell us and what we know.

Among these General Semantics articles, "What We Say and What We Do: A Case of Bad Form" is about forms of discourse. Nystrom argues a depressingly prescient case: namely, against politically correct but "unsane" uses of language. Here she is criticizing a form of speech—in this case, tyrannical speech—in any political guise, including liberalspeak. One can't help but wonder if the divisive us-them situation that defines current affairs—where "correct" emotional outrage is trumped by the crass conservatism of bullies—is the unfortunate apotheosis of this phenomenon.

Nystrom's approach to media through symbol systems informs what follows in "Symbols, Thought, and Reality: The Contributions of Benjamin Lee Whorf and Susanne K. Langer to Media Ecology." Here she discusses the relativistic orientation of postmodernism in terms of theoretical work in the sciences and earlier theories of knowledge. Once again, she reminds us that symbol systems are what human beings use to represent experience, to construct and convey thoughts, and to conceive of "reality." As such, what we experience and perceive—what we notice and recognize—is largely a product of the symbol systems we habitually employ.

It is in this regard that Nystrom pays tribute to Benjamin Whorf—in opposition to those who dismiss him as a "linguistic determinist"—with a strikingly clear summary of what Whorf brings to the study of language and mind. In contemporary scholarship in the field of media and cultural studies, Whorf has endured as something of a straw man for debate, while the compelling work of philosopher Susanne Langer (along with the study of symbol systems and how such systems relate to nature) has been ignored altogether. This essay is Nystrom's typically grounded, thorough, and generous attempt to correct that.

What follows a gleeful little conference paper on science-fiction horror movies, a semiotic analysis of "primal" fears. The concerns here are the other side of Langer's hypothesis—about what we leave behind on the other side of a door left slightly ajar in the passage from infancy and childhood to (ahem) rational being-ness.

Section II, Media Ecology, begins with Nystrom's Generalizations—articulated in a series of undated course notes ("Some Characteristics of Media," "Some Generalizations about the Biases of Media," "Nystrom's Laws of Media Change," and "Some New Generalizations")—from which all things media ecological flow. The first two follow closely from her 1973 dissertation *Toward a Science of Media Ecology: The Formulation of Integrated Conceptual Paradigms for the Study of Human Communication Systems*, which synthesized the work of theorists from diverse disciplines in order to construct a theoretical framework for the field of Media Ecology—its subject matter and its questions. The resulting framework integrated systems theory with the understanding of human communication as a complex "ecology" that exists through and in symbol systems, media, and technologies.

The following articles in the Media Environments section are presented chronologically and, dealing as they do with television and other electronic media, provide various approaches to analyzing new media. They also convey a sense of the changes that occurred in her concerns and attitudes.

The first piece, "Immediate Man: The Symbolic Environment of Fanaticism," was published in *ETC* in 1977, and reprinted in 2002 in response to the 9/11 call to war—an immediate, knee-jerk emotional response if ever there was one. However, today more than ever we can see how the biases of speed and the image-based presentational mode underscore the habits of mind associated with electronic and digital media. Nystrom's description of the habitual mode of thought associated with Immediate Man—"gestalt, nonanalytic, immediate, present-oriented, non-reflective, and emotional"—reads like a character study of our current political leadership.

From a contemporary point of view, "Television and Truth" could be renamed "Reality TV Explained!" Here Nystrom delineates the differences between presentational and propositional language and, in so doing, outlines why images elude the categories "true" and "false." Again, because of its presentational biases, the idea of "truth" on television (as with "truth in advertising") tends to be misleading; what audiences look for is "authenticity" or whether someone comes across as "genuine" or "real." (Which explains, among many other things, why the host of a reality TV show might be respected for his attitude—his authenticity—rather than for his grasp of events or facts, for his integrity or beliefs.)

It sounds almost quaint: "What Television Teaches about Sex." Does anyone even talk in those terms anymore? Instead, stifling a yawn, we hear the ongoing complaints of too much sex and violence. Debates about age-ratings, profanity, "explicit" images and so forth have usurped the sorts of questions Nystrom poses. "How can young people help but be confused about sexual impulses and their expression, when the messages they receive through the traditional institutions of society are so thoroughly contradicted by the messages they receive through a medium as engrossing and compelling as television?" Indeed. Today, of course, it is broadcast television that has become the "traditional institution"—and we are left to ponder what sex education might mean to a generation raised on social media, sexting, and Pornhub.

Nystrom once told me that she wrote "Literacy as Deviance" because she was so sick of all the bitching about television. This essay was oddly popular among Media Ecology grad students—perhaps because they understood the abstract reasoning she drew on to make her argument: That, alas, literacy isn't only time-consuming and difficult, it is unnatural. Or maybe they simply appreciated how this piece captures so neatly the conjoining of the rational mind with the wiseass.

The final essay in this section, "The Crisis of Narrative," is another one that I've used often in my classes. Students like it because it deals with something they can relate to—which is too much information—without trivializing the fallout from the overwhelm. The piece nicely explains how humans are able to carry and to call forth information through narrative. Indeed, humans remember information because it has context, and that context is narrative, the means through which ideas resonate and evoke meaning. Although largely concerned with the content of narrative, it implicitly addresses the types of narrative different media environments sustain. This piece could also serve as an introduction to Volume 2, which includes a series of brilliant lectures given at an obscure Australian conference, in addition to the entirety of Nystrom's unpublished "theory of everything" monograph: *Human Symbolic Evolution: A Study of Tales, Tools and Social Change*.

Dr. Carolyn Wiebe
Brooklyn College, NY

Prologue

Narrative: The Ecology of Tales, Tools, and Social Change

(undated, c. 1996). Excerpt from *Human Symbolic Evolution: A Study of Tales, Tools, and Social Change*. [Unpublished manuscript.]

When I was very young, and evening came, my mother would gather us up (my sisters and I) and tell us a tale. It was her way, I think, of knitting us up and soothing us down for sleep. I do not much remember the earliest tales, except that they had rabbits and moons, and sometimes bright angels and talking beasts. The later ones, of emerald cities and a lion that sang, I found again, with joy, when I could read. But the best tales were those my mother invented, for she would weave *us* in.

Times change, of course, and children grow too big for laps and mothers' tales. But the need for a story does not wear out with other childhood things. It grows along with children and expands as their world expands. By the time we are quite grown, we will have made or learned—and forgotten—many kinds of tales, though we call them by other names. For what are histories, but tales of the human past? And scientific theories, but tales of the natural world? And religions, but the stories of a people and their God?

In the main, this book is about our stories and why we tell them, and how they are related to our technologies and to social change. It is *not* a book about literature, though that will play its part. It is about our personal stories and how they shape our lives; about tribal and national stories and how they shape our political conduct and goals; about world stories, and the role they have played and have yet to play in deciding the future of our kind. This is also a book about how different types of stories—personal, national, and world stories—are interwoven and shape one another. It is a book, you might say, about the *ecology* of tales.

But it is also a tale *of* ecology, of the dynamic balances among technologies of different kinds, and how those technologies shape our narratives and thus the social world. And that is a sprawling tale indeed. For technologies are the material ways in which our species reconstructs the world, and in the process reconstructs itself. The story of tools is grand and gripping because, like the best of my mother's tales, it is a story not about angels or beasts or moons, but a story about *us*. It is the special *human* story, for it was tools that led us out of the savannahs of our ancient past and set us apart, to be so all alone. And it is rarely good for people to be set apart, to imagine themselves as kings. For that can make us heedless and cruel and, in the end, lords only of desolation. So the tale of tools is also terrible, because we cannot see how it will end.

But that is all the more reason for telling it. We are, after all, the makers of our tools. So we are not mere characters in their story. We are its authors, as well. We have choices to make about what will come next and after that, and therefore, how it will end. To make those choices wisely, we need to know how the story of tools has unfolded so far, and what patterns it has been following. For unless we see those patterns clearly, we are likely to let them dictate what we will add. When I was a child we played a game that will make clearer what I mean. One person would start a made-up tale, take it a little way, then stop—usually in the middle of some important development, like this: "So with the bear hard on their heels, the children ran and ran, until they came to a …" There someone else would take up the tale and move it on: "… forest. But the bear came ever behind. At last the children could go no farther, so they decided to …" There the story passed to the next child, and so on. The object of the game, of course, was to keep the story going, and ever new. And the aim of each player was to shape the tale in a direction he or she liked. The less experienced players rarely managed to change the story much from the point where they got it, for they had not yet learned to see the pattern in a tale, and where it would lead, and how it might be changed. So they accepted the tale as it had been told so far and merely continued along its lines. To such a player, a story about bears and children and a chase *remains* a story of bears and children and a chase, and all that changes is the details. But the better players could see the pattern in what had been told, and grasp its directions and limits. And because they knew how stories worked, they could change that basic pattern and direction: get rid of the bear, shift from chase to enchantment, go from forests to castles or fairs.

Our relation to the development of tools, and their development of us, is something like that. Our generation has come in, so to speak, at the middle of a tale that has been unfolding for centuries, and it is our turn to add the next piece. If we wish to keep the tale going, we had best find out what it has been about, and exactly where we are. We may discover something in the tale that frightens us—too many bears, too much dark—and wish to make a radical change in course while the story is in our hands. But that can only be done in certain ways. Children in a forest cannot decide to board an ocean liner and sail to France. That would bring the storytelling to an end as surely as "And so they died." For it would violate the basic rule of coherence, and there would be no point in continuing the game. Everybody would go home. Any change we wish to make, in a story about children or the unfolding story of ourselves and our tools, must fit within the dynamics of the tale. If children do not know that, or do not care, it is small matter. Their storytelling, after all, is only a game. If, through naiveté, they err and end it, the bear, the forest, and the chase will melt back into thin air. Our technologies will not. Or if they do, they will take our species, and all the planet, with them. We are *living* our part in the story of tools, not just telling it. The course we take while the story is in our hands will affect the future of our species. If we make a mistake that ends the tale, there will be no going home. Outside the *human* tale, there's no place else to go.

My purpose is to describe a pattern I see in the history of tools and people, and examine the dynamics of change. The pattern I will be trying to sketch is extremely large—as large as the history of our species is long. It has to be large, because I want it to outline the *human* experience in all its connectedness—not just the ancient Greek experience, or the Medieval experience or the American experience. Not just the digging stick experience, or the printing press experience or the assembly-line experience, either. Not even just the male or the female experience. As important as all those are to the people who are living, or have lived, within them, they are only parts of the larger human tale. And it is the pattern of the whole tale that we must try to see.

Sorry to say, there is a price to be paid for a vision so broad. It is not given to mortals to see widely and intimately at the same time. So you will find the outline here sadly lacking in detail. I regret that sacrifice, for I am well aware that only narrower views can reveal the rich detail that gives the human experience its texture and vibrant color. Closer study of a part of the human story would provide a deeper understanding, it is true. But it would also of necessity exclude a great deal and, in the end, make our differences from each other and other times more notable than what we have in common. We need views of both kinds. The one I have taken here stresses inclusiveness and connectedness, for that is what I sense we most need, now more than ever. To achieve such a view, I will be striding across the human past in great leaps and bounds, taking whole eras and continents in a single step. And to tell the truth, I will not be looking too carefully where I tread. Sometimes I will be walking mostly in the dark. If, in the process, I do violence to knowledge in some field I should not have entered, those who labor there will rightly tell me.

My only defense for trespassing, and too great speed, is urgency. I said earlier that our generation has come in at the middle of the tale of humans and our tools. But that is not quite true. We may in fact be perilously close to the end. It all depends on where we take the story from here. My race across the past and territories not my own is not spurred by confidence but by dread. If we cannot get a clear view of what our story has been, and where it stands, and how to correct its course, my mistakes in this account of it will not matter much.

I am not the first, of course, to undertake a telling of the human tale of technologies and their meaning for the past and the future. The last great account was provided more than a century ago by Karl Marx in *Capital*. And there are many, I know, for whom that tale is the only one we need. I do not agree. Noble and broad as it was for the time, Marx's narrative was shaped by the world he tried to explain, and by his position in it. We live in a different world, and it requires a different tale. For in 120 years, the story of technologies has taken several turns, and we are standing in a different place, from which different things can be seen. And the most important is this: that there are tools of two different kinds—technologies of production and technologies of information. Marx saw, and rightly so, that people must eat to survive. And so he placed at the center of his account the tools we use to produce our bread. His tale is the story of tools of doing. But that is only half the tale. For what profiteth a man if he seizes his neighbor's hoe but has no knowledge of how to use it? Or builds himself a factory but cannot tell his children how to run it? Or invents a product to make himself rich, but cannot let anyone know? Without the tools of *telling*, the tools of doing are useless. If we had no techniques of knowing and telling, we would not need an account of our past. It never would have changed. Change results from the interactions of doing and knowing—of means of production and means of communication. And narratives—tales—play a critical role in those interactions. An account of human history in which thought and telling trail wanly after triumphant power, carrying its bags, is unbalanced. It reduces to subservience half the human world.

And that is another reason why Marx's tale does not suffice, at least for me. It is a busy tale of getting and doing, of heroic struggle in the quest for power. Marx said it was the human tale, and I know he was on the human side. But it doesn't seem to be *my* side. It seems, if I may say it, a distinctly *male* perspective. Perhaps that is why talking and telling are so disdained, seen merely as the servants or dupes of power. They were, in the 19th-century view, women's ways—the ways of Eve, weak and deceived, not of sturdy, toiling Adam. It is no coincidence that in Marx's time, if not our own, tales were disdained as the business of old wives, not of young and daring men.

The time has come, I think, for a wider account than Marx's of the story of humans and change. Not a female account, for that would be just as one-sided, but an account that weaves together male and female, tools of production and tools of information, technologies along with tales, in one connected whole. It will not be necessary, in such an account, to re-tell the part that Marx has already told. No one can surpass, I think, the breadth and accuracy of his account of tools of doing, and their part in the human world. His tale is not wrong but incomplete—as mine will be from the perspective of the future, if we have one. My object here is to tell the other half of the tale—the story of tools of knowing and telling, of technologies of information—and to weave a larger narrative in which both halves will fit.

This book, you see, is also a kind of tale—a new story about our story. Before you begin it you are entitled, I think, to know some things about it. It asks you to accept, for example, certain premises and rules. Every story does. If one begins, "Once upon a time, there was a boy who could fly," and you insist that is no good because boys *can't* fly, there is not much point in your listening to the rest. It will all follow from that. The story in these pages does not require such a leap, but it has premises of its own. And the first is this: For all our differences from other living things, humans are part of the same pattern on which the larger tapestry of life is woven. We do not stand outside it, as something totally new, but are part of the whole. And Nature favors us no more than others in the great design. We need to account for ourselves only because we have survived. Those who have not do not require a tale.

This book begins, then, with a view of humans as a species that has survived. And it starts from the premise that we have survived in the same way as have others who accompany us still on this whirling ball as it travels through space: not through the special favors of a benevolent Nature or laws bent this way or that to our advantage by an arbitrary god. We have survived, as others have, because our species has found ways to solve problems of adjustment to change. Some of the change is a result of natural laws and phenomena—like the climate—that seem to have little origin in our own behavior. By far the greater bulk, in human affairs, arises from our own tinkering. In either case, change is inevitable. And it presents us with a continuous set of problems—problems of adjustment to change. In that respect, our situation is no different from that of other beasts, and for millions of years our story was the same as theirs: those genetic variations that provided some creatures with better "solutions" to environmental problems enabled them to flourish; those that proved inadequate left others disadvantaged, and they died. Evolution, one might say, is the story of life's biological solutions to problems created by change. As biological creatures, we are part of that long tale. But not entirely.

For somewhere along the way, humans developed the capacity to invent, and through invention, adjust our environments to ourselves. History, one might say, is the story of humans' *technical* solutions to problems created by change. Sometimes our solutions involve new ways of doing, as when we establish a new form of government or modify our cultural habits to make new arrangements for the raising of children. Sometimes they involve new ways of thinking, as when we construct new criteria for judging what we call "facts." And sometimes they involve new material creations, like digging sticks, or wheels, or money or computers. But whether they are new forms of economic and social organization, new methods of thinking, new tools of labor or new media, human techniques and technologies are always *responses* to something, and that "something" is problems—problems that arise from change. No less than biological evolution, technical evolution is driven by pressure of change and the requirement it imposes on living things: to adjust or die. It follows from this that our technologies must always lead back, at no matter what remove, to attempts by our species to solve problems of adjustment, and so survive. Thus the first premise of this tale—that our species has survived, as others have, because it has found ways to solve problems of adjustment to change—leads to several further rules for how it will unfold. The first is that our story must always explain technologies as solutions to problems; the second, that those problems must always lead back to the struggle of our species to survive.

But that is not all. There are two more premises this story requires, or there would be no need for a tale. If human solutions were perfect, we would have invented once, and that would have been enough. History would be a tale of decreasing complexity, with precious little to explain. But it is not. So the second premise is this: that humans are not perfect, and neither are their solutions to problems of change. Every technique and technology, therefore, suffers from some inadequacies. These are, themselves, a source of additional problems, and require further change. This may be called "The Premise of Imperfection" and, with the next, will give this story a peculiar twist.

The third and final premise we may call "The Premise of Ecology." It asks you to accept the view that all elements in a complex system (like human life) are interconnected, and in ways that we do not always see. Thus a new way of getting or doing or thinking or telling that solves some problem always itself *introduces* change, giving rise to new problems in places where we may least expect them. Let a man make a hoe to ease his planting, and it will change the surface of the earth and all that lives therein, sometimes to his sorrow. That much we have learned to see. But there is more to it than that. For the hoe also changes the shape of the hand that holds it, and the muscles that work the hand. And if a man hoes long enough, the frame that holds the muscles will start to shift and curve, until the hoe has bent the hoer to the shape its use requires. Thus the tools of labor not only change the world to which they are applied, but change the laborer as well. So it is with tools of knowing, too. They change the knower as well as the known. And both kinds of tools, in both ways, create new problems that require further change.

The Premise of Imperfection and the Premise of Ecology lead to a rule for this story that may make it seem somewhat strange. Humans are justly proud of all we have accomplished. And we tend, looking back along our past, to read it as the record of what we have achieved. That is perfectly understandable, and no doubt good for morale. The trouble is that it directs our attention to the wrong thing: to solutions, not problems. And this blinds us to the forces that drive the engine of change. The premises of *this* story lead to quite a different tale: a tale that focuses on problems, not solutions; on inadequacies, not success. It may not build morale, but it will give us a clearer view, I think, of how we have arrived at where we stand, and of what lies just ahead. The premises are, in fact, so central to that end that I will ennoble them here by calling them laws—the Laws of Technical Change. They apply equally, I believe, to tools of doing and tools of knowing, techniques of production and techniques of communication. But because this book is more concerned with the latter, I will restate them here in the narrower case, as the Laws of Media Change.

The First Law is this: *Changes in communication techniques and technologies are attempts to solve information problems that threaten the ability of humans to survive.* This does not mean that our search for solutions is conscious and rational, or even that we are aware of what our problems are. New techniques and technologies may arise in any number of ways, including by accident. But they will not be recognized as useful, or developed, or incorporated into the life of the group or culture unless they offer solutions to some important problem. Thus we have a corollary to the First Law—namely, that those media changes will survive, and succeed most widely, that most efficiently solve the most urgent information problems of the largest number of people.

The Second Law is this: *Every attempt to solve information problems suffers from inadequacies. These inadequacies result in new problems, which are the impetus for further change.*

The Third Law is this: *Every attempt to solve information problems inevitably introduces change into the state of our information, and thus presents additional problems which generate further change.*

Those, I propose are the laws. Like laws in any field, they are exceedingly simple. All the rest is complexity. But it is in complexity that all the interest lies, and through complexity that this tale will weave its way. My object in what follows is, first, to refine these Laws of Media Change by examining four great developments in the history of human communication: the evolution of language, of writing systems, of printing, and of electronic information technologies. In the course of that examination, we shall look at the kinds of problems that arise in the ecology of information and the dynamics through which problems and solutions interact to drive change.

My intention is, finally, to tease out from the story of change one of its central threads—narrative—and to examine in greater detail the role that narrative plays in ecologies of information at every level of human organization, from individual to species. On the basis of that analysis, we'll be able to assess where we stand just now in the living tale of our species—and of our tools—and identify the problems we must solve if we do not wish to end it.

On Science and Truth: An Antic Dialogue

ETC: A Review of General Semantics, Vol. 38, No. 2 (Summer 1981), pp. 131–136. Reprinted by permission of the Institute of General Semantics.

Once upon a time, in a bustling kingdom quite ignored by men, a youngish ant (as these things are reckoned among them) sat thoughtfully upon a bit of hill, musing to himself. Nearby, a great work of construction was going on, and orderly lines of workers trooped here and there at the direction of engineers from whose plans a new bridge was taking shape, stunning in its boldness of design. One of these, in search of a perspective from which to judge the true lie of the bridge, climbed the very hill where the youngish ant sat, and came across him there.

"Ho, there!" he called, startling the thoughtful ant from his reverie. "What are you doing idling here? We need all hands below."

The thoughtful ant jumped to his feet in dismay, for he recognized before him no ordinary engineer, but one of the chief scientists of the kingdom, an ant known far and wide for his keen mind and penetrating wisdom. "I was not idling, sir," he stammered, blushing (he was a red ant). "I was thinking."

"Thinking, were you?" replied the scientist, more gently, for he had been a thoughtful ant himself, especially in his youth, and he liked to encourage young minds wherever he found them, "And what were you thinking about?"

"Well, sir, as I watched the work on the fine new bridge in the valley below us there, I thought of the fate of the one that stood there before—crushed in the great flattening of 1120. And I remembered the other great flattenings of our era—in 1092, in 1106, and again in 1113. In the last," he added in a low voice, "I lost all my family and barely escaped with my own life."

"Ah," murmured the scientist sadly, thinking not only of his own lost friends and colleagues, but of the long and frustrating years he had worked on the flattening puzzle, to no avail. Over the centuries of recorded antic history, science had steadily scored triumph after triumph in establishing the nature of the universe and bringing it under antic control. In his own time, the scientist had seen most of the remaining riddles resolved, except for a minor mystery or two. Those and, of course, the flattenings. It was his own great and driving hope to solve that final puzzle, and so bring under control the natural disasters that, with frustrating irregularity, had struck the kingdoms of his kind, apparently since antiquity.

The two ants sat musing for a bit, each in his own line. Then the scientist brightened. Perhaps in this untutored young mind some idea might have formed that would provide a clue to the puzzle. "Tell me, where did your thinking lead you?" he asked.

"My thoughts did not lead me, exactly," said the young ant slowly, "but rather burst upon me all at once, in a kind of intuition, or inspiration, or—I do not know what to call it, sir." He paused for a moment, then rushed on, emboldened of his idea. "It seemed to me suddenly that perhaps our universe is only a tiny and insignificant thing in a something so much greater it is beyond our imagining. And perhaps in that vast unknown there are forces, presences, beings of a kind we can scarcely conceive—far superior to us, and of a totally different design. And I thought that maybe, sir—just possibly—the flattenings and some of the other mysteries of our universe might have something to do with *them*."

The scientist stared for a moment in disbelief at this outpouring, then shook his head regretfully and turned away. Where he had looked to find mind, intelligence, and hope, he had once more encountered his perpetual enemies—ignorance and, worse, superstition. But he soon turned back again, for he had spent much of his life in trying to help his fellow ants live saner lives through scientific thinking, and he would not give up that effort now.

"Tell me more about this ... this notion of yours, young ant," he began, "for I find it curious indeed. But you must try to be more concrete in what you say, or I cannot make out your meaning. These 'beings' you imagine, for example, What are they like? Are they intelligent, as we are? Do they build, as we do? Do they speak, and move about, and store things up, and construct nests?"

"I cannot truly say, sir," the thoughtful ant replied, "for I have never seen one. But if they are greater even than the most highly developed of our kind, then they must surely have those attributes that set our highest classes apart from the lower orders—intelligence, speech, and engineering skills."

"Well, then, if they speak and build, surely their voices have been heard among us, and their buildings have been discovered. What evidence do you have of this?"

"Why, have you not heard, sir, ever and again, those vast and distant rumblings that disturb the upper air? Indeed, all around us are designs marvelous to behold—shining rods that reach so far into the sky that no ant has ever reached the top of one (or returned to tell the tale), and slick cold things not present to the sight, but barriers to our forward movement, unless we climb their sheer walls."

"But, my boy, you have only described the natural phenomena of the universe—its atmospherics and geology. Our science long ago explained the nature of these things, and how they came to be. Only a pagant hears voices in the thunder, or imagines that the perfect architecture of nature requires a master builder. Surely you can do better than that. Point to something I can see that gives evidence of your beings."

The young ant blushed again, for the reference to pagantism had pricked him deeply. But he persisted, for his new vision of a greater universe still shone clearly in his mind's eye, and he would not quickly give it up.

"I do not mean to mock our science," he began apologetically, "but surely there is much we do not understand. Do we not from time to time find great clumps of food that seem to have come from nowhere? I remember well the great feast of 1109, when all my village awoke to find a foodstone so large it took eighty of us a day to move it to the nest—and yet it had not been there the day before."

"Such events are well known to our physicists and astronomers," the scientist replied, "and while some details remain to be explained, the antropocentric theory of the universe accounts quite well for such phenomena. The universe, you see, is filled with objects of different kinds, held in their places by a force we call gravity. Under certain conditions, however, the forces that hold objects beyond our atmosphere in their normal places are weakened, and the mass of our world pulls them down to us. Most such objects burn up in our atmosphere—which is why such foodstones as we find are usually small. But others, of a greater mass and different composition, survive almost intact. Indeed, our biochemists have been able to predict quite well what kinds of things will be found in great masses, and what kinds only in small particles. But come, lad, I am curious. What have foodstones to do with your imagined beings?"

"I thought, sir, that perhaps, like us, they eat. And perhaps from time to time they cast food down to us, or let it fall."

The scientist chuckled bemusedly. "Then they are benevolent, these beings of yours! But if that were so, then we should be the recipients of a very torrent of foodstones, and we should live in paradise indeed. But you know this is not the case. Resolve this puzzle for me, if you can: Why should your beings sometimes throw food down to us and sometimes not?"

"I cannot truly say, sir," replied the younger ant, puzzled. "Perhaps that is their nature."

"Ah, yes," murmured the scientist mockingly. "And I suppose there is something in 'the nature' of these beings that accounts for the flattenings, as well. Tell me, where do they fit in this fantasy you would weave?"

Though he reddened again at the amusement in the great ant's tone, the thoughtful ant persisted stubbornly. "If the beings I have thought of are something like us—as I must imagine them to be, since the greater cannot be less than the smaller—then perhaps they move about as we do, on great feet and legs. And perhaps, in going about their great universe, they now and then stamp on us, wreaking havoc wherever they tread."

"Strange indeed are the beings you have created, young ant! First you say they are benevolent, raining foodstones down upon us, that we might live in plenty. But now, it seems, they are cruel beyond imagining, stamping wantonly on the young and the old, the rich and the poor, workers and builders alike. Does not this contradiction seem to you odd?"

"I must admit it does, sir. But perhaps these beings are so different from us that we cannot understand their ways."

"Since you admit there is a mystery here, let us leave the question of their character aside and talk of what science allows us to observe. You imagine, you say, that your supernatural 'beings' have—forgive my smiling—feet. Moreover, that like us, they walk. And that in their walking, their feet fall upon us, causing the great flattenings. Do I have it right so far?"

"Yes, that is what I imagine," the thoughtful ant replied.

"Well, then, tell me this. If things are indeed as you have imagined, then should we not find the flattenings regular in their shape, and similar in size? For if you look back upon your own footprints as you walk, you will see just such a regularity. Moreover, you will see an observable pattern to them, three on a side. But we have charted through the ages the shape and size of the flattenings, and no two are at all alike. Nor do they come in a pattern, three on a side, as walking beings would make. No, there is no evidence at all for what you have imagined."

"But could it not be, sir, that regularity and pattern *are* there, but we are too limited—too small, and our lives too short—to see them?"

"Your argument there might have merit, my lad, *if* our science depended alone on the senses nature has so generously provided us. But this is not the case. We have developed instruments finer than any eye, more powerful than any antennae, more sensitive than the finest hair on your body. And through those instruments we have become more than able to escape the limitations of our own bodies and senses. Those instruments, young ant, have brought all nature within our power to observe and understand. Yet not a one of them has ever recorded such 'presences' as you would construct."

"I have seen some of the marvels of our new technology, sir, and I do not mean to mock their power. But still, do we not build our instruments to our own design? Are they not the extensions of antic bodies, antic senses, and antic minds? We look through our instruments and think we see the universe. But perhaps it is only our own reflection we are gazing on. If my theory is true—"

"Ah!" broke in the scientist, much agitated. "So now you would elevate your … your dreamings to a theory, and use of it such a word as 'true'! I have been patient till now with your notions, pointless and foolish though they seem to me. But this I cannot permit. You may call your 'vision' a fantasy, or a tale to frighten child-ants around the nest, or a poem, or even a belief, and I will not object. But to call it a theory—well, that makes gibberish of the word, and we cannot talk to each other in such a language." With that he stood, and shook his head, and turned to walk away.

The younger ant sprang to his feet in dismay. "But wait," he called. "Do not leave me, sir, for there is much I do not understand. And I would learn."

The scientist turned back again, regretting his impatience. "Then I will help you, lad. Listen, now, and try to understand. When we call our statements 'theories,' we place them in the domain of science. But statements in that realm must meet certain tests, and the first is that they must be intelligible. For how shall we know whether a statement is true or false if the words it contains have no clearly defined operational meanings? You have talked to me of 'beings,' yet when I press you to define what you mean, you offer only vague abstractions. They are like us, you say, but *not* like us. They are all-powerful and benevolent, but then again they are careless and cruel. They speak and eat, build and walk, but, you say, their ways are so different from our own that we cannot detect any evidence of such activities. Do you not see that what you have said is so much nonsense, then? You cannot keep shifting the meanings of words and still claim to have an intelligible theory."

"Yes, I must admit that what you say is true," replied the young ant slowly. "I had not thought of it that way before." He sat silent for a few moments, pondering what he had learned. "But even if my statements are not intelligible," he asked hesitantly, "may they not still be true?"

The scientist sighed. How difficult it was to counter superstition and unreason! "Come, lad, use your mind. To say that a statement is true implies that, at least in theory, it can be tested. And a 'test' means that you must be able to specify some outcome that, were it to occur, would lead you to grant that your statement is in error—that is, false. For if you can imagine no outcome that would prove your theory false, then you have no genuine 'test' of your theory. Thus, statements that cannot ever, even in theory, be said to be false cannot be said to be true, either. And your statements, I am afraid, are of just this kind—irrefutable, and therefore not in the realm of science. For whatever arguments I have offered against your notions you have countered by saying that 'the nature' of your beings is unknowable to antic minds, antic instruments, antic science. To what purpose, then, should we bother our minds with them? That way lies madness, lad."

The young ant sat for a long moment, silent, as he struggled with these new ideas. Then at last he stood. "You are right, sir," he said slowly, for he was after all a reasonable and honest ant. "And I thank you for what you have taught me, for I see now how much I have to learn. Perhaps," he looked shyly at the scientist, "perhaps some time we may talk again?"

"I should like nothing better, young ant," replied the other, warmly. "But let us go down now and see how the work is going, for it is growing late."

The two turned and walked companionably down the hill, each busy with his own thoughts. And then there came a great rumbling, far above in the clear air. The young ant paused briefly, then walked on. Though his newly educated mind rejected it, he thought for a moment he had heard in the thunder a great and gusty laughter, faint and far away.

PART I
MEANING

Language and Symbol Systems

Media, Self, and Society: Notes on George Herbert Mead

(date unknown) Conference paper, Department of Culture and Communication, NYU.

In the 1920s and 1930s, the American social behaviorist and pragmatist George Herbert Mead addressed himself to the questions, How does reflective thought arise in human behavior, and how does society come to be incorporated in the personal self of the individual? In answering those questions, Mead put forward a comprehensive theory of mind and meaning, symbols, self and society that has major implications for students of culture and communication—and particularly for those concerned with the role of media in historical and cultural variations in consciousness. (Note that all references to G. H. Mead's work are my interpretations of his theories as presented in 1934, *Mind, Self, and Society*).

So far as I know, Mead's theory has never been refuted. While it has been criticized on philosophical grounds, it has successfully withstood such challenges and continues to provide us, I believe, with the best theoretical basis available for understanding how self-consciousness arises in children and how symbols and social interaction—and therefore media—are implicated in the process. While

Mead did not explicitly or systematically explore the significance of his developmental theory for the evolution and cultural divergence of consciousness in the history of the human species, he clearly intended his theory to have such application. It is my intent, therefore, to review Mead's developmental theory in brief, add some interpretations of my own and suggest some of its implications for our understanding of media, consciousness, and culture.

In attempting this in the brief time I have your attention, I will need to simplify Mead's theory. One way in which I will do so is by using the words "language" and "speech" and "words" where Mead would have used "gestures," by which he meant both the sounds and the non-vocal acts of the child. I do not use his word "gestures" because it too easily leads to the supposition that his theory is primarily about non-verbal communication, which it is not. But neither is it exclusively about speech sounds. So please add silently to yourself, when I say "sounds," the phrase "and other, non-vocal acts."

So to begin. What is it, Mead asked, that children are doing as they learn to understand the sounds of others and to modify the sounds they themselves produce? In brief, he answered, they are learning to correlate one part of a complex event, its audible part, with all that goes with that sound, including the changes in feelings of well-being that accompany it. The hungry infant, for example, spontaneously emits a cry of distress, hears its own cry, and simultaneously experiences a variety of changes that result in the relief of its distress. Thus the child stores in memory, as a linked pair, the sound and the complex of events and feelings that go with it, so that the repetition of the sound "summons" the memory and feelings of the whole event. In this way, the sound or speech part of an event comes to stand for or evoke the larger whole, and the whole, from the infant's point of view, is what the sound means—both when others make it and when the child herself produces it.

Now it is important to remember that speech sounds occur, in the child's early experience, only in the context of interactions with others. And it is in fact those others, like mothers and fathers and older siblings, who bring about the events and changes in feeling the baby experiences in connection with speech sounds. Thus what the child is learning—incorporating into memory and feeling as her "own" meaning of speech sounds—is in fact the behavior of others with those sounds: what others do, with what consequences for her, when they make such sounds, and how they respond to her when she makes them.

So begins, in infancy, the process Mead called "internalizing the other": incorporating into one's internal world, via speech sounds, the responses of others and evoking in oneself, by producing those sounds, the responses others originally made. And it is through this process that the child continually constructs and modifies the meanings of speech sounds: by internalizing the responses of others to them—and to her. In effect, then, a meaning is a prediction—on the basis of past experience with others, their sounds and their consequences, all internalized in memory—about how others will respond to a word or non-vocal act. And these predictions, called to mind or mediated through the agency of words, allow us to modify, before initiating or completing them, our own verbal and non-verbal acts—even when others are not present.

Several years ago, for example, I sat chatting with my sister while my nephew of about 11 months played on the floor nearby. Peter had already learned the meaning of several words, among them "hot," which we had come to use, in the lazy way families sometimes have, for anything he mustn't touch. For him it meant the whole set of events that went with the sound—a frowning adult face, having his hand pulled back from the dangerous object, and his removal from its presence—or its from his. Now as he played among his toys, his eye caught the bright steel gleam of a pair of sewing shears dropped by his mother when she rose to answer the phone, and he made for them at top speed. But as he began to reach for them I heard him say, not very loud and not inquiringly, but softly and quite definitely, "Hot. Hot. Hot." And he withdrew his hand. He did not lose interest in the scissors, you understand. Everything about his behavior indicated that he maintained a lively curiosity about them and a strong impulse to touch. But each time his hand went out, his own soft "Hot … hot" restrained it, until I went over, placed him back among the safer toys, and put the scissors away.

What happened here, as Mead would put it, is that Peter used the sound "hot" to call up in himself the response of others to him, certain objects, and his action, and used that "internalized other" to modify his own behavior. In just this way, children become, through the agency of words they say to themselves, *self*-conditioning: capable of governing their own actions by calling to mind the response of others, codified and triggered by a word. It is as though they, as though *we*, carry about within us not one "self" but two: a spontaneous, impulsive self that generates action—that reaches, for example, for the scissors—and another, an internalized "other" evoked by words, that responds to our action before we make it and sometimes (at least) stops or modifies it.

This is precisely what Mead proposed, and there are two important points to remark about it. The first is that the "internalized other" is the necessary precondition for self-consciousness, for to be self-conscious—reflective about yourself, aware of yourself as an object and interested in it—implies that somehow you can step outside of yourself, observe yourself from a point of view not your own. We know that we do this—that we are both actors and audiences for our own behavior. But we also know that we do not leave our own bodies, that actor and audience inhabit the same skin. It must be, then, that the "audience" for whom we act, the observer who sometimes applauds, sometimes hisses and boos, is simply another part of ourselves, an "other" whose responses we have learned through social interactions mediated by language and who is called up by every use, audible or silent, of a word. And it is through this "other" that we become capable of reflecting critically on actions that originate in different parts of ourselves.

The second point to remark here is that the "internalized other," the necessary condition for self-consciousness, is essential to language itself; that is, one cannot learn to speak without internalizing others and thus acquiring the capacity for self-consciousness. This means that in the evolution of symbols and self in the history of our species, the first necessary condition for self-consciousness was already established by the time our ancestors had fully developed language.

This is not to say, however, that language and the internalized other are *sufficient* to generate awareness of the self as an object or to give rise to the habits of introspection, either in children today or in the history of our species. My nephew, at 11 months, was not aware of himself in the sense of a little person inside who weighs alternative courses of action, projects their consequences, and chooses. What he did, from his point of view, was simply unconscious *doing*, in just the way that my walking, or reaching for a glass of water, are un-self-conscious doings. And they remain un-self-conscious until and unless they become problematic. If I should begin to trip myself at every other step, or experience a sharp pain whenever I reach in my usual way, then I may for the first time begin to attend consciously to what I am doing, and how, and try to analyze what is the motion that brings the stumble or the pain. And so it is, Mead argues, with the other within, and the self. They do not become objects of our attention, our consciousness, until they become problematic.

First let's examine the conditions under which the self and the internalized other may become problematic, according to Mead, and then turn to my own thoughts about the implications of those conditions for the history of consciousness and culture. Recall that in Mead's theory, the self is never a seamless, undifferentiated unity but a composite of at least two "parts": a set of largely biological needs and impulses, experientially and socially elaborated into a learned social self or internalized other that restrains and governs biological impulses and wants— *but is no less forcefully felt as "one's own*—with another set of equally and often more powerful wants. Depending on the character of the society and its arrangements for satisfying both sets of wants, the two parts of the self interact with varying degrees of tension. To take a simple example: If a society instills in its children a strong prohibition against urinating in public, so that the very idea figures in the nightmares of the young, but then fails to provide adequate public toilet facilities, the biologic and social self will inevitably conflict in moments of tension so agonizing as to be unendurable. But in societies where either that prohibition is not inculcated in the young or it is, but with ample means of securing "privacy," there will be little tension between the biologic and social "selves," at least on that issue.

The point is that, as the complications of living in larger and more diverse groups require more stringent social controls on impulse, the tensions between the biologic and learned social selves become more frequent and distressing. As they do, we give more attention to them, and, since those tensions are located, via the internalization of others, *inside* us, we become more attentive to our inner lives. Thus the heightening of self-consciousness and the development of introspection in both individuals and cultures in general is very much a function of the particular restrictions that the requirements of group living in different circumstances impose on impulse.

A more critical factor in precipitating self-consciousness is also related to the complexity and diversity of the society in which people live and therefore the consistency among the "others" whose responses the child internalizes. As a general rule, we may say, the smaller the number of others with whom the child interacts and the more consistently they respond to her, the more coherent will be the dictates of the internalized other, the less likely to be problematic, and therefore the less likely to come to conscious awareness. Conversely, the more diverse the social settings and others with whom the child interacts, the more likely they are to generate learnings that dictate contradictory courses of action and thus precipitate a kind of crisis of consciousness. To take a simple example: The child goes off to school wearing a jacket, with the repeated lecture of his mother—"And don't come home without it!"—ringing in his ears, along with all the unpleasant consequences, stored in memory, of what "coming home without it" means. But as he turns toward home at 3:30, he realizes that he has left his jacket in the classroom, which his teacher has told the children, over and again, they are never to enter after the school is closed for the day. What is he to do? The internalized other of home and family tells him he must get his jacket. The internalized other of teachers and school tells him he must not. The situation has all the characteristics of the Batesonian double bind: The child cannot escape the situation and cannot not act, but either course of action dictated by the internalized "other" will be wrong. Mead's theory implies that it is in just such moments of conflict between competing internalized others that their voices are heard as "other"—and that the awareness of self, as the lonely, autonomous "I" who must choose between them, arises. (The term "Batesonian double bind" refers to the concept originally put forward in Bateson et al., 1956, expanded in Bateson, 1958, and elaborated in Watzlawick et al., 1967.)

In small and cohesive societies with little differentiation of roles, like tribal cultures, where parents are also teachers and home and schooling and religious instruction and craftsmanship and art are part of a unified experience in which the same people participate, such moments of conflict between competing others seldom arise. If they do, they are worked out dialogically in the presence of the child—and so the internalization of competing voices and the concept of the self as a lonely, decision-making, autonomous "I" need never arise.

But in highly complex societies like our own, at the other extreme, where people function in dozens of different kinds of social structures and relate to different communities of others quite differently, the "self" is more a conglomerate than a partnership and the internal conversation more a babble of competing voices than a dialogue between impulse and a seamless social "other." If you are at all like me, you may have, overlaid on your "biological" self and the self developed through your earliest interactions with parents and siblings, selves internalized through your transactions with female friends, and male friends, and fellow joggers, and sexual intimates, and baseball fans, and churchgoers, and teachers, and co-workers. And you may have, beyond these, a homemaker self, a parent self, a consumer self, a community-worker self, a political-action self—to name just a few. And these social selves see the world and respond to it in quite different ways: use language differently, talk about different things in different tones of voice, use different standards of judgment and different kinds of reasoning, bring different kinds of facts to bear on issues and decisions—even dress differently, choose foods differently, and feel differently about the same things. Of course there is some consistency among our various selves; if not, we should be quite mad. But on many issues they are in serious conflict, and their competing claims on our attention, energy, money and, above all, time, engage us in wearing internal conflicts about what "I" want—or more accurately, which "I"'s wants are going to be satisfied in the limited time available between, say, Friday evening and Monday morning. It is no wonder that educated Americans are so fiercely self-preoccupied, so haunted and confused by the questions, "Who am I?" and "What do I want?" We are compelled to choose among so many competing alternatives, so many different "I"s.

My point is that we experience greater conflict among our "selves," and therefore become more "self" conscious, when we have internalized a variety of others who are quite different *from each other* in their responses to the world. And we are more likely to experience such widely different others in three circumstances: first, when peoples of different tribes come together in one settled place; second, when human activity and knowledge are segregated into different domains, each with its own concerns, vocabulary, ways of thinking and valuing, and rules for social and intellectual conduct. The more a culture divides up human knowledge and activity—separates "religion" from "school," "school" from "play," "play" from "work," "work" from "art," "art" from "science"—the more divergent these "discourse communities," as Mead called them, become, and the more divergent the "selves" we acquire as we move back and forth among them in the process of growing up.

Third, we internalize a greater diversity of competing selves, and therefore become both more self-conscious and more differentiated from one another, more unique in the internalized world that makes up the individual "I," when changes in communication alter *whom* we may engage across space and time and the conditions in which we engage them. Thus writing and reading, emerging along with citification, the confluence of different tribal groups in settled places, and the economies of surplus and specialization made possible by agriculture, eventually made accessible to previously oral and tribal peoples others who were not part of their own place and time. In this way, writing amplified the internalization of divergent others already underway as a consequence of citification, and intensified the conditions of emergent self-consciousness.

Printing, which exploded the variety and diversity of others people might choose to encounter and internalize through reading, allowed each to choose differently, and thus to become more different from one another in the selves internalized and more aware of their personal uniqueness, the individuality of their internal landscapes. By increasing in exponential bounds the availability of information and the rate of change in knowledge about the world, moreover, printing accelerated and amplified the specialization of knowledge and differentiation of roles already underway in manuscript cultures. Thus it intensified those conditions in which the social self becomes more fragmented and conflicted, and therefore more relentlessly an object of preoccupation and concern.

These processes were further amplified, as Eisenstein, Ong and others have pointed out, by the capacity of writing to make the symbolic self, the "I" of one's own speech and thinking, visible in a form fixed to the page for one's own scrutiny, as in journals, diaries and other autobiographical writings. Just as the glass and mirror-making industries of the fourteenth and fifteenth centuries heightened awareness and interest in the physical self as an object, so did printing intensify awareness and interest in the symbolic self, the internal self of the mind. As for the electronic technologies of our own century—what Mead's theories would most emphasize is the further explosion of communities of divergent others they allow us symbolically to engage and incorporate as part of ourselves. And as people's choices of symbolic others with whom to engage proliferate and diverge, so will the social worlds they experience through the media and the "selves" they develop.

Thus the realm of shared meanings, shared values, shared ways of thinking and assessing the world and one's own behavior may shrink until even people who share the same physical territory—a town, a city, a country—may find that they have very little in common. Thus changes in communication may make strangers of neighbors and so heighten the sense of the uniqueness, the autonomy, the aching aloneness of the individual self so that *culture*, in the sense of *shared* internalized meanings and values, disappears, to be replaced by—by what? By a collection, a mass of individuals so strange and unpredictable to one another that all they wish to do is flee.

But that is an end that Mead did not foresee. Living and writing in a time before the full force of the electronic communications explosion had made itself felt—not even television was yet available, far less the PC—Mead grounded his theory of symbolic interaction firmly in an assumption of continuing *real* interaction at the social level, where people encounter one another and their environment largely in the flesh and are intimately dependent on one another, not on machines, for the gratification of their biological, social and economic needs. He did not imagine the extent to which technologies would come to distance people from their work and its products, from the environment and its products, and from each other, and it would have been unthinkable to him that symbolic interaction, via technologies such as television and the computer, might come to displace, even *re*place, personal encounters in situations of co-presence. Far less did he imagine that if technologies made such things possible, people would come to prefer it so, and look forward with longing to the day when they might engage others and the world only symbolically, in what they mistakenly call "virtual reality," which is neither virtual nor real.

But even in these failures of the imagination—or perhaps failures to read correctly the signposts in the long history of humans, their symbols, and themselves—Mead's theory is important for the questions it raises for us now. To what extent *can* symbolic interaction replace co-present social interaction? With what effects on mind, self and society? What kinds of creatures must we become to live in the no-man's no-land of the hyper-real?

Study Guide for Nystrom, "Media, Self and Society"

(1) According to N., what did G.H. Mead mean by "internalizing the other"?
(2) According to N., how does this process work in early childhood?
(3) So far as you can tell from reading this paper, is "self-consciousness" the same thing as "consciousness"? If not, how are they different?
(4) According to N., what are the two parts of the "self"?
(5) According to N., what conditions are necessary for us to become introspective—that is, to become aware of our "inner life" and "inner dialogue"?

(6) According to N., what are the implications of Mead's theory for understanding the evolution of self-consciousness in human history?

References

Bateson, G., Jackson D.D., Haley, J., & Weakland, J. (1956). "Toward a theory of schizophrenia." *Behavioral Science 1*, 251–64.
Bateson, G., (1958). *Naven* (2nd ed.). Stanford, CA: Stanford University Press.
Mead, G.H. (1934). *Mind, self, and society: From the standpoint of a social behaviorist.* Chicago, IL: University of Chicago Press.
Watzlawick, P., Beavin Bavelas, J., & Jackson, D.D. (1967). *Pragmatics of human communication.* New York, NY: W.W. Norton & Company, Inc.

From Cry to Speech: The Shift from Signalic to Symbolic Functions of Signs in Human Evolution

(2001, June 15–16) Paper presented at the Second Annual Convention of the Media Ecology Association. New York, NY.

Of all the mysteries of human communication, none has held as long and fierce a grip on the imagination of scholars as the mystery of language itself—what exactly language is, how it works, and when and how it emerged in the long prehistory of our species. I want to offer here a tentative thesis that addresses some of those questions. Specifically, I will argue that in human evolution, first, language was rooted in the early use of signs as signals; second, that throughout most of evolution, our ancestors did not use true language—that is, fully symbolic speech—but learned, passed on acquired skills, and communicated via signalic speech; and third, that speech acquired its symbolic functions through a breakdown of the "signalic paradigm" precipitated by social and informational factors roughly 60,000 years ago. I will also try to show that language develops in the same way in young children, and that their passage from cries to speech, therefore, offers important clues about the factors that precipitated the breakdown of the "signalic paradigm" in the distant past.

Let me begin by explaining what I mean by the terms "signalic paradigm" and "signalic speech." In human behavior, signs function in two quite different ways: as *signals* that evoke complex behavioral routines, and as *symbols* that evoke conception or thought *about* their referents. Signs achieve their signalic function by a process similar to conditioning. That is, through repeated association, the observable part of a complex event or routine—a sound or scent or gesture—comes to trigger the entire complex of behavior in which the sound or scent or gesture is the perceptible part. Thus the "alarm bark" of a chimpanzee, for example, triggers in the feeding band the entire event in which that sound is embedded: the "jump-for-the-trees-and-swing-away" complex. And that is what the alarm bark signifies: the whole activity. In this respect, signals have a command function: they bring about the whole event in which they are embedded.

Part of what I mean by the "signalic paradigm," then, is the learning, use of, and response to signs as signals—that is, the use of a perceptible part of a complex event or routine to trigger the whole. This is the oldest, most pervasive, and most powerful form of learning and communication among all creatures, including ourselves, for the very good reason that survival depends on it. And creatures that live in bands characterized by complex social relations, like the chimps and great apes, use an extraordinary range and diversity of signs—cries and calls, stances and gestures, even scent markings—as *signals* to evoke and regulate behavioral routines essential to hunting, defense, mating, and social order. I make this point to counter the argument that full symbolic speech must have originated very early in human evolution because our ancestors would not have been able to elaborate tools, pass on learned skills, sustain complex social relations or move out of the African cradle without language. Not so. Contemporary studies of primate communication and of human learning both suggest that we have vastly underestimated the extent and complexity of the learning and communication that are accomplished, in man and beast alike, through signalic processes—that is, without the agency of true symbolic speech.

I use the term "signalic speech" to refer to the use of and response to vocal signs as signals—that is, as signs that evoke the entire behavioral routines associated with them. Symbolic speech, or true language, is something quite different. It is the use of vocal signs, not to evoke behavioral wholes associated with them, but to break complex wholes into their component parts and name them, so as to represent them in mind—to refer to, and communicate *about* them—without necessarily acting on them. The enormous advantage of language, of course, is that it permits us to construct and mentally represent, with a relatively small number of word-signs and rules for combining them, a virtually infinite number of potential realities not given by our creaturely experience. Through the agency of names, for example, we may take the horns from a goat, the mane of a lion, and the body of an eagle and reassemble them to create, in imagination, a creature to vex our dreams to nightmare. Or bend steel to the shape of a bird's wing, and fly. My point is that language permits us, by the magic of names and rules for combining them in diverse relationships, to imagine new combinations and relationships. And what the mind can imagine, the hand, sooner or later, may try.

There is no question that, at some point in our long past, our ancestors came to use and understand vocal sounds as symbols—that is, as words, as names to refer to things by—rather than as signals connected to complex behavioral wholes. But why, and how, did this paradigm shift in the functions of vocal sounds occur? Here, our own children's journey from cries to speech provides important clues.

Perhaps the strongest evidence that symbolic language originated historically in signalic uses of sounds is that it begins that way in children even today. As any parent can affirm, one of the first things infants learn is that the sounds they produce somehow bring about changes in their world. *We* know, of course, that it is only through the cooperation of parents that the baby's cry brings about change—from the discomfort of hunger or a wet diaper to the bliss of a full belly and a dry bottom. All the baby knows is that this sound goes with that happy change in state, and that when she produces the sound the world changes accordingly. Thus, there originates an important element in the signalic paradigm: a wordless behavioral theory, so to speak, that vocal sounds bring about change.

Throughout the first year of life, the infant experiments with sounds and the events they produce, and attends carefully to the sounds others make as they engage with her in various routines. And while the baby's signalic theory—that different sounds bring about different events—is not always reinforced (sometimes no one comes when she cries), it is reinforced often enough, in the intimate interdependency of the first year of life, to become a powerful primitive theory of language. Namely, that speech sounds bring things to pass, causing their associated events to happen. And when the baby begins to use recognizable speech sounds herself, she uses them in the same way: not as words to name the parts of events, but as signals to evoke the whole events in which the sounds are embedded. When she first says "juice," for example, the sound is not, for her, a noun; it is not a name for a thing. It is instead a command, meaning something like "Let there now happen all the things that happen when you make this sound and that result in my thirst being satisfied."

In the limited contexts of infancy, before children begin to walk, and assuming they are usually in the presence of familiar adults who have learned to read their needs and wants, signalic speech works quite well. By 15 months or so the baby will have learned a "vocabulary" of some 20 or so speech signals which suffice to "command" those events most central to its needs. But between 15 months and two years the child finds its signals quite inadequate to manage the increasing complexity of its physical and social world. A number of factors combine to create a signalic paradigm crisis—that is, the collapse of her behavioral theory that speech sounds command or bring to pass the events they are associated with. To begin, as the baby encounters a greater variety of foods and drinks, for example, her early needs differentiate into more complex wants, and into preferences for slightly different "events" hard to command through a limited set of signals. She wants, for example, not just the "juice" event, but apple juice, not orange, and in the blue cup, not the red. This is not a problem so long as the child is in the company of adults who have learned to read, through thousands of shared experiences, subtle differences in the baby's vocal and non-vocal signals, and can therefore respond appropriately.

But sooner or later, the toddler finds herself more and more in the company of others who do not share such a history of mutual experience—baby-sitters, visitors, extended family members—and they frequently fail to produce the specific "event" the baby thinks her signal is connected to. And even parents, for their own reasons, often fail to respond as expected. By now, of course, the child has learned that sounds by themselves do not produce events, but require the presence of others. And it more and more often happens that when "juice" is commanded to happen, others are elsewhere. So the toddler patters off in search of an adult, repeating "juice ... juice," maintaining in herself the expectancy of the event which is to follow. Sometimes it does, and sometimes (parents being busy folk) it doesn't. From the child's point of view, this must be frustrating and enraging. From ours, it is a critically important step in the acquisition of true language.

The act of using a sound to maintain an inner expectancy outside the presence of the situation or object "connected" to that sound is the beginning of the use of sound to summon and maintain an idea. It is the beginning of a word. The separation of adults and children from the same immediate contexts also plays a vital role in undermining the signalic paradigm. For it is being in the same physical setting with the child—seeing what she sees, hearing what she hears—that provides adults with the information they need to understand the child's signals and respond appropriately. When contexts are not shared, when the child comes from one room and the adult is in another, that information is not available. The child's speech signals are therefore ambiguous, and the responses of adults more likely to be wrong. Decontextualized signals, in short, don't work.

How the human mind abruptly abandons a non-working paradigm and reorganizes experiential data around an altogether different principle is one of the world's greatest mysteries. To my knowledge, we have only one first-hand account of the signalic paradigm collapse in children and the sudden insight that word-signs function as names, not commands—Helen Keller's account of her epiphany at the well in her garden. As she says, in one frozen moment, she suddenly grasped that her teacher's insistent finger signs were not part of the water-feeling event, not commands, but the name of the coolness flowing over her hand. Her account of the events that led up to that moment confirms in every detail the process I have described—her initial understanding of signs as signals, her intense anger and distress as the signalic paradigm failed again to work in a particularly frustrating set of events earlier that day. But Keller's account sheds no light on how, at the moment of reorganization, such a paradigm shift occurs. Suffice it to say that, somehow, it does occur, given the circumstances I have described. And what follows is an unprecedented spurt in verbal learning. Helen's teacher, Annie Sullivan, wrote in a letter that evening, "All the way back to the house, Helen was very excited, and learned the name of every object she touched, so that in a few hours she had added thirty words to her vocabulary." In the next two weeks, she added a hundred more.

I do not say that the paradigm shift from the understanding of speech signs as signals to their grasp and use as symbols—as names, which is to say, as *words*—is quite as dramatic and abrupt in normal children as in Helen's case. But the pattern of change in their verbal learning, from the incremental acquisition of a handful of signals over a period of several months to an exponential explosion in vocabulary at about two years, suggests that the paradigm shift is more sudden than gradual.

In the archeological record, we see a similar change in the pace of learning and innovation beginning at about 40,000 BCE and intensifying thereafter. Here we are looking at the development of tools and techniques, of course, not of vocabulary—for speech sounds leave no record. From the time Homo Erectus first moved out of the African cradle, some 1.5 million years ago, until roughly 40,000 BCE, the pace of tool development was incremental and agonizingly slow, and this is consonant with signalic learning and communication. But at around 40,000 BCE, the pace of change changed. In the following 20,000 years, our ancestors produced a greater number and diversity of new tools and tool-making techniques than had been produced in the entire million-and-a-half-year period preceding. And by 30,000 BCE, they began to leave definitive evidence of a new way of seeing and using signs—the earliest representations of animals and humans, first in carved figurines and then in paintings on cave walls. Both the acceleration of change and the use of signs as representations rather than commands strongly support a dating of the paradigm shift from signalic to symbolic uses of signs, and the beginnings of true language, to this period—that is, roughly 40 to 35,000 years ago.

And I would argue that exactly those factors that precipitate the signalic paradigm crisis in our own children—the increasing complexity of life and of needs, interactions with relative strangers who cannot read one's signals, the failure of signals to work outside situations of immediate and full co-presence—all these factors have their parallels in the ecology of human life specific to roughly 60,000 to 40,000 BCE. Time, alas, does not permit me to demonstrate that here. Nor to address the question whether some genetic variation in brain physiology and neurology prepared one human subspecies better than another for the paradigm shift from signalic to symbolic uses of signs. Was large-brained Neanderthal, perhaps, the ultimate extent of what could be achieved via signalic processing of signs alone? And was the smaller-brained Cro Magnon, our nearer cousin, favored by Nature with some trick of wiring that allowed for more abstractive seeing and an easier shift to symbolic processing when the signalic paradigm broke down? And by what processes did our ancestors move from the use of word-signs as names—which break apart the wholes of our creaturely experience—to fully grammatical speech, which allows us to reassemble it in ways not afforded by perception? I cannot address these questions here.

In closing, however, I feel I owe you at least one "So what?" And it is this. In talking about a shift from the signalic to the symbolic paradigm for understanding and using speech sounds, I have somewhat misrepresented the case. We do not abandon the signalic paradigm and our behavioral theory that speech sounds cause things to happen when the light dawns that the same sounds may also function as names, with a purely referential function. The same sounds serve both functions, even today. I call you by your name. And by your name I call you—that is, summon you. The symbolic functions of speech signs are only lightly and recently overlaid on their signalic functions, and we have never quite been able to separate them. Indeed, it is the priority and tenacity of the signalic paradigm that gives to speech its awesome and mysterious power. All word magic and superstition—from the calling up of demons by changing their names, to the custom in many cultures of hiding one's true name from others, to our children's and our own lurking belief that saying something may bring it to pass ("Bite your tongue!") rest on the signalic paradigm. Indeed, I would argue that it is not until the interposition of a secondary symbol system—writing—between speech sounds and behavioral response that the signalic paradigm begins to lose much of its residual power. If that is so, if it is writing that holds the signalic paradigm in check, and therefore magic and superstition at bay, then we have good reason to fear the current decline of writing culture. But that is an argument for another day.

Information Theory

Information Theory: Some Terms and Definitions

(n.d., course notes)
Entropy: A term which refers to the tendency of all systems to move toward a state of loss of differentiation of parts, randomness, chaos.
Negentropy: A term which refers to the tendency of *local* systems to exhibit, in the short run, increasing differentiation of parts, organization, and systematization.

Information: Knowledge one does not have about what is coming next in a set of symbols or messages. In quantifiable terms, information is a measure of the freedom of choice a sender has in selecting messages from a set of messages. The sender has greater freedom of choice when the set of possible messages is very "shuffled"—that is, randomized—or, to put it another way, when the probability of a particular choice is low. Therefore, the information contained in a particular message is related to the entropy (or randomness) of the possible messages from which the sender may choose. The more entropic the set of possible messages (i.e., the more "shuffled"), the lower the probability of a particular message being chosen, and the greater the information it contains.

Bit: A contraction of the term "binary digit," a *bit* is the name for the unit in which information is measured. Generally, the number of "bits" of information in a message is the number of yes/no questions one would have to ask to reduce the number of possible messages to one.

Feedback: A term which refers to the control of entropy through a process of using indications of the performance of a machine (or any system) as new information to bring *actual* into line with *expected* performance.

Redundancy: A term which refers to the characteristics of codes to include elements that "repeat" information contained in other elements. Redundancy in a code carries no "information," but is useful in controlling entropy—that is, the tendency for all messages to get disorganized in transmission.

Noise: Anything that distorts the message. An unavoidable result of entropy.

Supplementary Notes on Norbert Wiener, Information, and Relativism

Notes on Wiener, Norbert (1948) *Cybernetics: Or control and communication in the animal and the machine.* Paris (Hermann & Cie) & Cambridge, MA: MIT Press (2nd revised ed. 1961), and (1950) *The human use of human beings.* Cambridge, MA: The Riverside Press.

The relationship between information and order

The earliest (and still most fundamental) formulation of the law of entropy came from observations having to do with *heat*. That is why the "entropy principle" is expressed as a law of thermodynamics. Specifically, it is based on the observation that differences in temperature in different parts of a system always tend to equilibrate or "even out" over time. If we take as our "system," for example, a glass of warm water into which we place an ice cube, the initial difference in temperature between the ice cube and the water will reduce over time (i.e., the ice cube, as we say, will "melt"), and the system as a whole (the water in the glass) will reach a uniform temperature, in which there are no longer two *different* things or states of matter (ice cube versus water), but only one undifferentiated thing (or state).

The theory that explains *why* this happens is a theory of molecular (and also atomic) *motion* (hence thermo*dynamics*) that relates heat to differences in the *speed* at which the different "particles" of matter are moving (in the sense of both "traveling" and "oscillating" or "vibrating"). To vastly oversimplify, this theory asserts that the different states of matter are a function of the speed at which their component elements (or "particles") are moving. The molecules of water in a solid state (the ice cube) are moving at a slower speed than are the molecules of water in its liquid state (the surrounding water). But when the two come in contact (the ice cube is placed in the water), the faster-moving molecules (of the liquid water) "collide" with the slower-moving ones (of the solid or frozen water). In each such "collision," the faster-moving molecule *loses* some of its speed, and the slower-moving one is "speeded up" by the force of the collision. For another example of this inertial principle, picture what happens when a car moving at a high speed rear-ends one moving at a slower speed. The impact not only slows down the fast-moving car, but also propels the slow-moving car forward at a sudden increase in speed.

After countless such collisions and re-collisions of particles moving at *different* speeds, all the particles will either have been slowed down or speeded up to the point that they are all traveling at the *same* speed. None of their encounters, therefore, will have sufficient force to change each other's speed, and the system will "come to rest"—that is, reach a point of uniform distribution of inertial energies ("speeds") at which all the water molecules are in the same, undifferentiated state: not water and ice cube any more, but just lukewarm water.

But why should these observations of *thermodynamics* be held to have *universal* application? That is, why should "entropy" be said to be a characteristic of the *universe*? The answer to that is related to the "big bang" theory of creation, which says, in a nutshell, that the universe began in a tremendous *explosion* that propelled "stuff" ("energy") from a "center" at enormous speed. But the force of that initial explosion was not maintained. (If it were, we would not speak of it as an "explosion." It would be a *perpetual* explosion, so to speak—which is a contradiction in terms.) As the initial force dissipated, therefore, the energy it generated began to slow down. *But not uniformly.* Some parts slowed down ("cooled") more quickly than others, and to this day, the universe is composed of "particles" moving at different speeds. And it is their difference in speeds (as well as such things as the difference in the direction they "spin" from that initial explosive force) that makes them different from each other, and therefore capable of colliding and combining in novel ways.

So the universe, we might say, is a very large version of our glass of water, with energy in different states, some of which we call "matter," because its various components are still moving at different speeds, *and at the "atomic" and other levels they are still "colliding."* But as you will remember from our glass of water, each such "collision" results in speeding up the slower and slowing down the faster "particles," until they are all moving at uniform speed (and are therefore at the same temperature) and are therefore indistinguishable from each other—that is, all the same. The celebrated (or perhaps I should say "infamous") "heat death" of the universe does not mean it will die from too much heat. It means that the present *uneven* distribution of heat in the universe (i.e., variation in particles' speeds) must, over time, even out, become uniform. And at that point, it would make no sense to speak of heat, since "heat" only exists in comparison to something *different* that we call "cold" or "cooler," or "less heat." If it is all uniform, then *there is neither cooler nor warmer neither cold nor heat, neither "fast-moving" nor "slow-moving," and therefore no "moving" at all, and therefore no liquid versus solid versus gas, nor "matter" versus "energy," nor "life" versus "death," nor "something" versus "nothing."* It would *all* just be "something" (or "nothing," which in the absence of any difference is the same thing).

Let me pause in this explanation to note how uncannily the creation story in "Genesis" reflects these same ideas—not merely that the universe began in a burst of light, but that *existence* (no less than order) relies on, is in fact a product of, *differentiation*. Re-read the first chapter of the Bible and you will see that God creates the world, brings order out of chaos, by continually dividing (or differentiating) what was initially all the same. Thus He *creates by* differentiating light from darkness, day from night, firmament (heavens or space) from worlds (or planets), dry land from seas, grasses from trees, sea creatures from fowl, "creeping things" from "beasts," humans from other creatures, woman from man. Only after they are differentiated from one another can things be *ordered*—that is, brought into structured relations in which the "things" ordered retain their identity as different "things." What we should make of this correspondence between the ancient tale of Genesis and the modern tale of general systems theory and advanced physics is a matter for discussion later in this course. For now, let us return to thermodynamics and entropy and in particular to how *information* gets into this story at all.

As you may imagine, the Second Law of Thermodynamics, which expresses the principle of entropy as a universal law in any system characterized by initial differences in temperature/energy states (and therefore in the universe as a whole), shocked the scientific world by its implications. These were, after all, the implications that not only "local" systems (like glasses of water containing ice cubes) but living systems and the universe itself were inevitably "running down." Not the least of the shocks this idea delivered was a stunning blow to the ideas of continuous upward progress that had characterized both the scientific and social world of the 19th century. If all systems were inevitably doomed, over time, to "run down," then what happened to the ideal of continuous progress without loss? Thus both scientific curiosity and the philosophical implications of the Second Law drove many of the best scientists of the late 19th century to attempt to refute (or at least modify) it.

The most important of these attempts at refutation (or modification) was offered by James Clerk Maxwell (1831–79), who created a hypothetical situation—he called it a "demon"—in which entropy could theoretically be held at bay by segregating slow- and fast-moving particles in a container of gas. His thought experiment was ingenious, but flawed. And critiques of it paved the way for the most significant scientific and philosophical breakthroughs of the 20th century.

First, without going into detail, the reversal of entropy within Maxwell's imagined container requires the intervention of a "demon"—that is, of something *outside* the system. And, clearly, that something must itself have a source of energy—which would also be subject to "running down" unless *it* taps another source, and so on. And since the First Law tells us that the total amount of energy in the universe is *finite* ... need I say more?

More important for our reflections on the relation between order and *information* is a second observation about Maxwell's hypothetical system—namely, that in order to sort and segregate fast- from slow-moving molecules, and therefore defeat entropy, the "demon" would need a way to *see* (or otherwise gauge) the speeds at which the molecules are moving. That is, the demon would require *information* about the system in order to create or maintain order within it.

That's Important Point One: *Order depends on information*. And here comes Important Point Two. In order for the demon to get that information about the system—that is, to allow him to see the molecules and grab the fast ones—he would need to introduce *light* into the system, since we can only see what light is reflected off. And light is itself a form of energy. Important Point Two, therefore, is that *getting the information required to keep a system orderly* (i.e., to temporarily slow its progress to entropy) *itself requires the use of energy*. In other words, we don't get information "for free."

And now we come to Important Points Three and Four, which emerged from the study, not of thermodynamics, but of optics. The light which Maxwell's demon is required to introduce into the container of gas itself behaves like "particles." That is, it illuminates by bouncing off the gas "particles." In doing so, however, the light *alters* their direction and their speed. So Important Point Three is that *the requirements of getting information change the state of the system about which we seek information*. And Important Point Four is that *our efforts to get information about any state of affairs change it in such a way that we can never know with complete certainty all that we need to know in order to predict with certainty what will happen next*. In physics, this is known as Heisenberg's "Principle of Uncertainty" or "Indeterminacy Principle."

It is based on the following reasoning. To predict with certainty the future interactions of elemental "particles," we need to know *precisely* what is their *present* velocity (speed) and course (direction). To get this information, we need to reflect some energy (light, let us say) off them. But we know that the energy ("particles" of light) will change their velocity and direction. It is possible to calculate precisely, Heisenberg demonstrated, *either* the velocity of the "particle" at the moment you observe it, or its direction. *But the more precise the measure of its velocity. the less precise will be the measurement of its direction, and vice-versa.* We can never know both with equal precision. Therefore, *there is an irreducible measure of uncertainty, of indeterminacy, in our knowledge of the world.*

Does this mean, one might ask, that there is a fundamental uncertainty in the *world*—that is, in *nature*—or just in our knowledge of it? And to this question, contemporary physicists reply, **"We have no knowledge of 'the world,'—of 'nature.' The only 'world' that humans know is that world we have information of, and that is a limited world. We know only that world which our instruments and our symbols and our efforts to know give us. That is all we know and can know. And that knowledge, itself, is inescapably limited."**

That is the true "revolution" in science that Wiener (and other contemporary historians and philosophers and scientists) speak of: not any of its particular discoveries or inventions, but the conclusion that *scientists do not study "nature" or "the world"; they study the state of our information about the world, as our instruments and logics give it.*

Supplementary notes

I use quotation marks around such words as "particles," "speeds," "collisions," etc., to indicate that these words are no longer understood *literally* in contemporary science. The belief that the universe is composed, at the "atomic" level, of literal "bodies" (or "particles" or even "waves") on which "forces" act "at a distance," just as they seem to do on objects at the level of our sensory perceptions, is part of the mechanistic worldview now abandoned by physical scientists. The story of the dismantling of that worldview (often called "Newtonian") is too long and complex to be told here in any detail, but may be read in any number of excellent books, some of which I recommend below.

Let me try to sketch here in a few paragraphs, though, one set of events of particular significance in the shift from the "mechanical" to the "relativistic" or "contingent" conception of the universe and our knowledge of it, and from mechanical to mathematical models. A fundamental assumption of the "Newtonian" worldview is that everything in the universe can be reduced to (i.e., explained by) the operation of "forces" of different kinds on "bodies" of different sizes, from tiny, invisible atoms to planets and stars. It was assumed, in this view, that the "atomic" world, being essentially no different in this respect from the world of the "medium-sized" bodies our senses perceive, could be explained in the same terms. That is, one could see how things like billiard balls behaved in relation to each other and from this deduce how atoms, and planets and stars, behave in relation to each other.

But light posed an interesting problem. How did *it* get from one place or body to another across intervening space? Sound waves, it was known, needed to travel through the air. Heat worked similarly, "getting from" one object to another by heating up the air around the first object and then passing that warmed air by contact with the second object. The mechanical model, therefore, required some *medium* between objects through which forces could be carried or "propagated." The logical-seeming assumption was that light would also need to travel through a specific medium.

And so scientists postulated one: a universal medium—a neutral, tasteless, odorless, invisible *something* filling the spaces between distant objects (like planets and atoms) and "conducting" light from one to the other. This universal space-filling medium was called "ether," and it came to play an ever-more-indispensable role in explaining the mechanical operations on which the entire universe, it was thought, rested. But in time, curiosity about the nature and behavior of this medium grew, and the fact that no one could devise a way to *detect* it became more vexing.

In 1887, the American scientists Michelson and Morley devised an ingenious experiment to learn more about the "ether" and the earth's passage through it. If the earth is traveling through an "ether," they reasoned, this movement should set up an "ether current" (or "wind") blowing against the direction of the earth's movement, and such a current should have a differential effect on the time it takes a beam of light to reach a destination in the direction of the ether current vs. a destination "against" the ether current. With an arrangement involving the use of mirrors, Michelson and Morley sent a beam of light simultaneously "with" and "against" the direction of the earth's movement (and the "ether current").

Their results shook the Newtonian worldview to its very foundations, for they found no difference whatsoever in the speed of light. In the paradigm of the time, this result could have only two possible interpretations: either there was no ether, or the earth was not moving. There was simply too much empirical evidence from other sources to reject the movement of the earth, so Michelson and Morley's experiment sounded the death knell, instead, for "ether." And with the ether went a substantial portion of the Newtonian worldview—most important, the assumption that all the phenomena of the universe could be understood in mechanical terms.

In its place there eventually emerged the present view, in which phenomena at different "levels" or "sizes" require explanations of quite different kinds. Mechanical models, and explanations that make reference to our sensory experience of the world, can be used to explain things at the level of our sensory perceptions. But they fail us when applied to very tiny "things" (like atoms) or very large "things" (like galaxies and the universe as a whole). Those require mathematical models *that do not "translate" into sense perceptions*. Thus while physicists may still talk of things like "waves" and "particles" (as a matter of short-hand convenience, especially in trying to explain things to non-mathematical laypeople), they realize that these are nothing more than crude metaphors, and not useful as working models for understanding "what the universe is 'really' like." Nor do scientists believe that mathematics tells us "what the universe is 'really' like." What it tells us is simply how our measurements of different things are related to each other.

It was Einstein, of course, who ultimately offered the interpretation of Michelson and Morley's results that would finish off the Newtonian view, with its assumptions of a fixed observer capable of detecting absolute motion in a rigid frame of space and time. Through a stunning series of thought experiments, Einstein demonstrated that absolute motion *cannot be detected*, and that all measurements (and our measuring instruments as well) are affected by the position and speed of the observer in relation to what she/he is observing/measuring.

In Wiener's view, however, it was more the mathematical physicist J. Willard Gibbs than Einstein who ultimately lay the Newtonian view to rest. Einstein gave us the "relativistic" universe, but rejected the "probabilistic" view (or statistical conception of our knowledge) advanced by Gibbs, Heisenberg, Bohr and their followers in quantum physics.

Either way, what all this adds up to, once again, is a shift in the conception of what it is that humans can know: not "the world," but only the world as we happen to observe, measure, and codify it; and by observing, measuring, and codifying, change and limit it.

Finally, please understand that in my attempt to explain the thermodynamic basis of entropy simply, I have sacrificed precision. For example, "temperature" and "heat" are two different concepts (and measurements) in physics—but explaining the differences would have required a much longer piece. If you are interested in the details, I recommend the books listed below.

Mason, S. F. (1962). *A history of the sciences*. New York, NY: Macmillan General Reference (Re-issue edition).

Matson, F. W. (1964). *The broken image: Man, science, and society*. New York, NY: Brazillier.

Barnett, L. (1952). *The universe and Dr. Einstein*. New York, NY: New American Library (Mentor Books).

Einstein, A. & Infeld, L. (1938). *The evolution of physics*. Cambridge, UK: Cambridge University Press.

Born, M. (1956). *Physics in my generation*. London: Pergamon Press.

Heisenberg, W. (1962). *Physics and philosophy: The revolution in modern science*. New York, NY: Harper and Brothers

Heisenberg, W. (1958). *The physicist's conception of nature*. New York, NY: Hutchinson & Co.

The Shannon-Weaver Model of Communication, Information, Predictability, and Knowledge

Notes (n.d.) on Shannon, C.E. & Warren, W. (1949). *A mathematical theory of communication*. Champaign, IL: University of Illinois Press.

In its verbal form, the Shannon-Weaver model states that communication is a process in which

- The *information source* selects a desired message out of a set of possible messages.....
- The *transmitter* changes this message into a signal which is actually sent out over the *communication channel* from the transmitter to the receiver.....
- The *receiver* is a sort of inverse transmitter, changing the transmitted signal back into a message, and handing this message on to the *destination*.....

In the process of being transmitted, it is unfortunately characteristic that certain things are added to the signal which are not intended by the information source. These unwanted additions may be distortions of sound (e.g., in telephony), or static (radio), or distortions in the shape or shading of a picture (television), or errors in transmission (telegraphy or facsimile). All these changes in the signal may be called *noise*.

To understand Shannon and Weaver's theory, you have to get the ideas in the right logical order. This might help.

(1) Shannon and Weaver define information conceptually as knowledge one does *not* have about what's coming next in a sequence of symbols (or "messages").
(2) Technically, the amount of information carried in a message coming to you, therefore, is a measure of its *unpredictability*. If you can predict what the message will be, then you already "know" it, and the message itself carries no information for you.
(3) Therefore, the amount of information "carried" in a message is *high* when the message is unpredictable, and *low* when the message is predictable to the receiver.
(4) If the sender of the message is choosing from a large number of possible messages (e.g., like the set of all the numbers from 1 to 1000), and is *choosing at random*, then the receiver has little predictability about what the message sent will be. Therefore, when the sender is choosing at random—that is, when the symbols she is choosing from do *not* follow any rules of order, his/her choice is less predictable to the receiver, and any "message" the sender chooses will carry a *high* information value (because it was unpredictable).

But if the set of messages from which the sender is choosing is organized in some way, according to some rules, the receiver has a better chance of predicting what's coming next. For example, if the sender is sending the names of cards drawn from a totally shuffled (disorganized) deck, the receiver can't predict what's coming next. But if the sender is sending the names of the cards from an organized deck, then the receiver can predict that "three of hearts" will be the message coming after "two of hearts."

Therefore, when the set of possible messages from which the sender is choosing is organized, the predictability of any particular message is *high*, and the amount of information it carries is *low*. In other words, the amount of information carried in a message depends on how organized/disorganized the set of possible messages is. And since "entropy" refers to *disorganization*, we can say that the amount of information carried in a message is a measure of the entropy (disorganization) of the set of messages from which the sender is choosing.

(5) The sender's "freedom of choice" is greater when there are no rules for the order in which she must send symbols (or "messages"). In other words, the sender's freedom of choice is higher when the set of possible messages is *disorganized* (meaning "high in entropy"). And the predictability of the message will be lower for the receiver when the sender's "freedom

to choose" is high. Therefore, messages chosen with total freedom from a disorganized set of messages (an "entropic" set) are less predictable to the receiver and carry more information.

(6) "Noise" refers to anything that "scrambles" the message as it is being sent. It arises from the universal tendency for things to get scrambled (disorganized).

(7) "Redundancy" refers to the repetition of the message in several different parts or ways. "Redundant" symbols carry no information (if the original message "got through"), but are necessary to compensate for noise that may have "scrambled" the message.

To sum up: When entropy (disorganization) of a set of possible messages is *high*, then the sender's freedom of choice is *high*, the predictability of particular message to the receiver is *low*, and the amount of information carried by the message is *high*.

Ideas I Find Particularly Useful from Information Theory/Cybernetics

(n.d.) seminar notes

(1) The definition of information as something you *don't* know. (Because it gives us a new way of looking at the so-called information media—like TV. If you think of "info" as something you don't already know, then TV doesn't seem to be much of an "information" medium. Which raises the question, "Then, what *is* it?")

(2) The idea (from Wiener) that information's function is to help us adjust to changing environments—and his further point that incoming information has to be matched to "effector organs" through which we *act on it*. This raises the question, "What if we have tons of incoming info (sensory receptors) but few 'effector organs' (i.e., ways of acting on it)?" Doesn't this mean we'd be just as "disabled" as we are by having insufficient info? And when I look at the so-called Information Society, that's what I see as the problem.

(3) The idea that there is only a small window—between too much redundancy/predictability and too much ambiguity/unpredictability—where meaning is possible. Indeed, perhaps, where *life* is possible. The problem of cultures/societies/individuals, therefore, is to find the proper balance between redundancy/predictability and novelty/ambiguity/unpredictability. How do cultures achieve this balance? Do different forms of discourse

emphasize different "sides" of this relationship? What happens when a balance is *not* achieved?
(4) The idea that structures *reduce* information—and that we cannot survive too much "raw" info. Implications for further thought seems obvious to me. What structures do we require at present, for example, to "reduce" information?
(5) The idea that *differentiation* among things is essential to growth, novelty, complexity. Important because it suggests that attempts to "even things out" or "homogenize" class, status, haves and have-nots, culture may in fact have the effect of reducing the possibilities for growth and change.

Media, Meaning, and Behavior

Chapter 1: Environments, Ecology, and Evolution

(n.d.) Excerpts from an unpublished manuscript

This is a book about environments. But not those natural environments which visible pollution and the death throes of vanishing species have so recently, and so late, called to our attention. This is a book about symbolic environments—the environments that shape the human mind.

This is also a book about ecology. But you will not find in its pages much about the delicate balance of sun and rain, soil and species that the physical survival of our planet depends upon. This is a book about *media* ecology, and what you will find in it are some attempts to describe the complex relationships between communication environments and human values, perceptions, feelings, and behavior.

Finally, this is a book about evolution. But it is not about the physical adaptation of species to their natural environments. This is a book about cultural evolution—the psychological and social adaptation of people to their symbolic environments.

Now, perhaps you are thinking that the connection between media and ecology is too farfetched, that it requires a metaphorical leap which serious thought can scarcely support. But whether you find the step from media to ecology a long or a short one depends on the definition of "media" you start from. And that depends on the model of communication you have in mind.

If you conceive of communication in the conventional and now classic way originally derived from the work of 19th-century physicists and early 20th-century engineers, you most likely picture it as some more or less linear sequence of steps, in which something called "information" is passed in a steady stream of bits or chunks from one person to another and back again, with some modifications. In this model, a communications medium is simply the "message carrier," something like a boat (as one writer has put it) that ferries supplies from one place to another and returns with new cargo. In the "cargo model," the structure of the medium has *some* effect on the messages it carries; the capacity of a ship obviously limits how much it can carry, and its tendency to rock in transit guarantees that the cargo will arrive in a less organized state than when it was loaded. But by and large, the role of the medium in the cargo model is a passive one.

I do not say that this is a faulty construct for thinking about communication and media. Models, like maps, are designed with specific purposes in mind, and the one you choose depends on what you want to be able to do. A Mercator projection of the world may be perfectly accurate, but it won't help you to get from Times Square to Grand Central Station—any more than the best street map of New York City will help you to plot the shortest air route from Denver to Peking. What I have called the "cargo model" of communication, and described so sketchily above, has in fact been an invaluable tool for explaining the characteristics of communication at the most technical level. It has given us a precise vocabulary for talking about certain aspects of communication—for example, information, redundancy, channel capacity, efficiency, feedback, noise—and instruments for measuring such variables and their consequences in some, largely non-human, instances of information exchange. This is not the place either to elaborate on the complexities of the model or to catalogue its application. Suffice it to say that, without it, we would not yet have the kind of telephone or television or computer systems we do. But, having given us the modern telephone and television and computer, the information-transfer model of communication is powerless to help us understand our relationship with them. For in the end, the "cargo" model is not about the human communication experience at all.

Human beings are not, as Ray Birdwhistell has pointed out, black boxes with one orifice for emitting a chunk of stuff called information and another for receiving it. We are—first, foremost, and always—*meaning-makers*. And the processes through which we make meanings—of ourselves, of other human beings, and of the events which comprise our personal and social reality—are more complex than a model of technical communication can account for.

To begin with, meaning-making involves, at once, the present, the past, and the future, for every meaning is, in effect, an observation, a generalization, and a prediction. To take a commonplace example, imagine that you are reading this in a coffee shop. Just as you reach this line, the person seated next to you says, "Pardon me, may I have the cream?" If you are a normal, socially integrated American, your response is instantaneous and automatic: you look up, say "Sure," and pass him the pitcher. By your behavior, you reveal the meaning you assigned to his utterance. But how did you arrive at that meaning?

Well, first of all, you made a set of observations—beginning, of course, with the observation that you had been addressed and that the sounds directed to you took the pattern of a request. You also observed the position of the cream pitcher relative to you and to the speaker. (This may seem a trivial point, until you imagine what meaning you would have assigned the utterance if, when you looked up, you saw the speaker with a full cream pitcher in his hand.) You may also have noticed that the speaker had a cup of coffee or tea in front of him—or at least (if you didn't look) you assumed so. (How would your response have changed if the speaker had before him only a bowl of chicken soup?) And you certainly observed, although without reflection, that you were in a coffee shop. (Consider the change in your response if the utterance had been addressed to you in a crowded elevator.) But your meaning for the event did not arise solely from such observations. When you recognize that a particular arrangement of words constitutes a request, for example, you are not operating on present information but on a generalization about your past experience with sounds and the behaviors that accompany them. And it is not enough, for meaning, to know the dictionary definitions of words. Imagine, again, that the sounds, "Pardon me, may I have the cream?" have just been addressed to you in an elevator, or that what you have just heard in the coffee shop is "Pardon me, may I have a dream?" In either case, you would surely know the dictionary definition of the words used, and that they take the pattern of a request. But even more surely, you would have considerable difficulty in making meaning—that is, a response—to them. What you would have to do is search your repertoire of past experiences for a context in which similar words, organized in a similar pattern, elicited some response which seemed to satisfy the speaker and suit the apparent purposes of the situation. Failing to find any such context, or finding only one so markedly different from the context you are in that the response appropriate there (e.g., a psychiatrist's office) would produce an impossible situation here, you must give up trying to make meaning of the sounds addressed to you.

For meaning may be defined as an appropriate response—a response that, in a particular context, leads to a predictable, patterned set of interactions. The meaning you assign to "Please pass the cream" in a coffee shop includes not only your verbal response ("Sure") and your action (picking up and handing the speaker the cream pitcher), but a prediction that he will take it from you, probably acknowledge your action in some way (perhaps a "Thanks," or a smile, or simply a slight nod), and then make some use of the pitcher. If something radically different happens (he says, "What're you giving me this for?"), you must assume that you misunderstood the original request—that you assigned the wrong meanings to those sounds—or he did. In either case, so compelling is the need in humans to make meanings that you will not abandon the attempt, even when your efforts to find an appropriate response to the sounds you heard are fruitless. What you will do then is try to make meaning, not of the sounds, but of the person uttering them, or of your situation. You may conclude, for example, that the speaker is from another culture, with different rules for the relationship of sounds to responses. Or, if that prediction fails to produce confirming evidence, you may conclude that you are dealing with someone who is following a set of rules known only to him. And that is as close to a definition of madness as one can come. The point is that, even in judging your neighbor mad (and no doubt moving away from him), you have engaged in meaning-making—a response and a prediction about the pattern of transactions that are likely to follow, even if only that they are likely to be unpredictable and, therefore, better avoided.

Human beings cannot *not* make meanings. We may sometimes make inappropriate or mistaken meanings, or meanings that disturb and upset us. But make them we must, for they are the sole devices through which we establish order—a predictable continuity—in life. And without that, we could not long maintain either sanity or survival.

Meaning-making, then, is the core of human communication, the center from which any adequate model of communication must proceed. And perhaps the best place to start is with a definition. Communication may be defined, from the point of view expressed here, as all those processes through which people—or objects, events, machines, symbols—structure the meaning-responses of others.

Now, there are several points to be noted about this definition. The first is that it is *not* a definition of what might be called "effective" communication. The notion of effectiveness requires us to assume intent or purpose in communication, and some way of judging whether the meanings a speaker intended to structure in a listener were in fact those the listener made. It also requires us to assess in some way whether the larger purposes of the speaker or listener, or both, were achieved—mutual intelligibility aside. Since humans are, by and large, purposive creatures, and since we think of most of our behavior as instrumental—designed to achieve some desired end—it is not surprising that effective communication is of major concern to us. But it is only a subset of communication. There are many instances of communication—the structuring of meaning-responses—that are not purposive in the human sense. A day-old newspaper in front of your friend's door may structure your meaning, "Not at home," but it would scarcely be sensible to say that the paper intended to produce that response. A looming thundercloud may structure your meaning, "Rain. Better get off the beach," but you would not credit the cloud with such a purpose. Situations—like coffee shops and elevators—structure your meaning-responses, but we grant them "purposes" only through the roughest sort of analogy. Perhaps most important, and least recognized, the very symbol systems you use—language itself, gesture, writing, television images—impose by their form (not merely their content) certain limited patterns on the meaning you can make. Yet we do not say that the *purpose* of English, for example, is to make you conceive of time as inevitably divided into a past, a present, and a future—though that is undeniably one of its effects.

Even when communication takes place between generally purposive humans, much of what goes on cannot be judged intentional—at least, not consciously so. A sleeping child's restless cry sends its mother for a thermometer. The set of a husband's jaw warns his wife to tread softly this evening, in spite of his smile. My hostess's arrangement of space in a room tells me to behave with the greatest decorum, even while she tells me to "feel right at home." In each case, "intent" in the communication would be hard to demonstrate. But these are instances of communication—the structuring of meaning-responses—nonetheless.

Indeed, it may well be argued that the greatest part of our communication behavior, and the most significant for our habits of thought, response, and feeling, lies in the realm of the unintended, the not consciously purposive, the out-of-awareness. Such students of culture and communication as Edward Sapir, Benjamin Lee Whorf, Dorothy Lee, Claude Levi-Strauss, Mary Douglas, Clifford Geertz, Edward Hall, Edmund Carpenter, Gregory Bateson, Paul Watzlawick, Erving Goffman, Eric Havelock, Walter Ong, Harold Innis, and Marshall McLuhan—to name only a few—have argued persuasively, each in his own way, that it is those aspects of language, of situations, of communications technologies which we least consciously recognize that most firmly regulate our meaning-making. Hall calls these the "covert" aspects of communication, the "hidden dimensions" of culture. Douglas refers to the hidden "rules" that regulate cultural meanings. McLuhan and others talk of the "invisible environments" created by communication technologies, and of the hidden ways in which these environments structure our meanings. Whatever the labels they use to describe the non-conscious, the unintended, the largely unrecognized aspects of human communication, such writers seem firmly agreed on one point: In shaping the meaning-making, not only of individuals but of entire cultures, that which is outside of our awareness plays a far more important role than the overt content of "messages."

This brings us to a second point worth noting about the definition of communication proposed here, and it is a corollary to the first. Communication is not conceived of here as an exchange of mutually intelligible "messages," at least, not in the sense that a "message" implies some positive action on the part of a "sender." Of course, some communication does involve such action. But much does not. The letter you do *not* receive, the telephone call that fails to come as expected, the silence that greets your "Good morning!" are at least as significant in shaping meaning-making as messages you do receive. This is what Paul Watzlawick, Janet Bevins, and Don Jackson mean when they say, in their *Pragmatics of Human Communication* (1967), that people cannot *not* communicate. They may not talk, not write, not call, not respond, refuse to send or receive "messages." But so long as their *not* doing these things structures the meanings of others, they are communicating nonetheless.

In a similar way, communication (so defined) does not require that people agree on the meanings of symbols, objects, behaviors, or events. *Successful* communication—that is, a process in which people's meaning-responses are predictable to each other—does require a certain range of shared meanings or, at least, a set of shared rules for the making of meanings. But not all communication falls in this category—as the history of human misunderstandings make painfully clear. In the movie *Cool Hand Luke* (1967), Paul Newman plays a spirited convict on a Georgia chain gang whose refusal to be broken—or contained—drives the sadistic warden to increasing excesses of brutality. Trapped and defenseless after his last escape, Luke calls out wryly to his nemesis, "What we've got here, Warden, is a failure to communicate." A fatal mistake. The shotgun blast that ends his sentence is also its rebuttal—the proof that communication has been taking place all along. The point is that there is a difference between failures *in* communication and failure *to* communicate. To overlook the distinction is rarely fatal, but doing so gives us a severely limited view of the communication process.

The definition of communication offered here, on the other hand, is designed to provide the broadest possible view. It includes purposive communication, the conscious exchange of "messages," and the sharing of mutual meanings. But it also includes those processes in which human meanings are shaped non-purposively, by variables outside the conscious control of "senders" and "receivers"; it includes the structuring of human responses by non-messages—by silence, by events that fail to happen; and it includes all those human transactions in which predictions about the meanings of others miscarry, in which meanings and the rules for making them are not shared.

Nor is this definition confined to transactions between co-present persons. It includes interpersonal communication, to be sure. But it also includes those processes in which objects, events, situations, and symbol systems structure the meaning responses of individuals and of cultures. And it includes intrapersonal communication as well—those processes by which we make and modify our own meanings by what we call thinking, or talking, to ourselves.

You may be wondering at this point whether the definition of communication as the process of structuring meanings may not be *too* broad. After all, one purpose of a definition is to limit a concept, so that we may distinguish between one kind of process or object or event and another. What kinds of events, if any, does this definition *exclude*?

Primarily, it excludes all those instances of response-shaping that do not involve a human mind. What we often call animal "communication" is not included here; neither are the processes in which machines interact; nor are those transactions between human cells at the submicroscopic level, though such events have sometimes been labeled "intercellular communication." These processes, and countless others in which objects and organisms achieve a patterned interdependence, are excluded here because they do not involve meaning-making.

As I am using the term, *meaning-making* refers to a peculiarly human activity. It is not simply a patterned response of one organism to another—such as ants and bees, cats and dogs, elephants and dolphins are perfectly capable of making (as are machines linked in an interactive system). A human meaning is a prediction, a sort of hypothesis about future events or contemporaneous events not directly observed. Let us say a stranger turns toward me with a smile as I approach him at a cocktail party. My meaning for his behavior is not only a response—a smile in return and a continued approach—but a set of hypotheses: that if I speak, he will answer; that if I extend my hand, he will not strike me. Of course, such hypotheses are rarely consciously held, but we make them just the same. If we did not, we should never experience surprise or puzzlement at another's behavior. Surprise is the result of the frustration of an unconsciously held hypothesis—of a mistaken meaning. That we are rarely stunned by another's response tells us something else about human meanings: like all hypotheses, they are tentatively held. If the smile on the stranger's face changes to a look of puzzlement as I come close, I am not shocked speechless. My tentative hypothesis changes: he mistook me for someone else, and in a moment will probably tell me so.

Human meaning-responses, then, are hypotheses. They are tentatively held, and subject to change. And they imply the existence, if not always our conscious awareness, of alternatives. It is as though every human meaning is a set of "if … then" propositions: He smiled. If I do this, then perhaps he'll do that; or if I do that, perhaps he'll do this; or if I do the other, perhaps he'll do something else. Such a process—of holding in mind alternative futures, imagined responses, each with its own set of hypothetical consequences, and choosing from them a response—is not to be found (so far as ethologists have been able to demonstrate) in the transactions of animals. A bee observing the "honey dance" of another can give only one response to a specific set of signals. There's no "maybe this, maybe that—or maybe he's lying" about it. The same is true, in a somewhat different sense, for the most sophisticated of computers. A computer can be designed to produce a set of alternative responses to an instruction. And it can even be designed to "decide" which alternative to choose in a given set of conditions. But it cannot "decide," without specific instruction, that a given command was not "really" intended to be followed, or that a "false" instruction has been given to it and that all future instructions from this programmer are to be regarded with suspicion. Humans, however, make such meanings all the time. What is more, though we may not be conscious of our meanings when we make them, we can be *made* conscious of them, and of the processes through which we arrive at them. That is, humans have the capacity to reflect on their meanings, and through self-reflection can effect self-change. That is, in part, why books like this are written: to help us explain to ourselves how we make meanings, in the hope that, through awareness, we may achieve somewhat better control of our own thought and behavior. But you are not likely to find any books on "The Meaning of Meaning" written by computers, or a school of dolphins that offers seminars in cetacean behavior.

The processes by which animals, machines, and submicroscopic organisms structure one another's responses through exchanges of signals, then, are only superficially akin to the process of human meaning-making. And a definition of communication centered on the structuring of meanings must exclude those processes, interesting though they may be.

In defining human communication as the structuring of meaning-responses, I do not mean to say that this is the "real" or the "true" or the "only" definition that can be useful. But I do propose that this one allows us to study a very large segment of human behavior, conscious and unconscious, private and public, individual and cultural. And it focuses our inquiries on what is unique to humans. Like any definition, it rules out certain questions—for example, the question, How are humans, animals, machines and submicroscopic organisms all alike? If this is the question that heads your list of "Things I'd Like to Think About," you won't much like the definition of communication offered here.

But if it excludes some questions, this definition also focuses attention on certain others. For example, What are the variables that structure human meaning-responses? And what are the differences in those variables that *make* a difference in our meanings? And what kinds of differences do they make?

Some tentative answers to the first of these questions have already been suggested here. The simplest meaning-response, you will recall from our coffee shop encounter of the cream kind, depends upon the past experiences of the meaning-maker. It depends upon the social context or environment he finds himself in. It depends upon the language—the symbol-system or code—used in the transaction. And it depends upon the culture—the shared set of rules for the making of meanings—in which the encounter occurs. These, then, are the four great variables that structure human meanings: the personal history of the meaning-maker, his social context, his symbolic system, and his culture. You may note that these four variables in communication fall into two categories: variables in the meaning-maker and variables in his environment—situational, symbolic, and cultural. Studies of human communication fall similarly into two great categories: studies of meaning makers and studies of the environments, the milieu—in a word, the "media"—in which meaning-making is shaped.

Insofar as studies of meaning makers take as their focus questions about the effects of such variables as past experience, personality, and such characteristics as "intelligence" on the particular meanings individuals make, they may properly be regarded as a branch of psychology. And in the sense that studies of communication environments take as their focus questions about the structure and effects of social setting, symbolic systems, and cultural contexts on meaning-making and its human consequences, they may with some felicity be labeled *media ecology*. For ecology is the study of the structure of environments. And "media," as I am using the term here, are the social, symbolic, and cultural environments of which communication—the structuring of human meaning—is a product.

There are several points about this definition of communication media that I want to stress here, even at the risk of belaboring the obvious. For old ways of talking (and thinking) about communication die hard, and nothing less is required here than your accepting a new set of meanings for old and familiar terms. It is worth noting in this respect, however, that in defining a medium as an environment, I am giving the word, not a new meaning, but an older one. Long before it acquired its present usage—as a synonym for communication technologies such as television, radio, telephone, the press—a *medium* denoted, in biology, an environment; specifically, a nutritive environment in which a culture of living organisms may grow. It seems especially fitting to use the biological meaning here, rather than the mechanistic, for this is, after all, a model of human, not machine, communication. And that is in fact the first point to make about this definition of a communication medium: It does not refer to a television set, or a radio, newspaper, telephone, record player, computer. These we may call communication technologies. Of course, such technologies play a central role in *creating* communication media—that is, environments—and much of what follows in this book will be devoted to exploring that role. But they are not, in themselves, environments, any more than a single element, like a tree or a road or a river or a deer, is an environment in natural ecology. Similarly, a coding system or symbol system—a language, for example—is not a medium in this definition. Like a communication technology, a symbol system plays a vital role in constructing a communication medium. But it is only part of a more complex system which, taken as a whole, structures human meanings.

So much for what a medium of communication is not. What it *is* is harder to say—and this book represents only the beginnings of an inquiry into that question. As a point from which to start, however, perhaps this will suffice: A medium of communication is an ordered social and symbolic environment—a particular organization of people and objects, using certain symbols and communication technologies, having a certain organization in time and space, operating within a given culture—that structures the meaning-responses and consequently the thoughts, feelings, expectations, and transactions of its participants in particular ways. In this view, a school is a medium of communication. And a library. And a movie theatre, a coffee shop, a living room in which a family gathers to watch TV, an airplane, a teachers' conference, a study where a solitary man simply sits and reads. What distinguishes these as environments, as media, is not that they are different *places*. For the same place may become a different medium of communication—that is, structure meanings differently—by changing its organization of space and time, its use of symbols, its use of communication technologies, or any one of a number of other variables. What those variables may be, and how they structure the meanings, not only of individuals in different social settings but, at the broader level, the patterns of thought and response, the habits of mind, of a culture, is the subject matter of media ecology.

Media ecology, then, is the exploration of human communication environments—their structure and consequences for human thought, feeling, and behavior. Like any exploration, it begins with an idea: the notion that communication is not something people *do in* an environment or *through* a medium, but something that *results from* the transactions of meaning-makers *with* their media environments. With this idea firmly in mind, the media ecologist sets out to chart the important features of media environments—those that make a difference for human meaning and response. The territory is a large one, and all the more challenging because its limits are unknown. For guidance, she uses maps provided by explorers—linguists, anthropologists, psychologists, historians. But she cannot rely too heavily on these, for each is limited in its perspective and scope, and she seeks to chart the broader patterns of media environments, not their fine detail. Besides these, she is equipped with three indispensable aids: a boundless curiosity about the structure and dynamics of media environments, a reasonable degree of confidence in his or her own powers of observation, and a cheerful brand of courage that permits her to accept, even welcome, the possibility—more, the likelihood—that some of the turns she takes will be wrong. And what keeps her going is the simplest of motives: not that the task is urgent or grim, not that the goal is lofty or the stakes high—just that the adventure is fun.

This is a book about media ecology. It is not the map of communications environments that future generations of explorers may one day produce. Think of it, instead, as a set of rough notes from the field—some signposts, guidelines for other explorers to follow, or to change. Think of it too as an invitation. If the territory interests you and the prospect of an adventure without visible end sounds like fun, pack up your curiosity, your powers of observation, and your courage to be wrong. And come along.

Chapter 2: The Structure of Situations

Where are you right now? In a classroom or a study hall? In a library? A coffee shop? At home? At first thought, the question seems simple enough. Albert Einstein loved such simple questions—but he never stopped at first thought, or second. For him, the question "Where am I right now?" led from his study, to the planet, to the galaxy, and eventually out into the spaces between the stars where, as he returned to tell us, the question is not so simple at all.

We are not concerned here with the spaces between the stars, but with spaces, and places, closer to home: the social situations that structure human meanings. But even here, where the ground is firm and familiar, simple questions may turn out to be more complicated than we thought. For example: Suppose your answer to the question "Where are you right now?" is "In a coffee shop." How do you *know*?

Your first impulse may be to answer, "Because it says so." And that answer is not without merit. Cultures do invent labels for their situations—this is a library, that's a school, this is a restaurant, that's a church—and some situations put their labels prominently on display, in neon lights or stamped plaques or chiseled stone. But most do not. I know, for example, that I am "home." Yet there is no neon sign flashing above my door that says so. Nor do I need it to determine that I am "at home" and not "at school." So while signs—labels—may sometimes be helpful in naming a situation, they are not what the situation is.

It is tempting to say, on second thought, that home is a *place* that has a particular relation to other places and spaces—that "home" is the first apartment to the left of the elevator on the fourth floor of the building across the street from the church ... and so on. But this explanation—that "home" is a specific location—raises some problems. If I move, for example, that place will still be where it was. But I will no longer call it "home." Moreover, I can recognize at once that I am in someone else's "home," even though I arrive in the dead of night and have no idea of its location. And so it is with other situations as well. Most of us would recognize at once the situation called "a coffee shop" or "a classroom," without reference to signs or specific locations.

Perhaps we recognize situations, then, not by sign or location, but by the functions they serve. Home is where people live, a classroom where they learn, a coffee shop where they eat snacks (and pay for them), a party where they have fun. But a moment's thought shows the problems here. I "live" as much at the office as at home (at least, I spend as much time there); people "learn" in all kinds of situations we don't call classrooms; they snack (and pay) at street fairs, hot dog stands, even in their offices; and as for parties ... well, I put it to you: Are they always fun?

If we do not recognize situations by their labels, locations, or functions, how then do we know where we are? And what does it matter, anyway? We know where we are, I think, because we recognize—without even being aware that we are doing so—a set of *conditions*: conditions involving space; conditions involving time; conditions involving objects, symbols, and the transactions between people. And it matters because those conditions allow us not only to label a situation, but to predict how others will behave and what expectations they will have of us. In a sense, knowing *where* we are tells us *who* we are, and who are the others around us. For every situation requires of us a certain persona—a self, if you will—who talks in a particular way, uses space in a particular way, dresses and moves and *thinks* in a particular way. You do not talk the same way at a baseball game as you do in a classroom, or dress the same way for a funeral and a disco party. You do not handle your body in quite the same way in church and at the beach, or move about in space at a business meeting as you do in your bedroom. Nor do you *feel* the same way in the executive boardroom and your own bedroom. In a very real sense, we do not know *how* to speak, move, dress, think, feel—how to respond to the people, objects, and events around us—unless we know where we are.

Imagine, if you can, awakening out of a profound unconsciousness, such as only a deep anesthetic or traumatic head injury can produce, to utter darkness, unplace-able sounds and the touch of something against your skin. How would you respond? Most likely, with panic. Not just fear that you might be ill, injured, captive. But the panic of meaninglessness—of not knowing how to respond, how to feel, what to make of your sensations. This is why ambulance attendants and recovery room personnel make it a practice to tell patients returning to consciousness, at once, where they are. "You're in the hospital" reassures, not because it's not frightening to be injured or ill, but because it allows one to make meaning of one's experience—making certain things, even unpleasant things like pain, predictable. In this respect, even such a statement as "Lie still, you're my prisoner" reassures; it reduces the panic of meaninglessness to manageable terror, gives order, albeit a dreadful order, to one's thoughts, feelings, responses. It is interesting to note, by the way, that doctors do not tell reviving patients who they are. And no soap opera amnesiac, on first regaining consciousness, demands at once to know "Who am I?" We may manage things—shakily—it seems, without knowing who we are. But without knowing where we are, we cannot manage things at all.

And so we come back to the question, How do we know where we are? Or more precisely, What are the conditions that define a situation and, consequently, structure our meanings? How do you know you're in a coffee shop? What do I mean by "home"?

To begin with, I mean by "home" a space. Not just any kind of space, but a space with fixed boundaries that set it off from surrounding spaces. In my case, the boundaries that mark off "home" are of glass and concrete and steel—my windows, walls, and door. For others the boundaries of "home" may be of different materials—wood, brick, even leather or nylon or hard-packed snow. Whatever they are made of, fixed spatial boundaries are one condition of the situation we call "home."

A second condition, and it is related to the idea of boundaries, is that *access* to the space I call "home" is limited in a special way: I and no one else determine who and what may enter, and under what conditions. The conditions I establish may be very loose—I may leave my door always ajar and permit friends to come and go without notice as they please. Or they may be stringent—I may require that appointments be made and identification shown. But I am the sole person who establishes those conditions, and I may change them at will. Of course, if I shared my home with someone else—with husband and children, other family members, even a roommate—we would hold jointly the power to limit the access of others to our space. Indeed, this is almost the definition of a household: people who jointly control the access of others to a shared space with fixed boundaries.

But there is more to it than that. "Home" is also a space characterized by certain kinds of objects and not others—by sofas, soft chairs, beds, dishes and spoons, for example, not rows of filing cabinets, photocopies, and computer workstations. Not to say that "home" may not include these things. But such objects will be in the minority, not the majority. Moreover, the objects that characterize "home" are organized in a particular way in space. Folding chairs are not lined up in rows, for example. If they are, we recognize this as a special, and temporary, situation "at home" and give it a discrete label to mark the change of situation—for example, "wedding at home" or "meeting at home."

Not only is "home" distinguished from other situations by certain objects, arranged in particular ways; it is also defined by the condition that I determine those arrangements—and all of the arrangement of internal space within the boundaries I call "home." Moreover, I control the access of others to both objects and spaces within those boundaries—that is, I determine who may touch, even see, which objects and enter which spaces, and in what circumstances. So powerful are these conditions of the situation "home" and so intimately connected to the feelings we experience "at home," that any disturbance or any breach of such conditions makes us profoundly uneasy.

If you have ever returned home to find your door ajar, your furniture and belongings in disarray, every space invaded and object handled without your knowledge and consent, you will know, I think, what I mean. Even if nothing is missing, nothing damaged, one feels a deep distress, a pervasive malaise, a sense of loss—not of property, but of some aspect of self. The situation is not what it was, and as a result, you are no longer quite the same. For some people, this kind of violation of the conditions of "home" is so unsettling that they cannot remain in the same place, but must establish those conditions anew somewhere else. It is not so much the fear of another burglary, of damage to life or property, that impels them, but an inability to recover the sense of being "at home." This is an extreme response, no doubt. But it does illustrate the intimacy, and the power, with which the conditions of situations are tied to our responses, our feelings, our sense of self.

As we have seen, space (its boundaries, its arrangement, its conditions of access) and objects (their type, their arrangements in space, their conditions of access) are two of the major variables that distinguish situations and shape our responses. Another is *time*.

Just as they have spatial boundaries, situations have temporal boundaries—times when they begin and end. And situations are distinguished, in part, by the nature of these temporal boundaries—whether they are fixed or flexible—and how they are marked. Situations called "classes," for example, have relatively fixed temporal boundaries: they begin and end at a specific time, with relatively little deviation permitted. Situations called "parties," on the other hand, have more flexible boundaries: they may begin as little as ten minutes or as much as forty minutes after the hour announced (if, indeed, any hour is announced), and the precise moment they end is rarely specified. (Although any situation that extends beyond ten hours or so in time would most likely go by some name other than "a party.") The temporal boundaries of parties and classes, moreover, are marked in quite different ways. Classes end with a technical or formal signal: a bell rings, a buzzer sounds, a professor says, "We'll pick up from here tomorrow." Parties end less formally: the hosts begin to yawn; the glasses, plates, and liquor bottles begin to disappear; guests look at watches, exchange glances, edge toward the door.

What can we say of the temporal boundaries of "home"? Unlike its spatial boundaries, they seem so flexible as to be almost nonexistent. One of the conditions of "home" is that one may go there at any time and stay as long as one wants. I do not mean, of course, that it is *practical* to be at home at all times or to stay there forever. Other situations—work, school, shopping—make demands on our time that would be foolish to ignore. I mean that there is no time that "home" is barred to you if you choose to be there. With due apologies to Thomas Wolfe, if you can't go home again, then that's not home. (Which is part of what Wolfe meant to say, anyway.)

One condition of "home," then, is that its temporal boundaries are exceedingly flexible. Another is that the organization of time within those boundaries is also flexible, controlled solely by members of the household, and informally marked. To be "home" means, among other things, that I am "on my own time," that I can manage time as I choose. I may choose to rise early, write at my desk for two hours or so and breakfast late. Or sleep till noon, skip breakfast and not write at all. But it is my choice. Even people of exceedingly regular habits—those admirable creatures who arise, shave, dress, breakfast, write and exercise at the same time in the same order every day—have organized their own time at home, and can change it if they will. Moreover, even for such paragons of organization, the temporal boundaries of activities "at home" tend to be informally, not formally or technically, marked. No one punches a clock when he sits down at his desk at home, or signs an attendance sheet. These conditions for time "at home" define the situation, not only for "single" households, but for shared households as well. You and your husband or wife may agree to arise at seven, set limits on who will use the bathroom when and for how long, breakfast no later than eight, and leave by nine to drive to your in-laws. She may decide that your usual two hours with the Sunday paper have to be postponed until the lawn has been mowed; or he that your morning's work in the study has to be interrupted to pick up the laundry. But such arrangements of time are made by mutual (if sometimes grudging) consent; they are relatively flexible ("Give me another twenty minutes or so"); and they are informally marked (by a tapping foot or exasperated sigh, not a buzzer or bell).

To this point, it has been possible to talk about "home" without distinguishing between two very important conditions of situations—namely, whether they involve solitary individuals or more than one. Indeed, in this respect, "home" is unusual among situations: It neither requires nor excludes the presence of others.

And the conditions of "home" I have thus far discussed—conditions of space, time, objects—do not much vary for individuals or families. But humans are a gregarious species. Most of our situations not only involve but *require* the presence of others in some form or another. And the nature of the "form" in which others are "present" is an important variable in the structure of situations.

Consider a "class," a "meeting" or a "party," for example. These are situations that do not exist in the absence of other persons: There is no such thing as a class, a meeting, or a party of one. It is a defining condition of such situations that at least two people or, in the case of classes and parties, three, must be present. Moreover, to have what we normally call a class, meeting or party, the others must be *fully co-present*. "Co-present" means, here, not merely that one person may observe another, but that all persons in the situation may observe and *be observed by* the others. Co-present persons, in other words, are accessible to each other—and *know* that they are. According to this definition, a television talk-show host is not co-present with his home audience. A person watched by a hidden or unnoticed observer is not co-present with his watcher, even if both are in the same room. Two persons observing one another through a two-way mirror—each seeing but not knowing he is seen by the other—are not co-present, though only a thin sheet of glass stands between them.

The point in making these distinctions is that the different conditions to which they call attention *make* a difference in the way we define our situation and, consequently, in the way we behave. We do not respond the same way, or even feel the same way, when we are alone or unobserved (or think we are) as we do in situations of co-presence.

Similarly, the *extent* to which others are co-present defines situations and shapes our meanings. To be "fully co-present," as I am using the term, means that each person in a situation is accessible to the others through sight, sound, smell and, in particular, touch. Persons accessible to each other only through sound (as in telephone conversations), or only through sight and sound (as in screen-based calls or meetings) are not fully co-present. And this fact accounts for important differences in behavior—a point critical to our understanding of the impact of modern communication technologies on human meaning-making.

Nor is that the end of the matter. Fully co-present persons not only have mutual access to *each other* through the full range of their senses; they also have mutual access, in theory at least, to almost the same sensory environment. Each can see (though it may require a turn of the head) what the other sees, hear what the other hears, feel what the other feels (e.g., the temperature of the air), smell what the other smells. Of course, even fully co-present persons are subject to certain limitations with respect to sensory information. We cannot see our own faces while we are talking to others (except in unusual circumstances), and people vary in the acuity of their senses of sight, sound, and smell. But the slight variations in access to sensory information do not, generally speaking, alter the conditions of a situation significantly. Major variations do. Imagine, for example, a board meeting at which ten people are present. Nine of them can hear only what is spoken aloud in the room. The tenth wears a micro-receiver in his ear, through which he receives information and instructions from outside the room. This is a very different situation indeed from one of full co-presence, in which all have access to the same information within the temporal and spatial boundaries of the meeting.

Consider, as another example, dress. If I live alone, I may dress, or not dress, as I please. And I may enter any number of different situations *at* home—cooking, writing, cleaning, reading—in an unlimited variety of outfits: prepare dinner in a formal evening gown, do the bills in my underwear, go to sleep in my street clothes, watch television without a stitch on. So long as my situation does not involve the co-presence of others—that is, so long as others do not have access to me—dress is not a significant condition in defining situations.

Nor are several other variables—all of which may be grouped under the heading "personal demeanor." Makeup, for example, or the state of one's hair, one's beard—even variations in personal cleanliness—these do not make a difference in the definition of a situation, so long as one is inaccessible to others (or believes himself to be). Neither does carriage—how one holds one's body, arranges one's face, moves through space. Or, for that matter, relations with one's own person—how and where one touches oneself. Even such matters as handling objects—how one eats, for example—do not significantly alter a situation if one is alone and inaccessible. Working alone at home, I may slouch or sprawl at my desk, stare vacuously into space, wander idly about the room, scratch noisily wherever I itch, slurp my coffee, drink milk out of the carton and leave it where it stands. And it doesn't make a difference in telling me where I am.

Not so at a party. Or in a classroom. Or any number of situations marked by the co-presence of others. In co-present situations, dress and personal demeanor *are* significant in defining where one is and shaping meaning. We know we are in a fine restaurant, not a fast food shop, not only because space, time, and objects are arranged differently, but also because people are dressed in a certain way, move in a certain way, handle themselves and objects in a certain way. If you enter a restaurant to find people dressed in jeans and sandals, women with their hair in curlers, parents calling in strident tones to children running about the room, men eating, standing as well as sitting, and wiping their fingers on their shirts, you do not expect to pay (barring an accelerated rate of inflation) $12.95 for your hamburger and french fries—though they may be every bit as good as the *bifteck haché et pommes frites* at the French restaurant down the street. Neither do you expect to linger for an hour in quiet conversation over your coffee and dessert, nor to find a 50¢ tip greeted with outraged indignation. In these and countless other matters small and large, dress and personal demeanor structure your expectations and responses—your meanings—in situations where others are present.

So, too, does the use of language—not only speech, but writing, print, and the "languages" of gesture and touch. Who says what to whom, through what symbol systems, gives us important information about our situations. But just as important is *how* and *when* things are said—in what tone of voice, with what displays of feeling, with what accompanying gestures, and in what order. Suppose I were to show you a photograph of a scene in which twenty people—men and women of roughly the same age—are seated around a set of four tables arranged in a square. They are informally but not casually dressed, and have an assortment of papers in front of them and a pen in, or near to, hand. Their posture is relaxed, but each person is self-contained, drawn up fairly close to the table, and no one is touching anyone else. Their faces are serious—neither grim nor suffused with feeling, but attentive—and most eyes are turned, at the moment, to a woman halfway down the left-hand table. What would you make of this situation? Most likely, that it is a meeting of some kind—certainly not a party or purely social gathering, and probably not a therapy group. But what kind of meeting would be hard to say. Perhaps you notice, though, that there is somewhat more space around a man at one end of the table than between the others; moreover, the woman toward whom most people are looking is looking at him—as are some others. If so, you may suspect that the man so singled out—call him "M"—has a somewhat different role in the situation from the others. Perhaps this is an interview, and he is the candidate; or a hearing, and he is a witness or someone called to answer charges.

But now let us suppose I switch from photograph to silent film. You see M give a slight negative shake of his head in response to the woman addressing him, get up casually from his seat, and pace slowly back and forth at the end of the table, apparently talking. He pauses occasionally to gesture with a slightly raised index finger, and when he does, many of the others begin to write on the papers in front of them. As his eyes sweep the group during a fractional pause in his talking, two people tentatively raise their right hands, but he gives a barely perceptible shake of the head and keeps on; they lower their hands. At this point you would recognize, at the least, that this is not an interview or a hearing; that M is not answering charges by the group, but is in charge of it. In part, you would know this from his use of space and gesture, but more important, from the observation that he regulates the symbolic behavior of the others—their speech and writing. You might also guess, from the observation that they write when he speaks, but he does not write when they speak, that this is not a situation where information is being exchanged among equals; that M is providing information or instruction to the others.

Suppose, now, that the camera pulls back a bit, to reveal a chalkboard behind M's place at the table. On it is a list of some sort. Still talking, M moves to the board, takes a piece of chalk, and points to each item on the list in sequence, occasionally underscoring a word. The others divide their attention between the chalkboard and their writing. M puts down the chalk, turns to the others, stops talking, lifts his chin, raises his eyebrows slightly, and sweeps the group with his eyes. Several hands go up. He acknowledges one with a slight nod, and the person speaks briefly. When he stops, M speaks for a moment, then nods to another person, and the sequence is repeated. Finally, M erases the chalkboard, writes on it "30 minutes" in large letters, and distributes a stack of printed papers to the group. At his gesture, they clear away the other papers in front of them. M speaks once more, looks at his watch, and sits down at his place. Each of the others begins to write on the paper in front of him, but two lean toward each other and exchange some words. M looks up, taps the table, and when they look at him, gives a slight shake of his head. The two move apart, fall silent, and begin writing.

At this point, you would have no difficulty identifying the situation you have witnessed as a "class." Moreover, you would be able to specify three somewhat different situations within the class: a lecture (with questions), a brief question-and-answer period, and a test. You most certainly know who the instructor is, and who the students are. And you can predict with some certainty the nature of the transactions you would observe if the film ran to the end. You can even make some fairly good predictions about the thoughts and feelings of the students and instructor at different moments. Yet you know nothing, apart from the words "30 minutes," about the *content* of the "messages" exchanged here. Your understanding of, your predictions about, your meanings for these events is based, not on their content, but on their structure: who engages whom, and when, and in what order; who uses that space, and how; who organizes the use of time; who regulates the exchange of verbal and nonverbal "messages," and in what patterns; what symbols systems are used—speech, gesture, handwriting, print—and by whom; to whom those symbols systems are accessible. In situations of co-presence, these are the conditions that tell us where we are, and who we are, and who are the others around us.

This is not to say that the content is irrelevant in shaping our meanings. In the first place, the structure of a situation is revealed through its content—just as space is made "visible" through the arrangement of objects within and around it. And humans do not, after all, merely jibber random noises at each other in patterned bursts. It is the "content"—the publicly shared denotation—of symbols that allows us to determine, *within* a recognizable situation which object is wanted, for example, when someone says, "May I borrow your pen," or what response is expected when someone says, "Please open the window." In this sense, content allows us to make a finer set of predictions and responses within a situation whose meanings are already clear. If the camera in our imaginary classroom had zoomed in on the chalkboard to show the words "ego," "id," and "superego," for example, we would know not only that this is a class, but it is a class in psychology. And we could more accurately predict what other kinds of words the instructor and students will use, what kinds of questions they will probably ask, what they are likely to be writing about on their tests.

But content takes on specific meaning—that is, determines a particular set of responses and predictions—only within the structure of a given situation. What you make of "Please open the window" depends on where you are: addressed to you by the instructor in a classroom where all have equal access to the windows, it means one thing; by a stranger in a closed elevator, another thing; by a shabbily dressed man outside your car as you wait for a light, something else entirely. And if this is true for words, which do have publicly agreed upon denotations, it is even more true for nonverbal forms of behavioral "content," which do not. A smile, a touch on the arm, a wink of the eye—what do they mean? Outside of a specific context, a structured situation, it is impossible to say. In this sense, the "content" of messages is always subordinate, in human meaning-making, to the structure of situations. This is what Stanley Milgram means when he says, in another context, that "relationship overwhelms content"; what Erving Goffman means when he writes, of human communication, that its first priority is to "establish and maintain a definition of the situation"; what Marshall McLuhan means when he says "The medium is the message."

The structure of a situation, then, is a set of conditions that shapes the responses of people to specific events, objects, behaviors within it—to its content, if you will. And these conditions, the variables that define a situation and make a difference in response, involve

- space—its boundaries and internal arrangements
- objects—their type and arrangement in space
- time—its boundaries and organization
- access—to other persons, to space, to objects, to sensory information
- dress and personal demeanor, and
- transactional patterns—who says what to whom, through what symbols system, and how, and when, and under what conditions.

You will notice that I have not included here two characteristics of situations that common sense (not to mention the teachings of sociology and psychology) tells us ought to be mentioned—namely, roles and purposes. Indeed, no analysis of situations can be complete without reference to these two factors.

The notion of a "situation" rests on the concept of *order*—a pattern or arrangement of some elements that is different in some way from other patterns or arrangements. If situations were not ordered then we would not be able to tell the difference between one and another, because there would *be* no difference. They would all be the same. And human life would be chaos—which is to say, no life at all. Just the idea of a situation implies order—and order differentiation of parts. It makes no sense to talk of *arrangements* of elements if one cannot distinguish one element from another, if they are all one and the same. There would be no order in the universe, for example, if there were no difference between electrons, neutrons and protons, between hydrogen atoms and oxygen atoms. If they were all undifferentiated, all one, all the very same, they would not interact or combine in different patterns—for interaction and combination require that things be separable, differentiated from each other. It is the differentiation of parts that makes the universe run.

And it is the differentiation of parts that makes human situations run. You cannot have a "class" without some differentiation between "teacher" and "students." You cannot have a "play" without some differentiation between "actors" and "audience," a radio call-in show without a "host," "callers." and "listeners." Part of the definition of a situation is how many different parts it requires. This is *not* the same as how many people a situation requires, for a single person may play many different parts in the same situation at different moments ("fielders" are also "batters," remember), and many people may play the same part (e.g., wedding guests).

You will have realized by now, of course, that I am using the word "part" here as a synonym for "role." And by a "part" or a "role," I mean a pattern of behavior that differs in identifiable ways from other patterns of behavior in the situation, no matter who is performing it. To put it somewhat differently, a role refers to those aspects of behavior that remain the same in a given situation, irrespective of the personalities of the individuals enacting the role. Take, for example, the role of "pitcher" in a baseball game. Pitchers vary widely as individuals, of course—that's what makes a ballgame. But whether a pitcher kicks high or low, takes a long stride or short, talks to the ball or not, there are certain things he *must* do that distinguish him from, say, a third baseman. Occupy a certain space at a certain time, for example. Throw the ball to the catcher when there's a batter in the box. Take the ball back from the catcher when it's thrown or brought to him. Perhaps more important, there are things he must *not* do if he is in the role of pitcher. Throw the ball straight in the air and catch it while a batter's up. Run around the bases when the batter hits the ball. And so on.

In this example, I am using the word "role" to refer, not to a differentiated pattern of behavior within a *specific* situation—that is, a particular ballgame—but to a more generalized pattern of behavior in many different instances of a situation. When we talk about the role of "pitcher" in the situation "ballgame," in the *abstract* sense, we are talking about the respects in which thousands of different individuals, in hundreds of thousands of different instances of ballgames, behave alike—and differently from others in that class of situations. And this is the sense in which we use the word "role" when we talk about the roles of teachers and students in classrooms, of mothers and fathers in families, of doctors, nurses and patients in hospitals. In fact, to *label* a role—he's a doctor, a patient, a teacher, a lawyer, a student—is to say that this person behaves in certain respects like many other persons in similar situations, and differently from others in those situations.

But we can also use the word "role" at a lower level of abstraction to refer to differentiated patterns of behavior within a specific situation. Suppose you were to observe, unseen, a situation quite unfamiliar to you. Six adults sit around a table in a small, closed room. You cannot quite make out what they are saying, but you observe that five of them seem to direct most of their attention and talk to the sixth. Most of what they say takes the form of questions. The sixth responds, but never initiates a question himself. While he is speaking, it frequently happens that one of the five interrupts him. On these occasions, he sometimes displays confusion, but never irritation or annoyance. Sometimes the five speak among themselves, in apparently lively discussion. When this happens, the sixth never interrupts—nor does he ever interrupt when any of the five speaks to him. From time to time, one of the five—always the same person—redirects the attention of the other four to the sixth, and it is this person to whom the other four signal when they want to ask another question.

What can you say about this situation? Probably not much, given such scant information. Perhaps only that it's some sort of meeting involving six people—five rude and one polite. But you could also say that this is a situation involving three different roles: *A*—which consists of speaking when spoken to, answering questions, and controlling any demonstration of hostile feeling toward the others; *B*—which consists largely of asking questions of *A* and exchanging remarks informally with all others *except A*; and *C*—which consists of asking questions of *A*, exchanging remarks informally with *B*s, *and* of monitoring the use of time and the order of transactions between *A* and *B*s and among *B*s. You could also say that, in this situation, roles are *fixed*, not flexible; that is, the three roles are identified with specific persons, rather than shifting from person to person: *A* does not at any time shift to a *B* role, or *B*s to *A* or *C*, or *C* to *A*. These two aspects of a situation—how many different parts or roles it consists of and whether those roles are fixed or flexible—we may call its *role structure*. And variations in role structure do make a difference in the meanings we make in different situations.

There are three points I want to stress here about roles, for they are too easily overlooked or forgotten. The first is that one cannot talk about roles without talking about relationships. A role is not just a set of behaviors, but a set of behaviors in relationship to others. It is not possible to describe the role of "pitcher," for example, apart from his transactions with a "catcher" and a "batter," or the role of a "teacher" apart from his transactions with "students." Even when roles do not bear familiar labels, they are defined in terms of relationships with others. In the hypothetical situation described a few pages back, for example, the role of *A* is defined by his transactions with *B*s and theirs by their transactions with *A* and *C*. This does not mean, however, that a role is defined *exclusively* through interpersonal transactions. It is also defined through such behavior as one's use of space, relative to others; one's use of time, relative to others; one's access to objects, relative to others; even one's dress and personal demeanor, relative to others. But here too, the key point is that a role is defined as behavior *relative* to that of others in a situation.

The sentence you just read, stressed differently, is also the second point to remember: A role is defined as *behavior* relative to that of others. Not what people wish, or intend, or hope to accomplish, but how they *act*. A "doctor," for example, is not merely someone whose purpose it is to cure the sick, but someone who uses a certain vocabulary, handles certain objects in particular ways, occupies certain spaces at certain times, engages in certain kinds of transactions with others. That's how we know he's a doctor. In our culture, of course, "doctors" must also have engaged in certain transactions in particular contexts in the past—that is, must have acquired their vocabulary and skills in handling objects and persons in the situation we call "medical school"—and the state must certify those earlier transactions. It is only in this sense that Ferdinand Demara, "The Great Imposter," was not "really" a doctor. In his short-lived practice of medicine, he enacted the role of a doctor with a competence that apparently made him indistinguishable from others in that role. His undoing lay in the discovery that his *past* experience did not include the roles "medical student" and "applicant for a license to practice medicine." On the principle that role is defined by behavior, was Ferdinand Demara a doctor? Yes. Was he licensed to practice medicine? No. Joe Burns completed medical school, was awarded an M.D., and successfully applied for a license to practice medicine. He does not see patients or prescribe medications; does not read or write medical books or articles; does not study disease; does not associate with doctors, teachers of doctors, or medical scientists; never enters a hospital, clinic, or laboratory. He sells real estate. Is he licensed to practice medicine? Yes. Is he a doctor? In any sensible use of the word, no.

Roles, then, are *relative*—based on relationships with others. And they are *behaviorally* defined. Given these two points, you may find the third something of a contradiction. It is this: Even when we are alone and not observably "behaving" at all, we are engaged in roles. Just now, for example, I am in my role as writer. I am not engaged in transactions with *present* others, it is true. But I have a fairly clear image of others—of you—in mind as I write, and that image shapes my behavior. I strike out one word and use another because, in my imagination, you frown in puzzlement. I add three sentences because, in my mind, I hear you say "I don't see how that follows." Of course, my image of you is not entirely accurate. It cannot be, since it is an abstraction—a generalization based on my experiences with real others whom I imagine you to be like. And it is also a projection—of what I am like when I read. To write, then, is to engage in a kind of internalized dialogue, between one part of myself and another—the "other" composed of my own experiences in a different role plus a generalization about the experiences of imagined others outside myself. Writing, in other words, is a transaction, a situation in which one "plays a part" to oneself, or to an imagined other.

And so it is with countless other activities that we perform in private. In cooking, for example, there is one part of the self who beats the eggs, adds the spices, sifts the flour; and "another" who tastes, criticizes, adjusts. In arranging the furniture, there is one who drags the chairs here and there, moves the plants, adjusts a picture; and "another" who looks on, judges the balance, approves. Even when we are "just thinking," we are engaged in internalized dialogues: "I think I'll get some ice cream." "Better not, it's bad for your teeth." "But I haven't had any all week." "Yeah, but what about the diet?"

Sometimes the "others" with whom we transact internally are clearly imagined, *specific* others—as when we rehearse the stunning one-liner with which we tell off the boss. Sometimes they are less specific others, but still an identifiable group—the readers I have in mind as I write, for example, or the nightclub patrons you may have in mind as you dress. And sometimes the non-present others for whom we enact our roles are so abstract, so non-identifiable, that we do not consciously recognize their voices and faces at all. This—the unseen speaker and audience buried in the deepest part of the self, with whom we transact even when we are most alone—is what George Herbert Mead called "the generalized other": an abstraction of all the specific others with whom we have transacted since childhood. In a word, society—internalized. This is the other for whom I clean my house, even when guests are not expected; for whom I don clothes, even though I am alone.

Just as our behavior with co-present others follows certain patterns, so does our behavior relative to internalized or imagined others—although "behavior" here does not necessarily refer to observable action. In my role as writer, for example, I *think*—that is, use language to myself—in certain ways and not others. I make plans—that is, picture myself doing certain things, with certain objects (e.g., paper and pen), at certain times—that are different from the plans I make in my role as "cook" or "house-cleaner." I transact in imagination with people who behave in a particular way relative to my behavior—who ask certain kinds of questions, display certain kinds of affect, give certain kinds of responses. None of this activity—thinking, planning, visualizing—would be observable to others. But it is a form of behavior nonetheless.

From birth—indeed, practically from conception—humans are engaged in relationships with others. And so compelling are those relationships, so essential to our survival, that they are the primary fact of the human experience—the model on which all behavior, public and private, is based. In this sense, "private" behavior—*intra*personal behavior—is a metaphor for social behavior. We act to ourselves "as if" to others. And this means, in part, that the same variables that shape our meaning-responses in social situations shape our meaning-responses when we are alone. I said earlier that such conditions of situations as dress, demeanor and the use of symbols do not make a difference in our responses unless we are in the presence of others. But that is not quite true. So powerful is the metaphor of social behavior in shaping private behavior that we use symbols, demeanor, and dress to signal to *ourselves* what roles we are engaged in—who we are in relation to others—even when we are alone. This is why I do not write by candlelight, to soft music, in a filmy negligee, with a glass of wine close to hand. Not because it would be inconvenient or uncomfortable. I do not dress and arrange my environment that way because to do so would summon up in me, on the basis of social metaphor, a set of feelings and expectations, a line of thought, an image of transactions quite different from those I want to characterize my relationship with you. And it is for a similar reason that I do not tear my meat with my hands, throw chicken bones on the floor, go unwashed or wear the same clothes for weeks at a time, even if there is no one to see me. To do so would signal a different relationship with my culture; it would violate my sense of *who I am* in relationship to others in my society.

I realize that I am very close to saying here that feelings follow from behavior, not behavior from feelings. Indeed, that has been the whole point of this chapter thus far: that the structure of situations—their arrangements of space, time, objects, dress, demeanor, transactions, and role structure—determines our expectations, meanings and feelings. And to a much larger extent than we typically realize, that, I believe, is the case.

But is it the whole case? Do human will, intention, and *purpose* play no significant role in meaning-making and response? Are we nothing but the creatures of our situations?

We are not. Unfortunately, some might say. Because the world would be much neater if we were. And certainly the study of human communication would be simpler, if we could construct a totally deterministic model, a precise formula that says, "When variables A, B, and C in a situation take the form X, Y, and Z, then people will inevitably behave in ways 1, 2, and 3." Apparently, the longing for such a model, the wish for a formula that would reduce the complexities of human experience to letters and numbers and equations, is deeply rooted and widespread. Why that should be so, why so many people should so devoutly aspire to the ultimate proof that humans are, after all, only complicated machines, is something of a mystery to me. Perhaps it is a symptom of the desperate need for order and certainty in a time of overwhelming cultural change. In any case, you will find plenty of books—in psychology, sociology, communication—dedicated to that end, and filled with wonderfully assured assertions that, if X happens, Y must follow, as inevitably as the night the day. But this is not one of them.

It does seem clear to me, as I have said, that human meaning-making and response, feeling and behavior, are conditioned by the structure of situations. And most of this book is devoted to the exploration, specifications, and implications of that idea. But what seems just as clear and undeniable is the fact that people do *override* their situations. Teachers have screamed and wept in classrooms. Students have attacked their professors at doctoral orals. Mourners have laughed at funerals. And some writers, I am told, do their most elegant and profound writing in the bathtub. Moreover, people have *changed* their situations—deliberately redefined their conditions of time, space, access, and so on. These two facts—that people override situations and that situations change—cannot be accounted for in a model of communication that says meaning is the direct result of the structure of situations. And of course it is not. Meaning is the *product* of a situation and a meaning-maker.

There are two characteristics of meaning-makers that make the construction of a determinist model of communication forever impossible. The first is that every person has a set of past experiences—with others and with time, space, objects, and symbols—that is unique to him. And since meanings are predictions based on generalizations from past experience, no two persons will make quite the same meanings in the "same" situation. Second, people have needs. Not only physiological needs—for shelter, food and drink, motor activity, rest—but psychological needs as well: needs for affiliation, for continuity, and for change. Since humans are fallible, the social arrangements they have constructed over the centuries for the satisfaction of their needs are always less than perfect. As a consequence, we experience frustration—problems in the satisfaction of our needs. And these problems lead us to engage continuously in tinkering with our social arrangements, in modifying, adjusting, changing the structure of our situations. All this is another way of saying that people do have purposes. And purposes do, on occasion, override the structure of situations, making it impossible ever to say with certainty, "Given these conditions, here is the behavior that will result."

Still, for all that people are unique as meaning-makers and differ in their needs and purposes, there is an astonishing consistency in human behavior. The key to that consistency lies, I think, in the fact that, of all human needs, the need for order, for a predictable continuity in life, is the most urgent. So essential is continuity to human survival that we are, in effect, physiologically "programmed" to perceive it (or create it), through the capacity of the brain to abstract from experiences what is similar among them and to ignore the infinite variations that make each instant in time unique. Without that capacity, we would not be able to speak or to understand language, to "recognize" objects or persons, to communicate or cooperate with others. We would not, in fact, be able to survive at all.

The same need for continuity, for predictable pattern, that is reflected in the functioning of the human mind shows up, in social behavior, as an inherent conservatism. Not, of course, in the political sense, but in the sense that, in social affairs (which is to say, human affairs), consistency and pattern take priority over variability and too-rapid change. If it were not so, we should not be able to speak of "social order," of "culture," at all. For social order implies the subjugation of some individual purposes and needs to the greater good of maintaining a predictable continuity in life, without which none of us, as individuals, would survive.

To study the structure of situations, then, is to study the consistencies in human meaning-making and response. It is to abstract from all the variability of human experience and behavior those factors that seem to be present in all situations, and to see how differences in these factors seem to affect human expectations and response. The end to which we engage in such studies is not, of course, to learn what a "coffee shop" is, or a "library," or a "classroom." That we already know. It is, instead, to learn what leads people to respond one way in one classroom or library or coffee shop and differently in another. And just as important, what leads people in apparently very different situations—like locker rooms and bus terminals, or airplanes and professional conferences—to behave in some respects similarly. Increasing our understanding of these matters will not enable us ever to predict with certainty what conditions will produce exactly which response in a given group of participants. But it should give us greater insight into the variables that shape our meanings. And it may help us to know a little better where to tinker when our situations are frustrating the purposes we have in mind. As legitimate ends to inquiry, those, I think, should suffice.

Chapter 3: Exploring Space

Of all the factors that shape human meaning and response, that define situations, that tell us who and what we are, none is more compelling than space. Space is the universal backdrop against which the drama of life is enacted, the pervasive ground that shapes and makes visible the figures of human experience. Like any ground, and especially one so pervasive, space tends to disappear from our conscious awareness, to become invisible to us. But its very invisibility gives it the greatest power in shaping our behavior. And indeed, there is no aspect of human behavior that is not grounded in space. We define ourselves in terms of shared literal spaces: I'm an American, a New Yorker, an East Sider. We describe our relationships with others—"close" friends and "distant" relatives—in spatial metaphors. We cannot speak more than a few words without a buried reference to space, for our language is built on a spatial conception of experience: position, place, situation, extent, focus, progress—all of these rely on an image of space and of movement through it. We talk of events as though they occurred in space—*down* through the ages, *up* through history, *across* the years—and of our own psychological "positions" in spatial terms: we're "up" on ecology, "down" on nuclear plants, "out on a limb," "in on a secret."

We measure time by the movement of objects through space, and we mark it off in little black squares lined up in rows across and down our calendars. We even give such abstract notions as "the past" and "the future" spatial existence: If I ask you to show me, on a line, where "yesterday" is, you'll point to the left; for "tomorrow" to the right. If you are a speaker of American Sign Language, you'll indicate "past" by a gesture to the space behind you, "future" by a gesture to the space ahead.

Consciousness itself, or at least that form of consciousness that distinguishes humans from our fellow creatures, has its origins in space. What it means to be conscious, says Julian Jaynes (1976), is to narratize the actions of an "analogue I" in a "metaphorical space"—which most of us locate somewhere just behind our eyes. Even our definition of life is tied up with the movement of things in space: Those which perceptibly move of their own power through space—like plants and animals and microscopic organisms—we call animate; those which do not—like rocks and ice cubes and bricks—we consign to the world of lifeless things.

It is not surprising, then, that space should play a dominant role in human social experience. And, of course, it does. It is space—how it is bounded and who has access to it—that tells us in large measure how we are to behave and how others may be expected to behave in a situation. It is space that tells us what is the relative status and power of different persons within a situation, and space that reveals how people in a situation are, to use Erving Goffman's term, "teamed." The space between persons shapes our feelings—of allegiance, intimacy, solidarity, security, hostility, even our sense of humor—and the orientation of a people in space structures the kinds of transactions they are likely to have. Space even tells us what the purposes to be accomplished in situations are, and what attitudes or "mind sets" are appropriate. It is for these reasons that Edward Hall—who, more than any other contemporary writer, has brought space to the conscious attention of students of communication—calls space and its uses a "primary message system" of culture. As an anthropologist, Hall is concerned primarily with differences between cultures in their conception and uses of space. Here, however, I am concerned primarily with the uses and effects on meaning of space in a single culture—our own. But perhaps I should start where Hall does, with some attention to that aspect of space and behavior referred to by the word "territoriality."

Territoriality may be defined, roughly, as the set of rules that governs how members of a species divide up and share the space available to them, and the behavior through which they lay claim to and defend a space. In animals, those rules are based in the biological requirements of the species—how much food they require, and of what kind, and how they acquire it; how often they mate; and how they raise their young ones. So important are such rules to the survival of the species that they are encoded and transmitted genetically. Indeed, one might say that territoriality in animals is the mechanism through which the genes of a species ensure their own propagation and survival. If there were no such mechanism—nothing to trigger competition for food and adequate space in which to find it, nothing to trigger defense against the assaults of others on the person and, by extension, the space of animals, nothing to limit the access of others to females—the species would soon weaken and disappear, and along with it, the genetic material which it is the mission of species to propagate. However one looks at it—from the point of view of the species or of the genes it carries—territoriality is essential to survival, and the rules that govern it are programmed into the very stuff of life. That is why there is relatively little variation, within a single species of animal, in territorial behavior.

Not so in humans. Although *homo sapiens* is a single species, different groups—different cultures—vary widely in their uses of space. Not just in what Hall calls "personal distance"—the invisible "bubble" that each of us regards as our sovereign air space (although differences in the size of these bubbles are perhaps the most noticeable of cultural variations in the use of space)—but in how they mark the spatial boundaries of situations, how they grant and deny access to different spaces, how they arrange persons and objects in space. Humans vary in their use of space because, unlike animals, we are not dependent for our survival on a fixed set of relationships with our natural environment. Through our ability to use tools and symbols—that is, to think, to pass on the results of our thinking to future generations, and to convert our ideas into technologies—we have been able to free ourselves, over the millennia, from many of the constraints of physiology and environment. If some foods are not plentiful in the spaces we inhabit, we can grow or import or manufacture others. If our teeth cannot grind what is available, or our stomachs cannot digest it, we can invent machines to grind for us, and chemicals to do the work our stomachs cannot. We can even control, through thinking and technology, our reproductive behavior and, consequently, the size of the population that inhabits a given space. Of course, there are limits to the extent to which we can modify ourselves and our relationship with the natural environment without creating a host of physiological, psychological and social disorders. Just what those limits are, it is not yet possible to say, although students in a variety of new fields—environmental ecology, evolutionary psychology, genetic research—are trying hard to find out. But in the oldest, deepest and in some respects most powerful part of ourselves, each of us still carries the experiences—the genetically coded survival "programs"—of our animal ancestors, and there are some cultural variations in behavior, it would seem, to which those programs say "No."

So it may be with territoriality. Cultural variation in the use of space gives evidence that the "territorial imperative" in humans has weakened as we have loosened our dependence for survival on the natural environment. At least, it has become more diffuse, in the sense that, as a species, we do not observe one fixed set of genetically transmitted rules for the use of space. Instead, we learn some variation on those rules from our particular culture. Not formally, of course. No one says to the child, "When you wish to be intimate with someone, stand less than eighteen inches away," or "To show your dominance in a situation, occupy more space than the others around you." We learn the meanings of space and behavior in space informally—through observation, imitation and transactions with others. But as recent studies of neonates reveal, these learnings are among the earliest and most profound we engage in. Consequently, they are buried in those parts of ourselves least accessible to consciousness and self-modification. Even when we become conscious of our culture's rules for spatial meanings, even when we "know" that cultures vary in those rules and meanings, we are usually powerless to change our deep-seated feeling responses to behavior in space.

For example: I am an inveterate beach-goer. Along with several million other New Yorkers, I trek on summer Sundays to Jones Beach where, like most of them,

I seek the spot farthest removed from the nearest others, spread my towel tidily in the center of my space, mark its perimeters with my belongings—beach bag, sneakers, Sunday *Times*—and settle down in that tiny island of privacy that, for New Yorkers, passes for solitude. And surprisingly enough, so long as I am surrounded by people adhering to exactly the same rule for the use of space—namely, that in public places shared by strangers, one must maximize the distance between oneself and every other within the space available—I do feel relaxed, private, alone. But New York is a city of diverse ethnic composition, and Jones Beach is accessible to all. So it sometimes happens that a person or group from a different culture—with a different set of rules for space—will spread their towels just next to mine. It is not because they are too close to me, in terms of some fixed distance, that I begin to feel itchingly uneasy. The rule for space here is not that simple. Rather, it is that my new neighbors have not established *equal* distance from me and from the surrounding others *in the space available*; they are relatively closer to me than to others, and I am now closer to them than to my nearest neighbor on the other side. This situation inevitably provokes in me a ferocious battle. I regard myself as fairly sophisticated in my understanding of space and culture. I know that my feelings of uneasiness, tension, resentment are nothing more than conditioned responses to a particular set of learned rules for the use of space. I *will* myself to break that conditioning—to remain relaxed and comfortable where I am, not to move. But the tension grows unbearable, and in the end, the struggle never seems worth the effort. Sooner or later, with a feeling something akin to shame, I get up and move my towel—perhaps only an inch or two to the left or right, just far enough to equalize my distance from others on all sides. And once again I feel, among a million others, alone.

The point is that, though territoriality may be more diffuse in humans than in other species, learned and not genetically programmed, it is there nonetheless. And it is a powerful determinant of feelings and response, not only between cultures, but within different situations in the same culture. Consider, for example, some of the differences in feeling and response we experience in three different types of spaces in our own culture: "public" space, "semi-public" space, and "private" space. There are two related factors that distinguish these spaces, or situations, from each other. The first is who may have access to a space, and the second is the conditions under which access may be obtained. A "public" space is a space to which any and all members of a community have access; there are no conditions which one must meet to gain access to it. To put it somewhat differently, a public space is a space in which no individual may control the entry, exit, or behavior of others. Those controls on behavior "in public" that do exist are exerted through only two channels: by the state and its representatives and by the internalized set of shared social rules—norms—that regulate behavior from within the individual. The state, of course, regulates public behavior through its laws and the agents delegated to enforce them. It may determine, for example, when pedestrians may enter public roadways, where and when cars may turn left or right, how fast they may travel. The state may even regulate certain aspects of personal and interpersonal behavior in public space. It may require, for example, that people entering public space be clothed, conduct themselves with a certain measure of sobriety, refrain from forceful physical contact with one another.

But far more powerful, pervasive and rigid than the controls exercised by the state are the internalized social norms that regulate behavior in public. There are no "laws" to govern how one must hold one's body or compose one's face in public, or how long one may look into another's eyes, or what is the permissible speed and angle from which one may approach another from behind. Yet such rules do exist, and they—not public law—are the primary device for creating and maintaining order in public spaces. For public spaces, because they are accessible to all, are spaces shared by strangers. And the only thing that makes strangers predictable to us is their assumed agreement to a "social contract"—a contract that commits them (and ourselves) to repress individual impulses, to follow, not the dictates of the heart, but a set of common behavioral rules. Were it not for such a "contract," public space would be, not "any man's land," but "no man's land"—a space rendered intolerable by our vulnerability to all comers.

It is our vulnerability to strangers in public that makes the unwritten rules for behavior more rigid there than in semi-private or private space. The slightest deviation—a glance held a second too long on a streetcar, a stranger an inch too close behind on a subway platform—makes us uneasy. And for good reason. If a stranger cannot be relied upon in these ways to observe the unwritten rules of the social contract, then in what other unpredictable ways might impulse break through the veneer of civility to threaten our well-being?

Public space, then—space to which access by others is outside individual control, and not limited by any conditions of entry—is space that gives rise in us to a relatively high degree of tension. We are not normally *aware* of our tension in public space, but it is part of what makes us tired after such non-strenuous activities as shopping or riding the subways, part of what makes us sigh with relief when we get home. And it comes from two sources: the requirement to maintain rigid controls on our own behavior in public—to repress impulse and its expression—and the need to maintain both a heightened alertness to the behavior of others and a readiness to "fight or flee" when strangers break the rules of the social contract. And those rules are stringent indeed—escalating in importance as the number of strangers in a given space increases. Among them, for example, are such rules for behavior in space as the mandate to maximize the distance between yourself and others in the space available; to minimize the physical access of others to your own person (this is the rule that makes us prefer, in public spaces, corner positions, aisle or window seats, walls at our backs); to maintain, in closed spaces, clear and speedy access to an escape route (and so we prefer, in subways and buses, corner seats next to the door; in public elevators, corner positions near the buttons and door); to protect, when physical contact is unavoidable, your front (and so we hold briefcases to our chests, cross our arms and legs, hold newspapers before our faces); to avoid intruding parts of yourself into the spaces of others (and so we do not swing our arms or gesture widely in public spaces, do not wander as we walk, or slouch and sprawl when seated); even to avoid intruding such *extensions* of yourself as your eyes, your voice, your breath into another's space (and so we keep our eyes averted, our voices down, breathe through our noses, and turn our heads to cough or clear our throats).

Less easy to articulate, but no less compelling, are such rules for public behavior as the pace at which one walks, the characteristic angle of head and body, the way in which one focuses and moves one's eyes, even the way in which one holds the thousands of muscles that control expression in the face. Like the rules for behavior in space, these more subtle rules vary, not only between cultures, but among different groups within our own culture, depending on the nature of the space and population in which the group is characteristically immersed. New Yorkers, for example, spend a great deal of their time in relatively crowded public spaces. In the course of a given day, the middle-class working man or woman will enter spaces where literally thousands of strangers will have ready access to, if not direct physical contact with, their persons. To minimize contact, the New Yorker learns to maintain a fairly rapid and even walking pace, to incline head and body in the direction of his goal, to travel in a relatively direct line, to carry his body and possessions compactly, to keep his head up and his eyes moving to check on the location of others, and to maintain a closed but alert expression on his face. All of this gives the New Yorker a typical body set in public—a posture, an expression, and a way of moving among strangers so unconscious and engrained that he adopts it automatically *wherever* he enters public space, even when that space is far from his own city and characterized by quite different conditions. It is this body set, as distinctive as speech dialect and as difficult to change, that marks the New Yorker (or any inhabitant of a large and crowded city) as an "outsider" in public settings different from his own—like the rural South, the suburban Midwest, or the uncrowded cities of the West Coast.

And the reverse, of course, is also true: Any New Yorker can spot at once the stranger to the city. It is not so much the difference in dress and the tour map that give the visitor away; it is the purse dangling from hand, the wandering eyes, the looseness of limbs, the vague purposelessness of step that says, more clearly than words, "I'm not on home ground here... I don't know exactly where I am or where I'm going... and I'm not entirely *paying attention*." These messages, subtle as they may be, let the native know that here is someone not quite predictable, not to be relied on for all the terms in the social contract and, for that reason, best avoided. But the same messages also say, "I'm more accessible than others around me, less defended, more open to approach," and every environment has its share of those to whom such an invitation is irresistible. This is one reason why strangers to the city are more subject to annoyance, and to street crime, than are natives. Their behavior in public space unconsciously invites it.

So, too, on occasion, does their lack of knowledge of the meanings of *particular* spaces within the public domain. Just as a city of any size has districts known to its natives for their high concentration of fine restaurants, or theatres, or financial enterprises, so does it have districts known for their high concentration of prostitutes, or pick-pockets, or muggers. The native knows that, if he wants to do business with a jeweler, he should visit, for example, Sixth Avenue and 47th Street between 10 a.m. and 3 p.m. And if he wants to "do business" with a mugger, he should stroll through the Dog Run in Central Park between midnight and 7 a.m. Understandably, city tourist boards do not hand out maps marked "Here There Be Muggers" as guides for the unwary. Even if they wished to do so, the nature of public space would make the design of accurate "maps" impossible. For one of the characteristics of public space is that its boundaries are diffuse and not formally marked. There is no clear-cut line that separates the theatre district from the diamond district or the garment center; no barrier between one neighborhood and the next that permits entry to some and not to others. Such boundaries as there are have arisen out of tradition, are observed by convention, and exist largely in the perceptions of the natives of a place. They are vague, and subject to change over time. Because public space is not clearly bounded and segmented, it is difficult to know exactly what situation one is in at a given moment, whom one is likely to encounter, or what behavior to expect. These, too, are reasons for wariness in public, and for the strict obedience to the unwritten rules for behavior we follow there.

In all these respects, public space is quite unlike the spaces we call "private." In private space, the individual determines who may enter, and under what conditions; how long and under what conditions others may stay. In fully private space, moreover, the conditions of access may be entirely arbitrary. I may decide to deny you access to my home, for example, simply because I do not like your face, or your dress, or your mannerisms. I may ask you to leave because something in your behavior offends me, or threatens me, or simply because I choose to be alone. And I am not compelled to justify the conditions of access I establish to any higher authority. You cannot sue for access to my home on the grounds that I have excluded you on the basis of sex, or race, or religion, or age. It is part of the definition of private space that access to it is discriminatory, and subject to the whim of those to whom the space "belongs."

In private space, in short, we are not compelled to transact with strangers. Of course, we may choose to do so, as when I invite to a party the friends of friends, whom I have never met. But they are there only at my invitation, and may stay only at my sufferance and must leave if I say. Because we may decide who has access to our private spaces, and control the behavior of others within them, we are more relaxed, less wary, freer to give expression to our impulses in private than in public. And the better we know those to whom we make our private spaces accessible—that is, the more predictable they are to us—the less rigid are the rules governing their (and our) behavior. For, to paraphrase an old adage, social rules for behavior are made for the obedience of strangers and the guidance of friends.

The greater one's control over the access of others to one's space, the freer from restraint one may be, and the more impulsively one may act. In this sense, we are least free in public, and least restrained from impulse in those spaces to which we can deny access—with physical barriers like doors and locks. This does not mean that we are most human, or most ourselves, "behind closed doors"—for to be fully human means to be social, not isolated, and our social selves are as "real" as our primitive, impulse-regulated selves. But we do give greatest expression to our most elemental impulses—to the creaturely functions of our bodies and such uncontrolled passions of childhood as rage and ecstasy—in well-bounded spaces to which access by others is denied. It is for this reason that we tend, in public affairs, to regard what goes on "behind closed doors" with some degree of suspicion and mistrust. We know, though we may not be able to articulate it, that behavior in well-shielded spaces is controlled less by social than by individual wants and needs; that closed spaces permit the ascendance of the individual over and against the group, while open spaces subordinate the individual to the group.

Ranged between those most private spaces to which none but ourselves have access and those most public spaces to which any and all have access is a vast continuum of spaces and situations neither fully public nor fully private, but semi-public. These are spaces to which we do not personally control the access of others, but to which access is limited by certain conditions, established jointly by the state and the individuals to whom the space "belongs." A movie theatre is such a space, as is a college, a business office, a museum. How we behave and feel in such spaces depends on their relative position in the continuum between "private" and "public." And that depends on the complexity of the conditions that permit and deny access to strangers. A movie theatre, for example, is a relatively public space. Access to it is limited by only two conditions: One must be able to afford the price of admission and (in some cases) have reached a certain age. Since the price of admission is relatively low, and the age restriction screens out only the very young, access to movie theatres is almost as readily gained by strangers as access to the streets and sidewalks of a city. Consequently, we tend to feel and behave in movies almost as we do in public space: with wariness, restraint and little deviation from the rules for behavior among strangers. A college or university, on the other hand, is a much more "private" semi-public space. Access to it is limited not only by economic conditions—and these, of course, more stringent than those regulating access to movies—but by conditions of residence, age, prior experience of a certain kind, demonstrated skills, competencies and achievements, and goals of a particular sort. We are, in a college or university, still among strangers—in the sense that we may not know personally those with whom we share the space bounded by the gates of the campus. But we are among strangers about whom we know (or think we do) a great deal; they are persons not very different from ourselves. Consequently, they are more predictable to us, less threatening, and we may behave toward them with less wariness and self-restraint. In short, because access to spaces like colleges and universities is relatively stringently regulated, because entry guarantees, so to speak, demonstrated adherence to at least a minimal set of shared rules for behavior, those rules are more flexible, permitting freer expression of one's individuality.

And this we may state as a generalization about space, situations, and behavior: in spaces to which access is highly controlled, which have clearly defined boundaries through which people may pass only under stringent conditions, we tend to behave with less self-imposed personal restraint, greater individuality, less wariness, and more openness to others than in spaces to which access by strangers is easily obtained. Conversely, in easily accessible spaces, whose boundaries are diffuse and observed only by convention, we tend to impose strict restraints on our own behavior, suppress our individuality, and behave with guardedness toward others.

And here is a corollary to those generalizations: The more restricted the access to a space, the greater the feeling of *identity* among those who share it. This is another way of saying that our social definition of ourselves—that is, our sense of group identity and of social role—is very much a function of discriminatory access to space. We recognize this linguistically when we talk of "in" groups and "out" groups—a metaphor which defines group membership in terms of shared access to (and exclusion from) space. And we recognize it symbolically when we incorporate in our rites of passage from one social role to another ceremonies involving doors, thresholds, even steps forward across some invisible boundary line that separates initiates from non-initiates. The word "passage" itself refers to movement from one space to another, and in traditional cultures, where the relationship between space and social role is more firmly fixed than in ours, rites of passage—from boyhood to manhood, or girlhood to womanhood, or single to married status—always center around symbolic admission to restricted spaces. And though the role/space relationship has weakened in our own culture, it has certainly not disappeared.

It is conventional in middle-class homes, for example, to mark the newborn's transition from "extension of the mother" to "aware person in his own right" by moving him out of the parents' room and into a space of his own. We mark a young girl's subtle change in status from "child" to "female" by giving her a room separate from her brother's. The adolescent indicates his new sense of individual identity, of increased autonomy, by closing the door to his room and posting it with "Please Knock!" and "Keep Out" signs. The young man signals his entry into adulthood by leaving his parents' home. Indeed, almost every change in social role that marks the transition from infancy to childhood, childhood to adolescence, adolescence to adulthood is signified by changes in the growing person's access to and control over space. In a sense, to "grow up" means, in our culture, to gain access to spaces previously forbidden, and to increase one's personal control over the access of others to one's own space. To "grow old," unfortunately, often means the opposite—for people of advanced years often find themselves as restricted in their access to space, and as powerless to control the access of others to their own space, as young children. And it is this, in part, that leads us to perceive the elderly as childish.

The social roles linked to age are not the only roles in which access to and control over space play a major part. Sex roles in our culture, too, have traditionally been defined in terms of differentiated access to certain spaces. It was not so many years ago that the maxim, "A woman's place is in the home," accurately defined, spatially, what it meant to be a woman—or at least a respectable woman. It meant, among other things, that one was forbidden access to such exclusively male spaces as business offices, bars, and private clubs—and most certainly to such spaces as pool halls, locker rooms, and sports arenas of all kinds. Similarly, to be a man meant to share such spaces with other males—and to stay out of such traditionally female spaces as kitchens. In recent years, of course, all this has changed. And it is no accident that the earliest, most prominently publicized, and most fiercely fought battles of the women's movement have been battles over access to traditionally male spaces, McSorley's Ale House in New York, for example, and the "gentlemen only" dining rooms of private clubs. Even today, disputes over the access of women to certain spaces—football locker rooms, for example—arouse stronger passions and claim greater national interest and attention than do such seemingly more significant issues as "equal pay for equal work."

So it has been, as well, in every social revolution of the past half century. The civil rights movement of the 1960s began, symbolically, with the occupation by African Americans of such restricted spaces as "Whites only" lunch counters, public toilets, and bus seats. And its most dramatic battle occurred, not surprisingly, on a threshold, when Governor Wallace assumed his famous "stand in the schoolhouse door." The gay rights movement, too, has been intimately tied to demands for freer access to space—a demand codified in the slogan: "Out of the Closet!" Even the student protests of the 1960s centered around territorial issues—who would control access to buildings and administrative offices, whether or not the police should have access to the college campus, etc. In these and countless other cases, we consciously or unconsciously acknowledge that social roles and changes in social roles are tied to access to space.

While increasing one's access to space is a step toward social equality, the achievement of a strong sense of group identity requires something else: the restriction of access by others to the spaces one's group occupies. For to be a member of a particular group means not only to hold certain things in common with a given set of others, but to be unlike those "outside" the group in some respects. That is, our social identities are defined equally by what we are *not* as by what we are. Group membership, in other words, is both inclusive (of those who "belong") and exclusive (of those who do not), and one of the primary means of excluding others—of defining a group—is to deny them access to spaces the group shares. This fact often leads fighters for social equality into paradoxical—and seemingly hypocritical—behavior. On the one hand, they demand freedom of access to the spaces traditionally barred to them by others; on the other, they are compelled, in order to establish a heightened sense of identity and solidarity among members of their own group (without which the drive toward equality would surely fail) to restrict the access of others to spaces they wish to call their own.

I witnessed, recently, an incident in which just this dilemma confronted a group of gay rights leaders at a panel discussion on teaching lesbian literature. Several of the speakers (women all) took the position that male students ought to be barred from college courses on "the female experience in literature." When members of the audience protested that such a step would go contrary, not only to the principle of academic freedom, but to the avowed commitment of the panelists to achieving respect and equality for persons of all sexual preferences, one panelist replied that, if males were admitted, one of the purposes of such courses—namely, to provide women with a heightened sense of their own identity—would be defeated. Moreover, she argued, opening the courses to males—that is, to persons with backgrounds, experiences, and attitudes different from those of women— would compel female students to respond with greater restraint, less openness and honesty, to the materials and topics under discussion. On both points she was, of course, right. But so were the members of the audience who found her arguments hypocritical—especially since the same panelist had begun her talk with a bitter attack on the ways in which females had traditionally been denied access to "male" spaces within the culture generally and academe in particular.

She had argued, on the one hand, that "separate but equal" is, as the Supreme Court has ruled, "inherently unequal"—hence, unjust in matters of sex as in any other matter; and, on the other, that separation was necessary to achieve the ultimate end of equality for her group—hence, in this case, justifiable.

The dilemma is, as I have said, a thorny one, and it has been a major problem in every "liberation" movement of the past three decades. In this case, it was complicated by a more subtle dispute over space and roles that underlay the apparent source of disagreement—namely, whether a university is the sort of space that can legitimately be used to promote feelings of group identity based on sex or sexual preference. Theoretically, of course, it is not—any more than it can be legitimately used to promote feelings of group identity based on race, or age, or wealth, or political, or religious preference. Ideally, a university is a space dedicated to the promotion of only one social role—the role of dispassionate scholar, humanist and scientist. Consequently, the policies and practices governing access to university spaces ought, in theory at least, to exclude only those who are not competent (or interested) in the pursuit and advancement of knowledge. And presumably race, sex, wealth, etc., are not determinants of such competencies and interests. To the extent that, by accident or design, the university excludes anyone from its space on the basis of such characteristics, it promotes among those it admits a sense of social identity different from that it is designed to foster—and thus falls short of its ideal.

Of course, not everyone agrees that the ideal of the university ought to be what I have claimed for it. And even those who accept that ideal are quick to point out that, in practice, American universities (like other cultural institutions) have frequently served to promote among students, through their conditions of access, a sense of group identity based, not on scholarship or disinterested inquiry, but on maleness, or social position, or ethnic heritage. Whether this fact justifies the establishment of new conditions of access—conditions designed to heighten one's sense of female identity, or black identity, or gay identity—is one of the great questions of our age. And not many are willing to settle for the answer offered by the proponent of the "females only" courses. Confronted with the question, "Is it any more politically justifiable for your group to exclude others on the basis of sex than for others to exclude you on the same basis?" she replied, "It depends on whose political ends you support."

In a sense, she was right. Questions of territoriality—one's access to space and one's ability to restrict the access of others—are ultimately, at the cultural level, political questions. For space—who shares it and who is excluded from it—is intimately connected not only with one's sense of social identity, but with one's sense of power. It tells us, not only who we are, but how we stand relative to others in what H. D. Duncan calls "the drama of hierarchy." Nowhere is our tie with our animal ancestors more directly observable than here—in the relation between space and status. In our own culture in particular, displays of dominance and subordination, of superiority and inferiority, are inextricably bound up with access to and control over space. The powerful not only claim more personal space for their own—larger homes, larger offices, larger cars, more land—but have greater access to distant spaces—to the oceans of the world, on yachts and luxury liners, and to its most remote islands, on private helicopters and jet planes—than do those of lesser rank and power. So indelible is the link between space and status in our culture that persons who achieve far-ranging access to space inevitably have conferred upon them a measure of status, respect, even awe that far exceeds what might reasonably be due them on the basis of their achievements. In fact, the attribution of superiority to those who dominate space usually carries over into areas in no way connected to their specific accomplishments and talents.

There is nothing in the training of an astronaut, for example, or in the docking of a spacecraft, or in the taking of measurements on the moon that would prepare him to perform with unusual competence the job of a senator, or a bank president, or a religious leader. But astronauts have had an access to space that the rest of us, no matter how wealthy or talented in other respects, can achieve only in our dreams, and this, by itself, confers on them a power almost mystical in its scope and depth. Something of the same power adheres to all those whose exploits are related to the conquering of space. It is for this reason, I believe, that some of our most popular culture heroes have been pioneers of flight, like the Wright Brothers, Amelia Earhart, Charles Lindbergh, or explorers of uncharted territories, like Admiral Peary and Sir Edmund Hillary. Even among scientists, the most likely to capture public attention and awe are those whose work is tied up with space: Einstein, for example, and more recently such astronomers as Carl Sagan.

Status is conferred not only on individuals and social groups by virtue of their access to and control over space, but also on the built environment. Consider, for example, the offices in a corporation or a university that carry with them the greatest prestige. They are likely to be spacious, located in an outside corner of the building, on a high floor. They have large windows ("with a view") and solid, floor-to-ceiling walls and doors. They probably have heavy draperies and carpeted floors (to control sound), and independently controlled lighting and heating units.

They do not open directly onto "public" corridors, but onto anterooms guarded by private secretaries, who regulate the intrusion into the space not only of people in the flesh, but of such extensions of people as phone calls, letters, and packages. In one way or another, each of these features is related to control over and restriction of access to space. The corner placement, windows, and high floor provide the occupant with an extended command of visual space. The solid walls and doors as well as the secretaries restrict the access of others, their noises, and their messages. The carpeting, draperies, lighting, and heating systems provide for personal control over conditions within the space—the regulation of sound, temperature, light. Such an office, in short, grants its occupant a maximum of territorial control. And so it ranks high in desirability and prestige.

Apartments and apartment buildings are ranked in social value (and the prices they command) on the same basis: The greater the personal command over physical, visual, and acoustic space they provide, and the more barriers to access by others (like 24-hour doormen, elevator operators, visitor identification requirements), the higher on the social and economic scale they rank. Modes of transportation, too, vary in their desirability because of their differences in access to and command of space—a point too lightly treated by those who envision the replacement of automobiles by magnificent, orderly, and inexpensive public transportation systems. It is not just because subways are hot, dirty, crowded, and crime-ridden that those who can do so avoid them—although that would surely be enough. It is because, compared to a car, even the cleanest, coolest, and most efficiently operated subway provides its passenger with almost no personal control over space—where he will stop, or how he will get there, at what speed he will travel, or with whom. And it permits even less control over the conditions within the space—its temperature and ventilation, its light, its sound. Perhaps the strongest indication of the depth at which territorial concerns permeate our culture is the price we have been willing to pay—in traffic deaths, pollution, gas lines, traffic jams—for the personal command of space the automobile provides.

And it is a price we are likely to continue to pay. Not merely because an increased command of space is associated with higher social status—meaning the rank, respect, and prestige one holds in the eyes of one's neighbors. But because access to and control over space are critical factors in shaping our feelings about *ourselves*—our sense of autonomy, of potency or powerlessness. This is a point about space and status worth stressing here, for it is too often overlooked. Struggles for status are not some silly social pastime we indulge in to no more significant purpose than "keeping up with the Joneses," although the popular literature on the subject has managed to trivialize these matters to a point where status and its symbolic display are represented as little more than a sophisticated form of social gamesmanship. Spaces, places, objects, and activities are not inherently valuable "counters" in some game of "I'm better than you are." They *acquire* value because certain of them increase our sense of personal autonomy, potency, freedom, self-direction, and self-control. Nothing could be less trivial than that. And nothing is more directly tied to such feelings—about ourselves and about others—than our access to and control over space.

This is the case not only in matters of social status—that is, the relative rank and value of *classes* of people, jobs, living, and working arrangements—but in the conduct of our individual transactions with others as well. Perhaps because restriction in space is a condition of infancy and childhood, and because our earliest associations with power (the omnipotence of parents and other significant adults) have to do with an almost magical command of space, we tend to *feel* childlike again in situations where our access to space is restricted while others have far-ranging control. This is one reason, I suppose, why those of us who prize our maturity and independence detest visits to doctors and dentists. Think for a moment how unevenly the rights to space are distributed in such situations. You must telephone in advance, then ring at the door to gain admission even to the "waiting room." Once there, you may not wander about, but must sit quietly in place, barred from access even to the receptionist's space by a partition, from the doctor's office by another door, from the examining rooms by still more doors within doors. You may move from one space to another only by specific permission, and usually under escort. And when you are left in one room, you must stay there until someone comes to take you out. The doctor, on the other hand, has free access to any space within the situation. Moreover, she or he has non-reciprocal access to your person—to your most private *internal* spaces—that no one else, including yourself, has. And all this while you sit, in another echo of infancy, stripped to the buff or, almost worse, swaddled in those paper gowns that in their texture, discomfort, and disposability are like nothing so much as diapers.

Is it any wonder, then, that in our dealings with doctors the best of us are reduced to the state of mind of four-year-olds? And in this state of mind, we not only experience all the feelings of childhood—vulnerability, loss of autonomy, dependency—but we quite unconsciously confer on the doctor all the omnipotence and magical power that accrued, in childhood, to those who had mastered space. In short, the unequal distribution of rights to the access and control of space in doctors' offices (not to mention hospitals, where the territorial imbalance is even more acute) guarantees that the transactions between doctors and patients will be modeled, psychologically, on the transactions between parents and children. And it makes little difference, I think, that doctors and lay persons alike bemoan this state of affairs, and wish that patients would assume a more adult role in the management of their own illness. All the brave calls for a new metaphor of medical care—one in which the patient is an equal member of the "health care team" or an informed and demanding "consumer" of health care services—will amount, I'm afraid, to nothing, unless the territorial characteristics of the doctor-patient relationship are changed. For space speaks with an older and deeper language than any words, and what it says—about who's in charge, who's competent, who's impotent in a situation—conditions our feelings and responses at a level too deep for the best intended reforms to touch.

This principle—that allocation of access to and control of space governs our feelings about ourselves and others, and consequently the psychological character of our relationships—sometimes leads us into paradox. There are many situations in our culture that require, for functional purposes, an unequal distribution of rights to space. Schools, for example, could not achieve their instructional purposes very effectively if students were free to move about the classroom and halls at will, open and close doors when they want, sit or stand as they please, adjust the lighting, temperature, and sound in the room as they choose. And so these rights to classroom space, its conditions, and control of movement within it are reserved to the teacher. In fact, they play a major part in defining the role of teacher. To test this assertion, I have on several occasions at the beginning of a new semester sent a graduate student into a classroom with instructions not to speak to the students there, but merely to walk to the front of the room and adjust the position of the desk, stroll to the back and change the position of a few chairs, glance at the overhead lights and dim them, walk to the windows and open one, study the thermostat and seem to adjust it, then glance at his watch and close the door. This purely nonverbal display of territorial control has never failed to identify the imposter in the students' minds as "teacher"—meaning that they willingly confer on him the authority to regulate their behavior in certain ways—for example, to direct them to sit or stand, change their seats, take out or put away paper and books, and so on.

Of itself, the conferral of authority on teachers by virtue of their territorial dominance is not a problem. Except, that is, when it conflicts with the avowed aim of many teachers, particularly at the college level, to establish with students a relationship of equality or, at least, one in which students behave as mature, self-directing, and intellectually independent partners in inquiry. Wherever professors gather to discuss their work, I hear the lament that students seem disinclined to "think for themselves," that they are too dependent on the direction of their teachers, that they accept too easily what they are told. Yet few of my colleagues seem aware that the territorial rules of the classroom situation promote just those attitudes which they claim to despise, and at a level which verbal messages to the contrary barely touch. I do not say that awareness of the role of space in shaping relationships will solve the problem. But bringing it to the conscious attention of students (and teachers) may help to mitigate some of the undesirable consequences of the territorial structure of the classroom.

Of course, classrooms are not the only situations where the pragmatics of space may produce responses quite different from those we hope for. A more dramatic case can be found in the responses of airline passengers to in-flight emergencies—particularly, to survivable-type crashes on takeoff or landing, where fire or the threat of explosion requires their immediate action if they are to escape. One might expect, in such a situation, that the major problem would be panic—passengers jamming the aisles and doors in a mad rush to get out. But this is not the case. I have been told by trainers of flight attendants that the major problem in evacuating a damaged plane is that the passengers will not move to help themselves, but sit in helpless passivity, not even unbuckling their seat belts unless commanded to do so. (This is why the safety briefing at the beginning of commercial flights now includes a demonstration of how to open your seat belt. But here I'm afraid, the airlines miss the point. The problem is not that passengers don't know how to unbuckle their belts. It is that they do not do it for themselves when every second counts.)

What could account for such extraordinary passivity in a life-threatening situation? Merely to label it "the paralysis of terror" is not enough. The flight crew, after all, is equally threatened—and equally frightened. But the crew responds quite differently. Why? Part of the answer lies, I believe, in the relationship between territoriality, autonomy, and dependency. For perfectly sound reasons of crowd control, flight management, and security, the average airline passenger is severely restricted in his access to airport space long before he boards his flight. Once on board, his access to and control of space is even more limited. He must sit where told to sit, dispose his belongings as directed, move about only when given permission— and then only in designated areas. Moreover, he has no control whatever over the course, speed, and direction of his movement through space. The territorial message of air travel, in short, is "put yourself entirely in our hands." Having no alternative, the passenger does—psychologically as well as physically. One consequence is that he surrenders, along with all care, a great measure of personal autonomy, responsibility, and self-reliance, and his transactions with airline personnel take on a distinctly child-parent character.

In ordinary circumstances this relationship poses no particular problems; its only symptoms are an unusual degree of playfulness, or willfulness, or rudeness (or conversely, timidity) in the behavior of some passengers toward the cabin crew. But in a life-threatening situation, the same relationship is expressed in a helpless passivity, a total dependence of passengers on crew. In some cases, this state of affairs works to the advantage of all, since the same conditions which induce dependency induce an unthinking obedience to authority as well, and airline personnel are taught to issue to passengers, in such circumstances, clear and forceful commands. The problem arises when the cabin crew is disabled and there is no one to assume the responsibility the passengers have so willingly (and unknowingly) given up. And then, for many, the will to act autonomously returns too dimly, and too late.

I know of no easy solution to such paradoxes, where pragmatic considerations lead us to design environments whose territorial characteristics promote counter-productive human responses. Indeed, problems like this might not be solvable at all, if space were the *only* environmental determinant of human behavior. But happily, this is not the case. Space is a major factor, to be sure, and I have been at pains here to show the powerful role it plays in shaping public and private behavior, our feelings of group belonging, our social roles, our positions in the drama of hierarchy, our sense of potency or impotence, dependence or autonomy. But for all that, space is only one in a constellation of variables that define situations and structure human meaning-making and response. And while space speaks to us in a language too old and too deep to ignore, its imperatives may be counterbalanced by the operation of other factors in the structure of human communication environments.

Epilogue: The Semanticist's Joke

From (1978, September) "Waiting: The semantics of transitional space," *ETC 36*(3), 245–253. Reprinted by permission of the Institute of General Semantics.

There is an old story about a miserable peasant, in some totalitarian state, who was driven to steal from the factory where he was employed. The owners of the factory knew that he was stealing—although they didn't know what—and the edict came down from on high that the factory guards must catch him in the act. So each night, as the peasant left the factory, the guards would stop him and search the wheelbarrow in which he dragged his few belongings home. But they never found in the wheelbarrow anything more than what was rightly his own.

Night after night, the peasant came to the factory gates, and night after night, the guards searched his wheel-barrow with microscopic care—all in vain. At last the evening came when they could stand it no longer. "You have driven us mad!" they cried to the peasant. "We know you are stealing, but we cannot find what it is. Only tell us what you steal, and we will let you go in peace, and trouble you no more." The peasant looked at them for a long moment in silence, then gave his thin shoulders a shrug. "Wheelbarrows," he said.

Now this is, of course, a semantics joke, because the purpose of most general semantics inquiries is to make visible what the guards in the story, like most people, overlook: the container—the environment—that gives the content of human behavior its shape and meaning. This is, of course, no easy task, since it is a peculiar fact that the environments in which we spend the greatest part of our time are the most invisible to us.

The Genes of Culture

Attention Universe!

(1977, June). Foreword to Media and culture [Special issue]. *ETC, 34*(2), 131–132. Reprinted by permission of the Institute of General Semantics.

Symbols are the genes of a culture. In them and through them, we transmit what we know and, even more important, how we do our knowing. For with symbols, we not only discover knowledge, we invent the idea of knowledge. With symbols, we not only bind time, we create it. With symbols, we not only map the territory, we construct what is to be mapped. The evolution of culture is the story of the evolution of symbols. There is nothing more fundamental in general semantics than this.

In the middle of the 19th century, a mutation occurred in the structure of symbolic forms—a mutation no less significant for the human future than the sudden appearance, in genetic history, of the opposable thumb. That is to say, it set the species on a new course or, more likely, laid the foundation for a new species altogether. The precise date of this symbolic transformation is disputable. There are several arguable choices. My own preference is the year 1844, when a New York University professor sent the first electric message ever transmitted by the species, and thus changed forever the nature of time and space. His name was Samuel Morse, and the schoolbooks tell us his message was the reverential, "What hath

God wrought?" In truth, the message was something else. In fact, in the first flush of his exaltation, Morse tapped out, "Attention, Universe!" But either message is plausible and, taken together, they tell us something important about ourselves. The first speaks of our astonishment and wonder, and even of our fear of new powers and an uncertain future. The second speaks of our confidence in our symbolic creativity, through which we can make even the stars take notice.

Over the past 133 years, our confidence more than our wonder has dictated the shape of our culture. In 1876, Bell transmitted the first telephone message. A year later, Edison invented the phonograph. By 1894, we had movies. A year after that, Marconi sent and received the first wireless messages. In 1906, Fessenden transmitted the human voice by radio. In 1920, regularly scheduled radio broadcasts began. Three years later, a picture was televised between New York and Philadelphia. In 1927, the first talking movie. In 1928, Disney's first animated cartoon. In 1935, E. H. Armstrong developed the FM radio. In 1941, commercial television. And so on, through the LP record, the tape recorder, the computer, the digital clock, the laser, the maser, and, probably sooner than we think, the phaser.

Of confidence, there is no lack. It is time for some wonder. With this issue of *ETC*, we wish to stimulate interest in and inquiry into the meaning and implications of modern communications technology. Of course, we do not mean to say that the subject has not been addressed by others. Indeed, some of them have contributed articles to this issue. Rather, we mean to say that the transforming power of new media has not been a central concern of general semanticists—the very group most equipped, by training and interest, to observe and analyze the ways in which new forms of symbol-making affect perception, value, and judgment.

And so our intention, with this issue, is to put this matter high on the agenda of general semantics. Accordingly, you will find in the following pages speculations, theories, recapitulations, satire, and research—all about media and culture. None of it is really meant to answer questions. Rather, it is to make sure that we understand there are questions to be answered.

Steps to an Ecology of Learning

(1975, September). [Review of the book *Education for adaptation and survival*, by T.W. Weiss et al.] *ETC, 32*(3), 325–29. Reprinted by permission of the Institute of General Semantics.

Those few librarians and bibliographers who have managed to survive the knowledge explosion with their categories intact will not, I suspect, welcome *Education for Adaptation and Survival.* For what Messrs. Weiss, Moran, and Cottle have given us here is a work so broad in scope as to defy the most ingenious taxonomers of knowledge. Yes, this is a book about education. But it is also a book about philosophy. And about language. And perception, culture, and change. In short it is about, one might say, the ecology of learning—and that is no easy subject to classify. Nor is it an easy subject to organize a book about, especially if the book is not some weighty tome but a relatively slim (200-odd pages) and pleasingly lucid volume. So it is worth a few moments here to describe just how the authors have accomplished the task of organizing and integrating such a diversity of ideas.

Although they are not so labeled, the book is composed of three sections. The first addresses the central question, What are the functions of education and how are they best achieved? In their answer, the authors set forth the thesis of their work, which may be summarized as follows: The primary function of education is to help the individual adapt to his changing environment. This requires providing the student with attitudes and techniques for maintaining an accurate orientation to reality, for minimizing false-to-fact "knowledge," for checking his cognitive maps against the territory of experience. Such attitudes and techniques are to be found in the principles and procedures of scientific inquiry. And they may be acquired through the constant exercise, in one's schooling and personal life, of the methods of science and the principles of general semantics. There is, of course, more to be said about what I am calling Section I than I have written in these few lines. Indeed, the three chapters that comprise it make up, for me at least, the core of the book, and I want to come back for a closer look at them in just a bit. For the moment, though, suffice it to say that they set the context for the two sections which follow.

Section II begins with the assumption that the relationship between man and his environment (i.e., reality) is the central concern of all philosophies and that different philosophies are, in effect, different constructs of the man-environment relationship. The key to the differences in philosophical systems, and in their educational applications, lies in the answers they give to three major questions: What is the nature of "reality"? How do we know what is the nature of reality? And by what standards shall we judge whether our relationships with reality are "right" or "wrong," "good" or "bad"? In the three chapters that make up this section, the authors provide a cogent and lucid explication of the metaphysics, epistemology, and axiology of five major philosophies (idealism, realism, scholasticism, pragmatism, and existentialism), then trace the consequences of each for educational goals and methods. As an introduction to philosophy in general, and educational philosophy in particular, these chapters perform—with exceptional clarity and style—a valuable function in helping the beginning student of education to examine the premises on which his own behavior as a teacher will rest. But they do more than that. For the general reader as well as the education student, the middle section of *Education for Adaptation and Survival* explores the philosophical roots of science as a mode of inquiry, of problem-solving as a teaching methodology, and of general semantics as a strategy for adaptation and survival. This gives to the main argument of the book a measure of depth and power it might not otherwise achieve.

In the final section of their work, Weiss, Moran, and Cottle address the questions, What are the dominant "realities" of the environment confronting us in these closing years of the 20th century, how have they affected the schools, and how can an educational system founded on science as both an orientation and a mode of inquiry help us to adapt? This is not the place to provide the authors' answers, except to say that they focus heavily on the role of population growth and technology in altering both the structure of American society and the responsibilities facing our schools. Science and semantics, they argue, can play a significant role in assuring our adaptation, helping us to identify and articulate the goals toward which education must aspire if we are to survive.

Having indicated something of the scope and content of *Education*, I want to come back again to the first section of the book, for it is here that its major strengths, and some weaknesses, lie. Chapters 2 and 3 are of particular interest to the semanticist. In them, the authors discuss the role of language in behavior and articulate the basic principles of both science and general semantics: extensionality, awareness of the abstraction process, or multiordinality, non-identity, non-allness, self-reflexiveness, etc. In general these principles are set out with appealing clarity, and the beginning student of science, language, and behavior will no doubt find them an excellent introduction to general semantics. But the thoughtful reader will also, I think, find some problems here. One is an unfortunate tendency toward a somewhat careless use of words—particularly, words like "really," "in reality," and "actually," as in "the way things actually are." In a passage intended to demonstrate the shortcomings of "prescientific" thought, for example, the authors conclude that "In reality... tomatoes are not poisonous but rather are a delicious fruit." In *reality*, of course, tomatoes are neither of these; they are not even "tomatoes." If this were the only instance of such lapses it would be a matter of small concern. After all, none of us, no matter how well trained in general semantics, can entirely escape the habits of our language. But there are too many instances of such talk here to dismiss lightly, especially in a book about language. One particularly unfortunate example occurs in a discussion of the ways in which "prescientific" man perpetuated false-to-fact information by talking about the world "not as it actually was but as he thought it was," The implication here, and it pervades these chapters, is that *scientific* man has somehow managed to escape the limitation of his own perceptions; that what scientists describe is not the world as they "think it is" but as it "really" is.

Messrs. Weiss, Moran, and Cottle don't need me, I'm sure, to lecture them on the inaccuracy—and the danger—of such an idea. There are plenty of sentences in their book to indicate that, if such an implication is there, it is there by accident—not what they "really" meant at all. But there are enough such accidents in these chapters to create the impression that science is not *a* way of looking at a reality, but *the* way to look at *the* real world. And to the extent that such a suggestion comes through, it weakens the book.

I find in these chapters, too, a second, and related, problem: some tendency to confuse disagreements over *fact* with disagreements over *value*. Take, for example, the following passage:

> Most people today would agree that the Spanish Inquisition perpetrated cruel and vicious crimes on their fellow men. Yet for members of the faith that instigated these practices, a suggestion that their leaders were misguided immediately calls forth an emotional reaction. The historical facts seem clear, but the visceral reactions prevent full acceptance.... Recognition of the effect conditioning has on one's viscera and a healthy respect for "fact" can do much to prevent animal responses.

Now it so happens I agree with the judgment that the events of the Inquisition were "cruel and vicious crimes." But I would hardly call such a judgment an "historical fact." Nor are "facts" the main issue here. What is at issue is the interpretation one ought to place upon the "facts," and that is a question of *values*.

The same confusion of factual disagreements with value conflicts is reflected, I think, in this passage:

> Yearly, nationwide publicity is given to people who refuse to have blood transfusions to save their lives because their faith taught that "Thou shalt not feed upon thy brother's blood." Even though these individuals may have families who need them, they steadfastly refuse the transfusions, paying more attention to the words that whirled around inside their heads than to empirical evidence. Teachers can help children avoid belief in prescientific dogma that contributes to non-survival.

I suspect that Jehovah's Witnesses probably know as well as "scientific" people what are the "facts" involved in blood transfusions, including the mortality rates for those who refuse them. Their argument with their doctors is not over facts, but how to weigh and respond to those facts within a context of values. And it is not sufficient to set up "survival" as the self-evident criterion for the "scientific" judgment of values.

Of course, most of us are so differently oriented from the Jehovah's Witnesses (at least in regard to blood transfusions) that it is easy to condemn their values as "prescientific," contributing to "non-survival." But such labels obscure the complexity of the issues here. To see them more clearly, imagine for a moment the following situation: You are stranded, badly injured and far from help, in a wilderness totally barren of life. Your only source of sustenance and, as hope of timely rescue fades, your chance for survival, lies in the bodies of your children, killed in the same disaster that has left you helpless. As the certainty mounts that starvation will outrace your rescuers, you confront the ugly choice that few men, thank God, have to face. How will you act, and why? Will you attend more closely to the "empirical facts" or to the "words whirling around in your head"? If you think the choice a simple one, if you opt too quickly and easily for the "scientific" and "survival-oriented" decision, you are, I think, either less than honest or sadly ignorant of the complexities of human existence. For what makes us human, in the end, is the "words whirling around in our heads," and the price for ignoring them—or at least certain ones of them—is exile from the human community. And that is no less a death—social, psychological and, in the end, no doubt, physical—than starvation. For the Jehovah's Witness, then, the question is not whether he will attend to the "empirical facts" (which include, after all, no guarantees of survival), but whether he will accept those "facts" at the cost of membership in that community which gives him social and psychological definition.

My point here, of course, is not to argue the case for refusing blood transfusions. It is that the question of *values* and how we are to assess them sanely is not addressed in a serious way in *Education for Adaptation and Survival*. The authors may easily be forgiven the omission, since this is by far the most difficult question for any philosophy to answer, and many an intellectual explorer, on approaching it, has found himself in a bog with little firm ground on which to tread. But for that very reason, a few well-chosen words here on the subject of values and their evaluation from a scientific perspective would have been most welcome.

There is one last problem I want to mention here, not so much to criticize *Education for Adaptation and Survival* as to call to attention an issue which general semanticists have not as yet addressed. In their chapter on "Science, Sanity, and Semantics," Weiss, Moran, and Cottle argue that "When people talk sense they talk about those things that are perceived by the senses; that is, they can be seen, heard, felt, tasted, or smelled, not only by the person who experiences them, but by others who can verify them. Verification is essential for those who would be scientifically oriented." And in the same vein, "Being sane requires adjustment to the real world as it is and not as it is said to be. What men say about the real world can be made more sensible by continuous checking to see if what they say fits the facts as they are found below the verbal levels of abstraction." Yet, as the authors themselves point out, most of our "information" about the world is acquired, not through our senses, but second hand, through the mass media. Under the impact of mass-circulation newspapers and magazines, transistor radio, motion pictures, television, computer, LP record, and, yes, laser holography, "reality" has changed. We are living today as much, if not more, in a symbolic environment as we are in a sensory one. And it is very much an open question which environment, for most of us, is what we mean by "real."

Last year at this time, I couldn't get space on a flight to California for Thanksgiving; the airlines were booked solid at $380 a seat, a month in advance. We couldn't get a table for dinner at Alexi's; their reservation list showed a full house. Half my students came back from the holidays with Florida or Puerto Rico or Arizona tans. But all the messages of my symbolic environments said we were in a depression, that money's tight, that nobody's spending. Which should I trust? The evidence of my own limited senses, or the infinitely more powerful senses of the media? Which is the illusion, and which reality? The advice of the general semanticists—to check the symbolic map against the territory of experienced reality—was a good prescription in the old days. But I'm not sure it works any more. How shall I know if that walk on the moon was "fact"? How shall I know if Vietnam is over? How shall I know if inflation is growing or waning? There *is* no territory, no sensory experience, against which to check our media maps, in today's symbolic environments. The best we can do is check map against map against map—ABC against NBC against the *Times* against the *US News and World Report*. And if they all agree? Well then, that *is* the official definition of reality. Certainly, it is the only definition of reality that *counts*. Walter Cronkite tells us, every evening, that *that's* the way things were today. And how are we to doubt it, when ABC and NBC and the *Times* and the *Daily News* all agree? Mass information is about events so far removed from our own experience that there is little or nothing we can do to affect or even verify them. And so we feel, not informed, but helpless, hapless, alienated.

The problem I have outlined here cannot be resolved, I'm afraid, through the strategies suggested in *Education for Adaptation and Survival*. In today's symbolic environments, we need a new set of techniques for "making sense" of a world which lies beyond our senses, inaccessible to sensory verification. It would be unfair to ask of a book like *Education for Adaptation and Survival* that it attempt to develop such techniques. That is a task that must engage all of us. The supreme value of the work Weiss, Moran, and Cottle have given us is that in this, as in other things, it directs our attention to the *questions* we should be asking. And that, of course, is the beginning of everything—education, science, sanity, and change.

What We Say, and What We Do: A Case of Bad Form

(1979, Fall). [Published originally as "Not by any means: Doubletalk in the service of 'humane' ends."] *ETC, 36*(3), 257–260. Reprinted by permission of the Institute of General Semantics.

A few years ago, I attended a meeting at which Charles Weingartner, co-author of *Teaching as a Subversive Activity*, participated in a debate with a rather stern professor of education on the subject of methods of teaching. The professor was, in fact, more than stern. In arguing his case for what he called "humane" approaches to teaching, he was consistently dogmatic and authoritarian, and gave the impression that he had never entertained the possibility that any of his opinions might be mistaken. Toward the conclusion of the debate, Weingartner asked him a question which, as it turned out, was a kind of one-punch knockout. As I recall, the question was put without rancor but with wry astonishment. "Are you," Weingartner asked, "offering yourself as an illustration of the benefits that will accrue from the application of your ideas?"

I have thought of this question on several occasions in the recent past; for example, when reading some of the curious statements made by S. I. Hayakawa who, in addition to being a United States Senator, is probably the best-known general semanticist in the world. It is both reasonable and predictable for people to wonder if Hayakawa's current insights are the result of his lifelong study of general semantics. Is he offering himself, one may ask, as an illustration of the benefits of general semantics?

The contradictions between what people do (and say) and the principles they claim to believe in is a subject of endless fascination and permutation, and was the theme of Neil Postman's editorial in the Spring issue of *ETC*. His description of "semantic tyranny" at the NCTE Convention in Kansas City (1978) put special emphasis on the question, To what extent can a "humane" sociological doctrine impel people to abandon their commitments to the sane and responsible uses of language? Of course, this is the question to which George Orwell addressed himself throughout his life, and to which he provided, by way of an answer, an enduring metaphor: *1984*.

1984 does not denote a period of time but a state of society and a state of mind. The state of society Orwell warns us about is totalitarian; the state of mind, fanaticism. Orwell's point is that totalitarianism and fanaticism are not identified with particular political goals. They are ways of thinking and behaving from which no doctrine makes us immune. The specific targets of Orwell's attack include not only what we might call "semantic tyranny" but what Orwell sometimes called doublespeak. Semantic tyranny—especially in the realm of politics—is the attempt to control people's behavior through the manipulation of language. It uses a number of strategies, among them the formulation of public policies which revise the language for political ends, the application of prior restraint on what people may write and say, and the practice of censorship. Doublespeak is somewhat different. It is characterized by a use of language that disguises the purposes of a speaker or writer, a use of language that does not bear a clear relationship to observable situations in reality, a use of language that allows its user to pursue, simultaneously, contradictory ends.

Of course, many educated people have read George Orwell or, just as good, have studied general semantics, and are therefore aware of the potential for mischief and danger in the misuses of language. However, a problem arises for some—its name is hypocrisy—when their ardor for a particular doctrine demands only a one-sided surveillance of language usage: They do not and cannot offer their own language as an illustration of the clear and honest expression of ideals they find wanting in others.

The goings-on at The National Council of Teachers of English (NCTE) always provide good examples of this point, since the organization explicitly claims to oppose doublespeak, censorship, and other forms of semantic boondoggling. In fact, the Council actually has a committee called The Doublespeak Committee, whose purpose is to alert teachers and their students to semantic tyranny and doublespeak whenever they appear; that is to say, whenever they originate from "conservative" or "reactionary" sources. However, there has been some considerable reluctance on the part of some of the Committee's members to apply equal analytic rigor to the misuses of language when it appears in the service of "liberal" goals. Orwell, of course, would judge such a bias as a case of missing the point altogether. It requires no special disciplining of one's mind to find nonsense in the utterances of your political antagonists. The challenge is to find the same in your own.

Like Neil Postman, I can draw a pertinent case from an experience at an NCTE convention—this one in New York in 1977. I had been asked to chair a panel, co-sponsored by the Doublespeak Committee, on "The Language of Sexism," and I accepted in the belief that the meeting would be a forum for the exploration of different points of view on the issue. I was badly mistaken. One speaker, with whose ideas I was in rough agreement, dealt with persons who offered a different view by labeling them "willfully ignorant," "maliciously ignorant," "oppressive," "stupid," and, at best, "naive." There was much cheering and hissing at appropriate moments, meaning when speakers uttered, respectively, politically correct or incorrect views. To another speaker, a member of the audience timidly addressed the following question: Did she agree with Orwell's view that the manipulation of language for political ends is a totalitarian strategy? Her reply, which was warmly cheered by the majority of the audience, was, "It depends on whose political ends you manipulate for."

At the close of the panel's presentation, a woman announced that signatures were being collected to protest certain "tasteless" remarks made by a speaker who had addressed a luncheon meeting earlier in the day. Now, a petition of protest against another's use of language is certainly a reasonable procedure in a democratic society. But further inquiry revealed that the purpose of the petition was to support a proposal that all future speakers be required to follow certain "guidelines" in what they may say and how they may say it. This is the sort of edict to which Joseph Goebbels was so partial—always issued, of course, in the best interests of the future.

The tendency to believe that the sincerity and even correctness of one's goals exempt one from fairness and responsibility is widespread, by no means confined to organizations like the NCTE. For instance, just about every "right thinking" liberal has been outspoken in protecting the right of homosexuals to the expression of their views without the threat of losing their jobs. Yet, when the Gay Alliance demanded that Anita Bryant lose hers for the expression of her views, "liberal" voices by the regiment were silent. An even better example was called to mind recently by *The Village Voice*, a New York-based publication noted for its liberal leanings. During the course of an article on the limits of free speech, a writer referred approvingly to the shouting down of William Shockley when he tried to speak at a Staten Island college. Shockley, you will recall, believes that there are genetic differences in intelligence among races, a hypothesis that is probably shaky enough to fall of its own weight. Nonetheless, students who are assiduous in protecting their rights to express themselves acted energetically to eliminate Shockley's. Their reason? "People who built the movement to oppose Shockley believe there is a connection between ideas and actions... Opponents to Shockley's appearance believe that the issue was racism, and the right of people to live a human life, not free speech.... The ruling class will hide righteously behind the Constitution in defending its right to rule, but beneath the Constitution it holds a loaded gun." This opinion *The Village Voice* writer quotes with a measure of reverence and as the conclusion to his article, as if to imply that it says all that needs to be said.

A similar and even more recent case in point emerged as a result of a public letter signed by Joan Baez, in which she criticized the present Communist government in Vietnam for its oppressive policies toward some of its own citizens. These policies have resulted in the displacement, illness, and death of thousands, especially the ethnic Chinese. Apparently, Miss Baez believes that to the victim of cruelty it is a matter of indifference whether its source is a "capitalist" or "communist" regime. For this belief she has been severely reproached by many who were active in the anti-war movement because, as one of them put it, it is an "historical necessity" that revolutionary governments must act this way in order to free themselves of the past. How George Orwell would have loved that one! One might just as well say that the U.S. invasion of Vietnam was an "historical necessity," since large and powerful countries, historically, have found it necessary to take what they can from small and weak countries.

I believe S. I. Hayakawa once defined general semantics as the study of how not to make a fool of yourself. Note that he did not say it is the study of how to make a fool of others. What he meant to imply, I am sure, is that of all the varieties of deception, self-deception is the most pervasive and the most difficult to recognize, especially when we are in the thrall of some doctrine that is obviously "humane." The fact that one is in favor of equality of the sexes, or a redistribution of wealth, or greater sensitivity to the grievances of oppressed groups does not in itself mean very much or even tell a great deal about the person. Most tyrants have preceded themselves on the stage with announcements of their humane intentions—which is to say, "good" opinions may come from "rotten" people just as surely as "bad" opinions may come from "decent" people. In the end, if what we do and say are not illustrations of our principles, we are deluding ourselves and do no service to others. That is Orwell's message and, as I understand it, the message of general semantics.

Symbols, Thought, and Reality: The Contributions of Benjamin Lee Whorf and Susanne K. Langer to Media Ecology

(2005), C.M.K. Lum, (Ed.), *Perspectives on culture, technology and communication*. New York, NY: Hampton Press. Reprinted with permission. Original publication (Spring 2000), *New Jersey journal of communication*, 8(1), 8–22.

Toward the beginning of the 20th century, there arose an idea so powerful and so radical in its implications for our understanding of reality that it transformed every arena of scientific and humanistic study. This idea might most generally be summed up in the word "relativity." More specifically, it is the idea that the reality humans encounter is not what is out there, but the particular version of what is out there that our instruments of perception, exploration, representation, and communication provide. Since I take this to be the defining idea of the 20th century, as well as the central idea on which media ecology is founded, it is worth saying more about it before turning to the ways in which Benjamin Lee Whorf and Susanne K. Langer transformed it into a cornerstone of media ecology.

The Roots of Relativity

To begin, it should be said that while the idea of relative realities attained its most powerful expression and impact on human understanding in the 20th century, it did not originate in our own time. Plato knew, in the 5th century BCE, what Einstein demonstrated in 1905: that humans cannot encounter reality directly, but only from some position in relation to it and through instruments of perception and knowing that play an active (and transforming) role in our construction of the known. Plato's allegory of the cave is about as concise an illustration of the relativity of reality, of its social construction, and of the biases of the senses as one is likely to meet in 20th-century works on the same subjects. But for all its centrality to Plato's philosophy of knowledge, the allegory of the cave was just that, an allegory, an illuminating tale and not a scientific treatise. Its potential as a serious instrument of thought in itself was swept away, with most things Platonic, by the new broom of the empirical sciences with the coming of the Enlightenment.

The great achievements of Enlightenment science in early modern times, and the steady march of technological progress that resulted, rested squarely on Newtonian assumptions of a fixed and absolute framework of space and time, and of observers entirely capable of neutral and objective reports on what they read in Nature's book. While those assumptions did not entirely banish intimations of relativism in the 18th and 19th centuries, such intimations could not make much headway against the prevailing Newtonian paradigm of scientific objectivism. In that paradigm, the world was held to be ultimately knowable and (at least in theory) knowable in full, through instruments and procedures that in no wise affected the workings of the reality they investigated.

By the closing years of the 19th century, however, the Newtonian paradigm had begun to wobble more than a little under the weight of accumulating anomalies (Kuhn, 1962)—scientific findings that could not be made to fit coherently within the established frameworks, assumptions, and principles of Newtonian physics. These anomalies, arising out of the observation of the behavior of both very large bodies, like planets and solar systems and galaxies, and very, very small bodies, like electrons and other subatomic particles, led in the early years of the 20th century to the two great thought experiments that revolutionized not only science but our understanding of human knowledge and of its relationship to reality. The first was Einstein's question, "What would one see if one were riding astride a beam of light?" His answer was that what an observer sees depends both on her position in relation to what is observed and on the speed at which she is traveling. Nor is it only the hypothetical *observer* who is affected by relative position and speed of movement. Instruments of measurement are equally affected: Clocks slow down and speed up; yardsticks stretch and shrink with changes in speed of travel. Time and space themselves change as a function of the relative movements of objects and observers within them. There is, moreover, no place in which an observer can take a fixed stand *outside* these relationships, no position from which an observer can construct a detached, neutral, objective account of reality without including herself within it as a defining element of that reality. In short, there are multiple realities of which accounts may be given, and each is dependent on the stance of the observer in relation to it.

The second thought experiment was Werner Heisenberg's, and it emerged from attempts to predict the behavior of electrons in the shells of atoms. The Newtonian paradigm assumed that a complete understanding of the world could be built up, piece by piece, from the application of laws of physics to the interactions among the smallest building blocks of matter, thence to their interactions as larger units, thence to their interactions as still larger units, all the way up to the interactions of such great bodies as planets, stars, solar systems, and galaxies. To maintain that assumption, it was essential that the laws of physics be able to account, with perfect precision, for the interactions among the simplest building blocks of nature or all the rest would founder. Thus Heisenberg asked, "What would be required to ascertain the exact position and velocity of an electron in the simplest of nature's building blocks, the hydrogen atom, which contains only one electron in its shell?" His answer was that to obtain such information an observer would need to somehow make the electron visible. This would require bouncing a beam of light off it, since we can only see what light reflects back. But as Einstein had already demonstrated, light itself is composed of particles that affect the position and velocity of what they bounce off. Making the electron visible would alter its position and velocity in such a way that, while one might be calculated with near-perfect precision, the other could not. To put it simply, wherever the electron might be before it is observed, it isn't when it *is* observed. The requirements of observing alter the observed in ways that cannot be fully accounted for. Heisenberg concluded from this that there is an irreducible degree of uncertainty in our knowledge of the physical world, at the subatomic level at least. Since all the rest of our knowledge is built up from there, we can never attain the full and certain knowledge of reality that the Newtonian paradigm promised. The only reality one can truly have knowledge of, therefore, is that reality which the conditions of observing it require. The conditions of observing, moreover—the operations of our senses and the technologies used to extend them; the structures of the media (like light or sound) they require to obtain information—not only limit what we can know, but alter the reality observed in ways not fully predictable, so that what we know and what is out there are sometimes subtly and sometimes greatly different things. (Note that comprehensive and readable accounts of these ideas can be found in Barnett, 1968; Heisenberg, 1962; and Matson, 1966.)

From this brief account of relativity as expressed in the physical sciences, it should be clear why I say it is the central idea on which media ecology rests. Media ecology is the study of the ways in which our instruments of knowing—our senses and central nervous systems, our technologies of exploration, the physical media they require (like light, sound, electricity), and the conditions in which they are used—construct and reconstruct what we know, and therefore the realities that humans inhabit. To that extent, media ecology is deeply indebted, for its guiding assumptions and questions, to Einstein, Heisenberg, and their 20th-century colleagues in physics, who made relativity the defining concept of the modern era.

But there is something critically important missing from the physicists' account of relativity, and from the definition of media ecology just provided. That something has to do with the meanings of knowledge and instruments of knowing. In Einstein's and Heisenberg's accounts, and in Plato's allegory of the cave, the instruments of knowing referred to are primarily our senses and those technologies used to extend them, and knowledge refers to the sensory data received through such means. But sensory data themselves constitute only a tiny part of what is meant by knowledge. Without some way to record, sort out, categorize, organize, retrieve, and communicate what we see, hear, smell, taste, and touch, knowledge would consist merely of a welter of fleeting and fragmented impressions of what lies beyond our skins. To construct and maintain a coherent understanding of sensory experiences, we need something more than our senses. We need to *represent* experience to ourselves, so that what we know can be recalled and reworked and articulated and passed on to others in words, sentences, pictures, graphs, measurements, and other systems of codes and symbols. These systems of representation are no less vital instruments of knowing than our senses and their technological extensions. Codes and symbols also play an active role in constructing the realities we know—or think we do. Indeed, they play an even more significant role than do our senses and technical instruments, because codes of representation, starting with language, not only govern how we record and report what we see, but shape our choices about what to observe, and how to make sense of it. Heisenberg himself intimated as much in his well-known observation that "What we observe is not nature in itself but nature exposed to our method of questioning." Questions are a product of language and, in this sense, Heisenberg meant to acknowledge the power of language as an instrument of knowing that transforms our conceptions of reality. Einstein, too, acknowledged the pivotal role of language in shaping constructions of reality when he remarked that the greatest adversary to his theory that space and time are functions of a single phenomenon, spacetime, is language itself, which insists on dividing space and time into two different things.

It was neither Heisenberg nor Einstein, however, who placed at the center of relativity, and of media ecology, the idea that language and, by extension, all symbol systems for representing experience play a major role in how we construct reality and, as a consequence, conduct our affairs within it. That idea was given its most systematic and forceful expression, not by physicists, but by the linguistic anthropologists Benjamin Lee Whorf and Edward Sapir.

Benjamin Lee Whorf and Linguistic Relativity

The names of Whorf and Sapir are invariably linked in referring to their powerful hypothesis about the role language plays in shaping human conceptions of reality; that is, their thesis is known, alternatively, as the Whorf-Sapir or Sapir-Whorf Hypothesis. I give Whorf precedence here, both in naming the thesis and in singling out his contribution to media ecology, because although Sapir is the better known (and more academically respectable) linguist, it is Whorf who most fully articulated the set of ideas that constitute what has also come to be called the theory of linguistic relativity and the theory of linguistic determinism. The choice between the latter two terms to characterize the Whorf-Sapir hypothesis, incidentally, is not unimportant, since they reflect different readings of the theory and its implications. Before turning to the thesis and its interpretations, however, let me provide a brief sketch of the two men whose names it bears.

Of Edward Sapir, I will say very little, not because there is little to be said, but on the contrary, because his contributions to the study of language and culture were so extensive and distinguished that any attempt to sum them up in a few sentences would be both futile and presumptuous. Suffice it to say that he was, in the 1920s and 1930s, a leading linguist of the anthropologically oriented school founded by Franz Boas; an authority on American Indian languages; and a teacher of great distinction at the University of Chicago and, subsequently, at Yale University, where Whorf first came under his tutelage in 1931, although the two had met and talked several times at professional congresses of linguists in earlier years. (Note that the biographical data presented here have been abstracted from Carroll's introduction to and comprehensive bibliography in *Language, Thought, and Reality*, Whorf, 1956. All references to Whorf's thought and writing are to Whorf's articles collected in the same volume.)

Sapir's influence on Whorf's thought and work long predated their meeting, however. Sapir's (1921) important and widely read book *Language* could scarcely have escaped Whorf's attention, addressing as it did many of the issues with which he was already deeply involved. Among these was the relationship between language and thought, which Sapir argued were inextricably related, although not *coterminus*, to use his word (p. 15), and between language and culture, which he argued must be considered separately from one another (pp. 218–219). Generally, it may be said that, once they began to work together as teacher and student, Sapir exercised a moderating influence on Whorf's more radical thinking, while Whorf apparently persuaded the more scholarly, careful, and temperate Sapir that bolder statements on the relationship between language and thought were warranted.

For example, although Sapir's (1921) speculations in *Language* were rather moderately expressed, Whorf quotes him, by 1934, as saying, "The fact of the matter is that the 'real world' is to a large extent unconsciously built up on the language habits of the group.... We see and hear and otherwise experience very largely as we do because the language habits of our community predispose certain choices of interpretation" (Whorf, 1956, p. 134.)

As for Whorf, he was more than something of an anomaly among linguists. By academic training a chemical engineer, and by his own choice a lifelong fire insurance claims adjuster and administrator for the Hartford Fire Insurance Company, Whorf had no formal education in linguistics until he enrolled in Sapir's course in American Indian languages at Yale in 1931. But he was a voracious reader with a particular passion and gift for languages, a denizen of museums and libraries with university-quality collections on linguistics and American Indian cultures, and a tireless correspondent with Americanists and linguists throughout the U.S. and Mexico. By the late 1920s, he had already presented scholarly papers on such subjects as Toltec history and Aztec linguistics at learned congresses, and his scholarly output and reputation grew steadily throughout the 1930s and 1940s, with many of his technical articles on Aztec, Shawnee, and Hopi linguistics appearing in the professional journals of both linguists and anthropologists and in books compiled by such notable linguists as Harry Hoijer. In the two years before his untimely death in 1941, at the age of 44, Whorf brought his ideas before a wider, non-specialist audience in a series of three articles on linguistics, science, and logic published in M.I.T.'s *Technology Review*, and it was in these three pieces, together with his widely reprinted 1939 article on "The Relation of Habitual Thought and Behavior to Language," that he gave the thesis of linguistic relativity its most forceful expression.

Linguistic Relativity. In "Science and Linguistics," Whorf (1956) put the thesis this way:

> [T]he background linguistic system (in other words, the grammar) of each language is not merely a reproducing instrument for voicing ideas but rather is itself the shaper of ideas, the program and guide for the individual's mental activity, for his analysis of

impressions, for his synthesis of his mental stock in trade. Formulation of ideas is not an independent process, strictly rational in the old sense, but is part of a particular grammar, and differs, from slightly to greatly, between different grammars. We dissect nature along lines laid down by our native languages. The categories and types that we isolate from the world of phenomena we do not find there because they stare every observer in the face; on the contrary, the world is presented in a kaleidoscopic flux of impressions which has to be organized in our minds—and this means largely by the linguistic systems in our minds. We cut nature up, organize it into concepts, and ascribe significances as we do, largely because we are parties to an agreement to organize it in this way—an agreement that holds throughout our speech community and is codified in the patterns of our language. The agreement is, of course, an implicit and unstated one, *but its terms are absolutely obligatory*; we cannot talk at all except by subscribing to the organization and classification of data which the agreement decrees.

This fact is very significant ... for it means that no individual is free to describe nature with absolute impartiality but is constrained to certain modes of interpretation even while he thinks himself most free.... We are thus introduced to a new principle of relativity, which holds that all observers are not led by the same physical evidence to the same picture of the universe, unless their linguistic backgrounds are similar, or can in some way be calibrated (pp. 212–214, original emphasis).

I cite this passage in its entirety because it contains most of the significant ideas that comprise Whorf's thesis. But it does not contain all of them. A fuller reading of his collected papers suggests the following elaboration. Every language is a particular way of cutting up and reassembling the reality experienced through our senses. Our senses alone give no instruction, for example, about where one thing ends and another begins. We can say, "See that cup." But no one has ever *seen* a cup that is not part of some larger whole: cup-in-the-hand, or cup-on-the-desk, or cup-on-the-shelf. The same is true for the hand, the desk, and the shelf. Each is connected in sensory experience to something more. But through the agency of *naming* we can cut the connections, separate the cup from the hand or the shelf, and through *grammatical conventions,* we can reshuffle nature at will: take the horns from a goat and the mane from a lion, the head of a man and the legs of a horse, and imagine a creature to vex our dreams to nightmare. In short, through words we can make a world our senses cannot enter, a place biology cannot even understand. And words, for all their power, cannot encompass what biology understands. Language *represents* experience, or part of it; it does not *replicate* experience. Indeed, that is where the power of language lies: in the fact that it is a code, not a replica of the world known through the senses. Through words we can construct a universe we cannot hear, see, or touch. We can call to mind times that do not exist to our senses, the future and the past, and invent things like cups and tables, unicorns and gargoyles, that nature has never produced. Because language is a *code,* it operates according to rules that are not the rules of our creaturely experience, of the sensory-motor-biochemical world. And that world cannot be made to fit within the structures and rules of language. The reality given by language is fundamentally different from the reality given by sense data.

Words and Worldviews. Whorf argued that no two languages cut up reality in exactly the same way. To begin with, each has a somewhat different lexicon or set of words it uses to call attention to one or another distinction that is important in the lives of the people who use that language. And we habitually attend to those distinctions our vocabularies make. There is nothing startling about this observation or about the fact that, even among speakers of the same language, there may be large differences in vocabulary. One would expect, for example, that people who ski will use more words for different types of snow than will ordinary city-dwellers for whom the generic "snow" (and perhaps "slush") will suffice; and that people who work with textiles for a living will have a larger set of words for different kinds of weaves and fabric surfaces than those who do not. Nonetheless, it is important to note that the vocabulary distinctions any language provides never reflect the infinite gradations of difference in nature. Each person, for example, is unique in her feelings of sexuality and their enactment. At the moment, however, English provides only a small set of words—masculine, feminine, homosexual, gay, queer, lesbian, bisexual—to categorize a much larger spectrum of variations. In so doing, it tells us which differences this culture thinks it is important to pay attention to and which may be safely (for social reasons) ignored. Of greater importance, it suggests that these are the real categories of sexuality into which nature is divided, and *this* is more Whorf's point: that the lexical categories language provides condition the ways in which reality is conceptualized.

Still, Whorf gave only passing attention to lexical differences among languages, except to point out that the vocabulary distinctions available to a speech community condition the attention given to differences among things and, conversely, the tendency to treat things named by the same word as the same. Of far greater importance in his thesis is the nature of the units into which different languages carve up the world—that is, *how* they construct their words and the grammatical categories into which different phenomena are sorted. English (and most European languages), Whorf pointed out, cuts up reality into hundreds of discrete, autonomous things: cups, tables, chairs, cats, dogs. It also distinguishes grammatically among such "things" *(nouns)* and what we conceive of as actions or processes—running, growing, loving, and going *(verbs)*. Moreover, English has a set of grammatical rules that permits the transformation of almost any verb into a noun; thus loving becomes love, growing becomes growth, and thinking becomes thought. These grammatical features of English, he argued, play an important role in the tendency of English-speakers (and speakers of other languages with the same features) both to conceive of reality as a collection of discrete objects and to objectify (i.e., make into things) phenomena that are not thing-like at all. What could be less like a thing and more a dynamic process than, for example, an explosion? English allows us to disguise the process as a thing by the simple technique of assigning it the form of a noun. This in turn leads us to talk and behave as though relationships, activities, and processes exist in the material world in the same way as do other "things" in the grammatical category of nouns, like cats and dogs and apples, and to search for them there—as when people search for love or success or power, or resent their inequitable distribution, or mourn their loss.

By contrast, the radically different languages Whorf studied—Shawnee, Aztec, Hopi, Nootka—form their words in a process Whorf called polysynthesis. In those languages, each word consists, not of a single unit with a discrete semantic meaning, like dog or apple, but of a core semantic root embedded in a relatively large set of prefixes, suffixes, and other morphemes that indicate particular states, relationships, intensities, conditions of observation, and the like. In other words, such polysynthetic languages cut up experience into less autonomous or isolated pieces than does English (and other European languages); they incorporate in their words a larger part of the sensory, social, and interactive surround. This aspect of their grammatical structure, Whorf argued, favors a way of conceptualizing reality that focuses more on relationships and contingencies than on isolated entities and their actions, as English speakers conceive it.

Structures of Grammar and Thought. Such languages as Hopi do not permit, according to Whorf, the objectification of such non-spatial and subjectively experienced phenomena as duration (the sense of the passing of time) or of feelings, wishes, hopes, thoughts, expectations, and the like. Indeed, to speak of these requires an entirely different grammatical form from that used for objects with perceptible spatial features, and the different forms may not be used interchangeably, any more than we may use English verb tenses interchangeably—for example, say "He ran to the store" to indicate something that *will* happen tomorrow. Just as English speakers *must* choose a verb form that indicates whether something has happened in the past, or is happening now, or will happen in the future, speakers of Hopi, for example, *must* choose a verb form that indicates whether the event/thing spoken of lies in the realm of the objective world (i.e., things perceptible to the senses at the moment of speaking) or in the realm of the subjective (i.e., things remembered, imagined, hoped for, but not-now-present-to-the-senses). This grammatical distinction between the objective and the subjective realms extends, in languages like Hopi, even to ways of counting. In English, cardinal numbers (one, two, three, four, etc.) can be used to count both perceptible collections of objects, like chairs in a room or pieces of chalk held in the hand, and purely imaginary collections, like a set of days (which no one has ever seen standing together in a cluster, like so many trees or houses).

Hopi grammatical structure, on the other hand, does not permit the use of cardinal numbers for counting such imaginary collections. It requires, instead, the use of ordinals to count remembered or anticipated successions of events. The Hopi speaker cannot talk of ten days or six years, but must speak of the tenth coming of the day or the sixth coming of the spring. This grammatical requirement, Whorf argues, reinforces a construction of reality in which events-in-time are understood not as a progression of units along some imaginary line extending from the past into the future (as the structure of English leads us to conceive them), but as a continuous *cycle*. In this worldview, such Western conceptions as the idea of progress are not only very difficult to express, but more important, difficult (if not impossible) to *think*. So, too, are such notions (and behavioral compulsions) of English speakers as the preoccupation with saving time, spending time, wasting time, investing time, and the like. Such preoccupations arise in large part from the linguistically founded conception of time as a *thing* that exists in the real world as a set of units that may be counted, collected, stored, and otherwise handled just as any other set of perceptible objects.

The cyclical conception of time codified in the linguistic structure of Hopi is closely related to the cultural history of its speakers. The Hopi are an agrarian people, at least in origin, closely tied to the cycles of the seasons and of planting, reaping, and cultivation of the earth. Thus, the question arises, "Which came first: their language and the habits of thought and behavior it engenders, or their cultural activities, which shaped the development of their language?" This is a question about how language and culture originate and evolve, and it has an important place in our attempt to understand ourselves. But it is not a question that Whorf was concerned to address in detail, except to stress that language and culture grow up hand in hand and are inextricably intertwined. From the point of view of the present, however, how different languages attained their grammatical structures is largely irrelevant. Every human child is born into a language community that already has a fully developed linguistic system in place. Every child, in the process of learning to speak, learns along with her language the particular *way* of cutting up and reassembling reality that the grammatical structure of her language requires. Having learned that way, reinforced every time we speak, write or think, we unconsciously project it onto reality ever after. Thus, to one extent or another, we all become prisoners, not of our senses, but of our language.

Linguistic Relativity or Linguistic Determinism? The key question is to what extent language imprisons thought. As I noted earlier, there are some who have read

Whorf's thesis as an argument for linguistic determinism. That is, they understand him to be saying that: (a) *all* thinking is linguistic, (b) every aspect of a language imposes equally inescapable constraints on thought, perception, and behavior, and therefore (c) language totally dictates (or determines) thought and culture. Pinker (1994) is one contemporary writer on language and thought who represents Whorf's thesis in this way, and he ridicules the absurdity of such a set of ideas (no doubt to bolster the serious significance of his own, by comparison). Indeed, such a position *would* be absurd. But this is more Pinker's construction than Whorf's. In the long excerpt cited earlier, Whorf is careful to say that the kaleidoscopic flux of our sensory impressions is organized *largely* by the linguistic systems in our minds, and that we cut nature up and organize it as we do *largely* because we are parties to an agreement codified in the patterns of our language. *Largely* is not the same as *entirely*, and Whorf was of the view that underlying all the variations of languages there are more fundamental processes of mind. As he put it,

> [T]he tremendous importance of language cannot, in my opinion, be taken to mean necessarily that nothing is back of it of the nature of what has traditionally been called "mind." My own studies suggest, to me, that language, for all its kingly role, is in some sense a superficial embroidery upon deeper processes of consciousness, which are necessary before any communication, signaling, or symbolism whatsoever can occur (p. 239).

Whorf hoped that the study he called *comparative linguistics* might eventually lead to the discovery of a universal set of sublinguistic or superlinguistic mental processes that, transformed as they may be by the varieties of different languages, would provide clues to those commonalities that bind us as members of a single human family. In this respect, he anticipated the Chomskyan project of searching for universals underlying the diversity of human tongues. But his own project had a different thrust: to demonstrate that the grammatical structures of widely different language groups provide a ready-made set of patterns that give very different shapes to the habitual modes of perception, conception, and elaborated thought of their speakers.

The phrase that most troubles determinist readers of Whorf's thesis, in the frequently quoted passage cited earlier, has to do with the "absolutely obligatory" terms in which different languages codify thought. If this is taken to mean that *every* aspect of a language is absolutely obligatory, then the thesis is not only deterministic but exceedingly easy to refute, since nothing could be more obvious than the *choices* speakers (and writers) must make in composing every utterance. Nothing obligates me to use the word "use" rather than "choose" or "select" in the sentence I am now writing, and I might have written "instead of" in place of "rather than." Indeed, writing and speaking (not to mention thinking) would be a great deal easier if *all* the terms of language were equally obligatory. But that is not what Whorf says. It is the grammatical structures and categories of language, not word choices, that he characterizes as absolutely obligatory for elaborated thought. The grammatical structure of English, for example, requires us to indicate in the form of every verb the time it refers to—past, present, or future. We cannot choose *not* to do so. The grammar of Hopi, by contrast, has no tenses, but imposes different requirements—among them, not only the use of different verb forms to distinguish between objective and subjective events and phenomena, but the use of different endings to indicate whether utterances are reports, expectations, or generalizations. English grammatical structure requires us to articulate thought in sentences composed of substantives (or subjects) and predicates, leading us to conceive of the world as composed of actors and their actions—even when there are no actors in any sane sense of the word. (What exactly is the "it" that is doing the activity of raining, for example, in the sentence "It is raining"?) Hopi grammatical structure does not require verbs to have subjects, and thus constructs a different picture of reality.

Can we think *outside* the grammatical structures of our own language—fully grasp an alternative reality where time, for example, has no past, present, or future? Can a native speaker of English genuinely apprehend, and accept as an entirely reasonable construction of reality, the idea that a rosebush and the *thought of* a rosebush are not two independent things but are simply two different stages of a single phenomenon, so that the one inevitably affects the other? No doubt one *can* think such thoughts, and Whorf would have been the last to deny it. Were it not possible, he would not himself have been able to make sense of the Hopi or Aztec or Nootka constructions of reality—nor would his readers be able to understand his attempts to explain them. But it is intensely difficult to think in such ways for more than a few moments, and we do not *habitually* do so.

Language and Culture. Habitual thought runs quickly and lightly along the tracks that linguistic structures provide. If it did not, it would be a continuous struggle to think and speak at all and people would find themselves continually at odds with their own culture. For the worldviews languages codify are expressed and reinforced not only in speech but in countless other symbol systems, cultural practices, and social institutions. The objectification of time that characterizes the linguistic structure of English and other Standard Average European languages, for example, gives rise to mechanical clocks, calendars, digital watches, time cards, daylight saving, lateness penalties, datebooks, appointments, and hundreds of other artifacts, practices, and cultural values derived from the projection of time into an imaginary visual space, where it may be carved into units and counted.

Of course, linguistic structure alone is not the cause of such techniques and cultural practices. As other media ecologists have pointed out, in particular, Havelock (1976), McLuhan (1964), and Ong (1982), the development of writing systems, beginning some 3,500 years ago, also played a major role in the spatialization and objectification of subjective experience. Writing permits the commitment of thoughts, expectations, feelings, and the sense of the passage of time to a fixed, visible form outside the body, as marks on stone, clay, and paper. It projects subjective experience into visual space, and by fixing it there, allows it to be observed and analyzed. One may not be able to see ten sunrises standing in a row like so many trees; but one can certainly see ten *marks* representing those sunrises on a stone, and count the marks just as one counts any other collection of perceptible objects. It well may be that the availability of writing systems, rather than linguistic structure, is the key factor in the objectification of time and the spatialization of the subjective that characterize cultures that write.

Indeed, McLuhan and Ong, among others, have suggested that many of the characteristics of the Amerindian worldview that Whorf attributes to linguistic structure are better explained by the fact that the cultures Whorf studied are (or were then) primarily *oral* cultures; that is, cultures that did not develop writing systems of their own or come to rely on writing until recent times. Whorf did not live long enough to respond to that suggestion. If he had, he might have replied that the development of writing was itself influenced by the structures of the spoken languages of the cultures that played major roles in the evolution of writing from its logographic forms (in Sumeria and Egypt) to its syllabic forms (in West Phoenicia) and ultimately, to its unique alphabetic form (in Greece). While he did not extend his inquiries back that far, Whorf (1956) does remark that much of the reference to the nonspatial by spatial terms and linguistic structures was already fixed in the ancient tongues, most notably in the Greek-influenced Latin from which most of the spatializing Standard Average European languages derive (pp. 156–157).

Whorf would have been quick, in any case, to grant an important role to writing in the intensification of such pre-existing linguistic biases toward spatialization. He understood that language and other systems of representation interact in exceedingly complex ways with social, environmental and technological conditions to create and continually transform the ecologies of culture. He says so quite clearly in his brief answer to the question why and how the Western European worldview and the Amerindian attained their distinctively different forms:

> In the Middle Ages the patterns already formed in Latin began to interweave with the increased mechanical invention, industry, trade, and scholastic and scientific thought. The need for measurement in industry and trade, the stores and bulks of "stuffs" in

various containers, the type-bodies in which various goods were handled, standardizing of measure and weight units, invention of clocks and measurement of "time," keeping of records, accounts, chronicles, histories, growth of mathematics and the partnership of mathematics and science, all cooperated to bring our thought and language world into its present form.

In Hopi history, could we read it, we should find a different type of language and a different set of cultural and environmental influences working together. A peaceful agricultural society isolated by geographic features and nomad enemies in a land of scanty rainfall, arid agriculture that could only be made successful by the utmost perseverance (hence the value of persistence and repetition), necessity for collaboration (hence emphasis on the psychology of teamwork and on mental factors in general), corn and rain as primary criteria of value, need of extensive preparations and precautions to assure crops in the poor soil and precarious climate, keen realization of dependence on nature favoring prayer and a religious attitude toward the forces of nature, especially prayer and religion directed toward the ever needed blessing, rain—these things interacted with Hopi linguistic patterns to mold them, to be molded again by them, and so little by little to shape the Hopi world-outlook. (Whorf, 1956, pp. 157–158)

Whorf was not in fact a linguistic determinist. He was, rather, an early media ecologist. He understood and argued persuasively that humans do not live in the objective world alone, but in symbolic environments of thought, communication, and culture built upon systems of *representing* experience—the earliest and most fundamental of which is language. Whorf's most urgent and insistent point was that language is not a neutral container or conveyor of ideas, but an instrument of thought that has a distinctive structure of its own, and a different structure in different speech communities. These structures of language are interposed between people and reality, and just as the astronomer's telescope, the biologist's microscope, and the physicist's beam of light bring different realities into view and transform them, so do the different structures of language construct different conceptions of the world. In particular, the structure of every language codifies a *metaphysics*—a set of assumptions about the nature of space and time and the relationships among objects and events within space and time. These conceptions, in turn, direct attention to certain aspects of experience and suggest different social arrangements, different cultural practices, different inventions to solve particular problems as we conceptualize them. Social arrangements, cultural practices, and inventions feed back into the patterns of language, transforming it, in turn, in a continuous process of language, thought, and culture change.

Whorf himself did not generalize these foundational principles of media ecology to all systems of representation and communication. His passion and scholarly concern was language, and except for brief references to such other symbolic forms as painting, music, dance, and architecture, and to the medium of radio (relatively new on the scene in Whorf's time), he did not pursue the question whether different forms of symbolic representation and communication might cut up and reassemble reality in ways very different from language, in ways specific to the structure of each medium. But Whorf's work played a major role in moving that question to the forefront of inquiry, and thus laid the groundwork for the development of media ecology.

Susanne K. Langer and the Symbolic Transformation of Experience

One of the first to recognize the significance of the larger question implied by Whorf's work, and to address it systematically, was Susanne K. Langer. In the first of her major works on symbolic philosophy and aesthetics, *Philosophy in a New Key* (1942), Langer argued that the "new key" of her title (i.e., the new question at the center of philosophical inquiry in the 20th century) is the question, What is the nature of symbolic representation and how does it function, in its various transformations, in the constructive process of human thought and response? In a set of volumes that became the core of her life's work—in particular, *Philosophy in a New Key* and its successor, *Feeling and Form* (Langer, 1953)—Langer aimed to answer to that question. In the process, she set forth not only a comprehensive theory of symbolism, but an analysis of the different symbolic structures and functions of discursive language as well as painting, sculpture, architecture, literature, music, dance, drama, and film. Her work had worldwide impact on the philosophy of art, and it is still considered essential reading for students of aesthetic philosophy. More to the point, it is essential reading for students of media ecology, or should be, since *Philosophy in a New Key*, in particular, advances a number of ideas that are vitally important to the understanding of differences among various codes and modes of representation and their consequences for human thought and response. Here the focus will be on the central argument of Langer's work in that volume, rather than on the detailed analyses of specific artforms in *Feeling and Form*.

Signals, Symbols, and Mind. At the core of Langer's thesis is her argument that neither the human capacity for language nor our capacity to express feeling in such forms as ritual and dance is the distinguishing feature of the human mind; rather, these capacities grow out of a more fundamental activity that distinguishes humans from other creatures. That underlying activity of the human mind is the process of abstracting experience and representing it *in symbols that evoke conceptions*—that is, that *call ideas to mind*. This process of transforming experience into symbols is radically different from what other creatures do with signs. Signs—which may generally be defined as the entire set of things which indicate, to some creature or person, something else or some larger state of affairs—serve two quite different functions. (For clarity of explanation, I have revised Langer's use of "sign" and "signal" in *Philosophy in a New Key* according to her later use of those terms in *Feeling and Form*, and her acknowledgement that this usage is more accurate. See Langer, 1953, p. 26, n 1.)

One function is to *signal* the existence of some state of affairs, as when a chimp barks to signal the approach of an intruder to the rest of its tribe. Signals serve as behavioral triggers or commands; they function as a stimulus to a conditioned response, so that the receiver behaves in response to the sign as it would in response to the actual presence of the intruder. In this respect, one might say that the meaning of a signal is the *behavior* it triggers. The signalic function of signs is widespread among creatures of all kinds, and it is entirely utilitarian and survival-oriented. We ourselves may respond to signs as signals, as when we pull to the side of the road at the sound of fire-engine sirens, although the engines are not yet in view. But humans may also respond to signs *symbolically*. In their *symbolic* function, signs do not trigger overt behavioral reactions, but *call ideas to mind*. If the sound of sirens leads someone not to pull over, but to reflect on fire engines and their vivid colors, or on the brave deeds of firefighters, or on the irony that fire both gives life and destroys it, then she is responding to the sign (the sound of sirens) as a symbol, not as a signal. While she is doing so, she is likely to be run down by the engines, but that is not the point. The point is that, in humans, signs may function either as signals or as *symbols*: as instruments for *thinking about* things they call to mind. The meaning of a symbol is not the reaction it calls into action, but the *conception* it calls to mind.

So far as is known, other creatures do not use signs as symbols. Chimps or gorillas may be taught to use a particular sign (from American Sign Language, or even on a keyboard) for "banana." But it has not yet been demonstrated that they can use these signs as symbols; for example, to reflect on the virtues of bananas or their relative dietary value as compared to, say, fish. Their object in signing "banana" would seem to be to bring the banana into their hands, not the *idea* of bananas into their minds. (There is, of course, a great deal of debate on this issue at present. Here I represent Langer's view of the matter—as well as my own.)

Langer's point in distinguishing between the symbolic and signalic functions of signs is to rebut the view that human language is merely a complex elaboration on the signaling systems used by other creatures, and, like those systems, serves primarily communicative and utilitarian ends. That line of argument, she contends, leads inevitably to the privileging of discursive, propositional language over other forms of symbolic representation, since it is this form of representation that has made possible logic and science and all their utilitarian benefits. This view also relegates the arts to a minor and somewhat accidental position in the spectrum of human symbolic progress, since they do not seem to serve the destined utilitarian ends on which language is based (according to this view) and to which it must inevitably lead. By arguing that language is *not*, in its origins, an outgrowth of utilitarian signaling, but is, like the arts, a manifestation of the human mind's tendency to transform experience into *symbols*, Langer places the arts and discursive language on a par, as two different forms of that symbolic activity that characterizes all human thought.

Langer argues that the distinctively human need to transform experience into symbols has generated two quite different modes of representation. Both are equally symbolic, and both reflect the higher activities of mind. But the two modes are quite different in their forms and structures, in the spectrum of human sensibility they represent, and in the responses they engender. Langer calls these two distinct patterns of codes the discursive and presentational (or non-discursive) modes of symbolic representation. Discursive symbolism, according to Langer, is comprised for the most part of true or propositional language and of mathematics. These coding systems differ both formally and logically from the codes of presentational symbolism, which comprise what is usually called the arts: painting, photography, music, dance, sculpture, architecture, literature, drama, and film.

Digital Symbols and Discursive Forms. The major logical difference between the two modes derives from the ways in which they represent their objects, that is, the conceptions they call to mind. The discursive forms of true language and mathematics, to begin, represent ideas in discrete units, sometimes referred to as digital symbols, which have no natural or structural correspondence to what they represent. (Note, however, that Langer does not use the terms "digital" and "analogic" symbols, although she does consistently refer to presentational symbols as "analogues." I have introduced the terms "digital" and "analogic" for purposes of providing a clearer explanation and more current terminology.)

A digital symbol is a purely *arbitrary* mark or sound associated with a concept and applied to things and events as a name for them. There is nothing about the form of a digital symbol (its particular shape or noise or color or length or size or anything else) that corresponds to any perceptible characteristic of what it stands for. People simply *agree* to use this sound or mark or whatever to stand for something else (conceptions and the objects, events, etc., they denote). One cannot tell by looking at the letters "man," for example, whether the object denoted by those marks is big or little, straight or round, animate or inanimate. One does not change the *form* of the symbol to indicate a change in the form of what it denotes; one does not write MAN in bigger letters to indicate a big man, or use long words for long things and short words for short things. It is purely a matter of convention, of social agreement, to use *this* (digital symbol) to stand for *that* (conception, object, or event). As Whorf and other linguists have pointed out, different cultures have developed, over their long histories, very different agreements and conventions about what sounds and marks will stand for what concepts and name what things. That is why, if a Russian tries to describe her cat in *words* (digital symbols), listeners will not understand her (unless they speak Russian), nor a German who describes his house in his language.

Words are not the only kinds of digital symbols. *Anything* can function as a digital symbol, simply by our agreeing to make it do so. People can agree to let the color "red" mean stop and the color "green" mean go, or the sound of a bell mean "stop" and the sound of a siren mean "go." On road maps, we can let the color "black" mean two-lane roads, the color "red" mean major highways, and the color "green" mean throughways or toll roads. How would one know that? *Because the agreements about what digital symbols stand for can be made explicit.* If one looks at the top of the map (the key) it will indicate that black line = two-lane road. A dictionary is a culture's equivalent of the map key for its lexicon: It makes explicit the concepts that words stand for and gives examples of the things and events that the words name or denote.

The individual units of discursive forms like true language, then, are arbitrary digital symbols that both bring to mind or *connote* certain abstract conceptions (like the conceptions associated with the word "dog," for example) and *name* (or *denote*) things in the world of experience that fit those conceptions (like the specific four-legged, tail-wagging, cold-nosed bundle of fur that barks you a welcome home each evening). But that is only the beginning. To construct their representations of experience, discursive forms also rely on *syntax*.

Syntax is a set of rules for indicating the relationships among things denoted by individual words. The important point is that these rules, like word-symbols, are a form of *digital* symbolism, in that the rules are a matter of cultural agreement or convention. Different cultures have different ways to indicate different relations among things. In English, for example, the order in which things are named tells us what is the subject (or doer of the action) and what is the object (or receiver of the action) in a given situation. Generally, the rule is, "Name the doer of the action first, then the action, then the thing acted upon." This rule lets us know that when someone says, "The dog chased the cat," they mean the dog was running after the cat (because that's the order in which they named them). In some other languages, the *order* of the words doesn't make any difference. They have a different rule—like "attach a particular ending to a word to indicate that it's the subject, and a different ending to indicate which one is the object." It is possible to make these rules for how to indicate relationships among named things *explicit*. That's what I've just done: told you the rule in English for how to indicate the subject and object. If you study a foreign language by using a textbook, the textbook will teach you the explicit rules for indicating various kinds of relationships in that language.

These characteristics of true language—that it uses digital symbols whose meanings and rules for indicating relationships can be made explicit—give it an enormous capacity for precision in representing experience and communicating it to others. Syntax, in particular, allows the representation of complex *situations* with great specificity and distinction between one situation and another. Syntax allows us to assert that "this pattern of symbols corresponds to that situation in the real world." It allows us to make *statements* that others can decode by following the explicit rules, then verify or refute by looking at the world. But there is a catch.

Truth, Falsity, and Propositions. The catch is that not all statements can be verified or refuted (falsified) by looking at the world. There are some statements, for example, that are not *about* the world outside our skins and what is going on out there. There are many statements, for example, about what *ought* to happen in the world. These are usually called prescriptive statements, to contrast them with descriptive statements. Commands, too, are a form of prescriptive language. Logicians have pointed out that prescriptions, whether they are commands or statements about what ought to or should happen, cannot be verified or refuted by looking at the world because they don't indicate anything that is happening or has happened. One cannot say of such statements that they are either true (meaning, they correspond accurately to something that is happening in the non-word world) or false (meaning they do not correspond to what is happening outside our skins).

Second, we do not always make the meanings of our words so explicit that they indicate very specific things to look at in the world outside our skins. In other words, it isn't always clear what someone intends to *denote* by her words. If I say, for example, "There is a purgle in the top left corner of this page," and you do not know what the word "purgle" denotes, you cannot judge whether one is there or not, because you don't know what to look fo. The same thing is true about a great many regular words like "ghost," "soul," "intelligence," and "beauty." Unless the speaker makes his meanings so explicit (i.e., makes them public) that we can be sure we are looking for or at the same thing, there is no way to determine whether it is there or not. In short, one cannot say a statement is true or false unless one knows precisely what the words used in it *denote*.

The same thing would be true if one doesn't know the rules for decoding the statement as a unit; that is, if it does not follow the conventional rules of grammar or syntax. If someone puts her words in an any-which-way order, one would not be able to tell what she means to assert, or even whether an assertion has been made. We cannot say that something is true or false if we don't know what it means. In order to assert something in English, one must arrange words in such a way as to *predicate* something about a subject; that is, say something *about* it.

Finally, one cannot say that something is true or false unless there is some conceivable way to *test* it; that is, some imaginable procedure one could use to verify or refute it. If I say, for example, "No more than 23 angels can dance on the head of a pin at the same time," and specify precisely what I mean by an angel (e.g., a being exactly like a human, but invisible), and the dimensions of the pin, you would still need to know how you could find out whether that is true or not. If the answer is, "There is no way to find out, because angels never do it when someone is there, or when any kind of mechanical device is around," then it makes no sense to say the statement is true or false because there is no way to verify or refute it.

In the tradition of other symbolic philosophers, Langer uses the term "propositions" or "propositional utterance" to refer to representations that satisfy the foregoing criteria. Propositions are *statements* that can be said to be true or false because: (a) they use symbols that have explicit, public denotations; (b) they conform to syntactic rules that can be made explicit; (c) they propose or assert (i.e., predicate) something about something; (d) they are *descriptive*, not prescriptive; and (e) they are in principle subject to tests of refutation and verification.

All this is necessary to understand because Langer argues that *propositional utterance is both the symbolic form and the mission of true language and of discursive symbolism in general*. The discursive forms of symbolic representation, comprised of true or propositional language and mathematics, are the codes through which people conduct rational thought and reasoning, and through which they build up scientific and logical knowledge of the world.

Analogic Symbols and Presentational Forms. True language and mathematics are not, however, the only forms in which the human mind expresses its need to transform experience into symbols. Langer argues that the discursive forms of symbolic representation constitute only a fraction of our total symbolic experience. The larger part takes a different form, which Langer calls the non-discursive or presentational mode of representation, and it differs from the discursive mode in many important respects. To begin, the presentational forms of representation—like drawings, paintings, photographs, music, dance and the other arts—are not composed of digital symbols, but represent their objects (i.e., what they call to mind) *analogically*. Unlike a digital symbol, which is totally arbitrary, an *analogic* symbol represents in its *form* some important characteristic(s) of the object it stands for, in such a way that when the characteristics of the *object* change, so does the form of the symbol. Pictures, sketches, and drawings are good examples of *analogic* symbols. If I want to send my sister a sketch of a new dining table, and the table is round, the shape I draw must also be round. If the table is square, the shape of the marks I make on the paper must be changed to reflect that difference. If two different tables need to be represented, a cocktail table and a dining table, then shorter marks are made for the legs of the first and longer marks for the legs of the second to correspond to the different lengths of the legs on the objects. The way the path of a road is represented on a road map is also a good example of an *analogic* symbol: the line that represents the road changes in length and direction as the road changes in length and direction. Analogic symbols do not have to represent *every* feature of something to call their objects to mind. Some analogic representations are very detailed, as photographs tend to be, and some (like road maps) are very abstract, meaning they leave out most detail. The important thing in analogic representation is that some features of the *symbol* must correspond to some features of the *object* the symbol calls to mind.

To be more precise, an analogic symbol represents in its form the *structure of relations among parts* that the mind abstracts from sensory experience. The familiar visual symbol of the smiley face, for example, brings to mind a human face, not because real human faces are composed of three black dots and a curve, but because the structural relationship among the dots and the curve in the symbol corresponds to the structural relationship among eyes, nose and mouth that the mind abstracts from the sensory perception of human faces. And it is the whole structure of relations among the elements of the symbol that is significant, that is meaningful, not the individual dots and lines of which the symbol is composed. To put it another way, the individual units or elements of which analogic/presentational symbols are composed do not have independent meanings outside the particular structure of relations in which they are presented. The smiley face, for example, is composed (in part) of three dots that are exactly alike, yet the two that are at the top of the drawing call to mind eyes, while the one in the center calls to mind a nose. In a totally different arrangement of lines and curves, the same dots might call to mind, instead, the pips on a strawberry, or raindrops falling from a cloud.

In short, the elements of which presentational symbols like drawings or musical chords are composed are *not* the equivalent of words, which carry over their meanings from one context to another. It is quite impossible to say what a dot means generally in pictorial representation, or a straight line, or a curve. Similarly, it is impossible to say what the sound of a C-major chord calls to mind, or the sound of a piccolo or snare drum, outside of the context of their relations with other chords and instrumental sounds in a particular composition. That is, the individual elements of a complex presentational symbol like a painting or piece of music do not have independent, fixed connotations, as words do. Neither do the elements of a dance, a painting or a symphony *denote* specific things and events in the experiential world. Musical sounds, for example, in particular combinations and relationships, may *connote* (call to mind) certain ideas and feelings—for example, rising excitement or a sense of a resolution of tension—but they do not point to this or that event or object in the phenomenal world, as names for them. That said, different musical sounds in a particular piece *can* be used to refer to or denote specific things. For example, in *Peter and the Wolf* certain instrumental sounds and melodies denote the character Peter, while other sounds and melodies refer to different characters in the musical story. But people must be told this, in words, in a written program that accompanies the music. Without that guide, one could not guess from the sounds alone that they denote particular characters or events. Nor do the same instruments refer to the same characters and events outside that particular musical composition.

Similarly, the visual composition alone in Picasso's *Guernica*, for example, does not denote or refer to any particular set of events. Its elements, in their specific arrangements, connote or summon to mind ideas/conceptions/feelings of discord, imbalance, destruction, chaos, grief, but they do not name any particular objects or events to which those feelings (and the symbolic elements of the painting) apply. Indeed, without the title of the painting (a word) and an accompanying linguistic text, one would not be able to say what the whole refers to or denotes.

Presentational Forms versus Statements. Because the units of which presentational symbolism is composed have neither fixed connotations nor explicit denotations, there can be no such thing as a dictionary in which one might look up the meanings of dots or lines or curves, or of the sounds produced by violins or piccolos, or of the different positions in which a dancer might hold her arms. Nor is there the equivalent of a grammar book where one can learn the explicit rules for building up the units of visual or musical representation into larger structures of meaning. This is not to say that paintings and symphonies and ballets do not *have* a structure. But it is a kind of structure entirely unlike the structure of propositional language and other discursive forms, and it does not lend itself to analysis into independent parts with fixed meanings and explicit rules for combining those parts into statements.

Langer argues that the presentational forms of representation do not *make* statements. They present subjects, structured symbols that call to mind conceptions and feelings, but they do not predicate or assert anything *about* their subjects. A striking landscape photograph, for example, may call to mind many different ideas—about the monumental permanence and substantiality of mountain peaks, the insubstantiality of clouds and the ever-changing quality of light, or about the relative endurance of nature compared to humankind or the magnificence of the Creator's awesome design. But the photograph itself does not assert any of these things. Such is the power of our tendency to think in *language*, as Whorf noted, that we may formulate into sentences the wordless conceptions to which paintings and photographs, music and dance and sculpture give rise. But the statements are not there in the work itself. Even the symbolic form of film, for which the metaphor of a language is often used, does not make statements (although its characters might when they speak). Film is not a medium for messages, assertions, statements, or propositions. Neither is painting, photography, music, dance, architecture, or sculpture. Their symbolic form does not permit them to assert or state anything because their elements do not have fixed connotations or denotations. The structural relations in which they arrange their elements are not the structural relations of linguistic syntax.

For these reasons, Langer argues, the presentational forms of symbolism fall outside the realm of expression to which the words "true" and "false" apply. If McDonald's *says*, in a television commercial, that its hamburgers weigh one-quarter of a pound (before cooking), that is an assertion in the realm of propositional utterance; it may be subjected to tests of verification or refutation, and on the basis of the outcome one may say that the statement is true or false. But there is no way to test a series of images in which children roll in the grass with a lawn full of puppies in front of a McDonald's sign, or smile and snuggle against their parents while eating french fries. Such images do not assert anything, such as "McDonald's provides puppies to play with" or "french fries cause children to snuggle against their parents." Thus the images themselves cannot be said to be true or false. One may like them or dislike them, be moved to laughter or tears by them, associate good feelings or bad feelings with them. But one cannot argue with them or refute them, because they are not in the symbolic realm of *discourse*.

Discourse is defined by a specific set of formal and logical properties of representation, found in a limited set of codes, particularly true language and mathematics. The mode of symbolic transformation that characterizes such other codes as images, music and dance has neither the forms nor the functions of discourse, argument or reasoning. For that reason, Langer warns us not to use the metaphor of languages in referring to photography, film, painting, music, or dance, since it implies that these forms are language-like in their structures and functions, and obscures the much more important point that, in fact, they are vitally different.

Presentational Forms and Feeling. If the presentational forms of representation are *not* language-like, if they do not serve the functions of discourse, rational thought, argument and reason, what functions do they serve? What exactly is it that they represent, and why do we need them? Langer's answer to these questions is concisely indicated in the title of her sequel to *Philosophy in a New Key* (1942): *Feeling and Form* (1953). To reduce it to a sentence, her argument is that the presentational forms of symbolism articulate the life of *feeling*. They provide, in their structures, symbolic analogues of what our eyes can see, what our bodies experience, what our ears hear, and all the feelings, sensory and emotional, that arise from our encounters with the world as very complex biological creatures. We need such modes of expression and communication because *the ways in which language cuts up and reassembles the world are not the same as the ways in which we experience the world through our senses.*

We are, despite all our rational linguistic achievements, creatures of biology and sensation. Our deepest feelings run together, concatenate, reverberate, and cross semantic and neurological boundaries in ways that no digital system of words or mathematical symbols can ever adequately represent. In its technical sense, a digital system of codification is a way of sampling the full range of some phenomenon, such as a sound wave or a light wave, rather than reproducing the entire spectrum of variation along the wave. Propositional language is like that: a sampling of what we experience, a highly selective and compressed code that represents only the peaks and troughs of the continuous wave of our bio-sensory-motor experience—the bits and pieces that have proven essential, in the history of our culture, to surviving and getting on in the world. All the rest of the wave of our creaturely experience is voiceless because it has no words into which to fit. There is no adequate way to speak, in digital, propositional language, about how gravity tugs at our senses and weighs us down, and how winter and rain and certain slants of light seem to add to that weight, while the greening and brightening of spring somehow frees us. The tongue stutters and stammers in our attempts to express our deep autumnal sense of—of what?—of things passing, slowing, dying, falling, darkening, spiraling down, coming to rest, and of the inchoate feelings of longing, mourning, yearning that come with the changing of the light. But the cello's voice in Max Bruch's *Kol Nidre* somehow sings of this, and dance gives expression to our feelings of weight and weightlessness, falling and rising, tension and release, oppression and freedom, grief and joy.

In short, Langer argues that the presentational forms offer, in their structures, complex analogues of sensory experience and feeling, of all that cannot fit within the sparse and parsimonious structures of propositional utterance. They also call forth a different mode of response. Where true language fosters analytic reasoning and linear thinking—the taking of things apart and the reconstructing of ideas in logical and grammatical sequence—the presentational forms foster the instantaneity of *recognition*, of gestalt apprehension, for the meanings of pictures, music, dance must be grasped as wholes or they cannot be grasped at all. Propositional utterance—true language or discourse—fosters the delayed response, not only because its elements are strung out one at a time in such a way that successive elements modify the meanings of preceding ones, but because *the criterion of its merit is its truth or falsity.* That requires time for tests of verification and refutation, the search for evidence in the non-word world to which propositions purport to correspond. Thus language also directs our attention outward to the world beyond our skins. The criterion of merit for the presentational forms, on the other hand, is not their truth or falsity, but their *consonance with the structure of our sensory experience and feeling*. They direct attention inward.

The discursive and presentational modes of symbolic representation complement one another. Taken together, they permit us to do what neither mode can do alone: transform the entire range of knowledge and experience, thought and feeling, into symbols, and so give articulated expression to the fundamental activity of human mind.

Codes, Modes, and Media Ecology

Langer wrote *Philosophy in a New Key* in the early 1940s, and completed her analysis of the different forms of presentational symbolism in *Feeling and Form* in 1953. She did not foresee the proliferation of new forms of representation that would emerge with the maturing of television in the decades that have followed, and therefore did not address many of the questions that occupy media ecologists today—for example, how people choose between the different modes of response and assessment required by discursive and presentational symbolism when confronted with mixed forms such as the docudrama and the infomercial. Neither did she speculate on whether the increasing immersion of young people in presentational forms might lead to a rearrangement of habits of thought and response that would leave an older generation of discursively conditioned teachers puzzled and frustrated by their students' apparent difficulties with logic, reasoning, argument, and the niceties of evidence. Of computers and their unique symbolic forms, Langer had nothing to say—although she did move the terms virtual space, virtual time, and virtual reality out of the domain of physicists and into the common parlance of humanistic studies of symbols, codes, and media. Indeed, *Feeling and Form* is almost entirely about virtual space, time and reality and how they are constructed and manipulated in different symbolic forms. Her analysis there is as vital for understanding the role of computer-mediated forms in the construction of reality and response as it is for understanding the more traditional forms of representation and their unique functions.

I have focused on *Philosophy in a New Key* here not only because it is, as Langer herself wrote, a prerequisite for understanding the later work, but because it first charted the ground on which so much of media ecology stands. In it, Langer extended Whorf's insights into the relativity of language to a much larger set of codes and modes of representation. She argued that language is not *the* way in which humans construct reality, but *a* way, and that different systems of symbolic transformation codify different aspects of the spectrum of human experience. She raised for the first time, in a systematic way, the question, How does the *structure* of different symbol systems constrain what they can express, and shape the nature of human response?

As Heisenberg said, all that we know is a result of the questions we ask. Benjamin Lee Whorf and Susanne Langer are foundational to media ecology, not because their analyses of the languages and other symbolic forms are adequate or complete or correct in every respect. They are foundational because they asked the right questions.

References

Barnett, L. (1968). *The universe and Dr. Einstein.* New York, NY: Bantam Books.
Havelock, E. A. (1976). *Origins of western literacy.* Toronto, Canada: The Ontario Institute for Studies in Education.
Heisenberg, W. (1962). *Physics and philosophy.* New York, NY: Harper & Row.
Kuhn, T. S. (1962). *The structure of scientific revolutions.* Chicago, IL: University of Chicago Press.
Langer, S. K. (1942). *Philosophy in a new key.* Cambridge, MA: Harvard University Press.
Langer, S. K. (1953). *Feeling and form.* New York, NY: Charles Scribner's Sons.
Matson, F. W. (1966). *The broken image: Man, science, and society.* Garden City, NY: Doubleday.
McLuhan, M. (1964). *Understanding media: The extensions of man.* New York, NY: McGraw Hill.
Ong, W. (1982). *Orality and literacy.* New York, NY: Methuen & Company.
Pinker, Stephen (1994). *The language instinct.* New York, NY: William Morrow and Company, Inc.
Postman, N. (1999). *Building a bridge to the eighteenth century.* New York, NY: Alfred A. Knopf.
Sapir, E. (1921). *Language.* New York, NY: Harcourt, Brace and Company.
Whorf, B. L. (1956). *Language, thought, and reality.* Cambridge, MA: The MIT Press.

You Are Who You Eat: Monsters and Meanings

(1991, 31 October—3 November). Paper presented at the 77th Annual Conference of the Speech Communication Association. Atlanta, GA.

Thank you, and good morning everyone. Unlike my co-panelists here, and probably most of you, I am glad that our meeting was scheduled at this dim and unholy hour, for my topic is movies and monsters, and they are best spoken of while thought is still overcast by shadows, and minds are still cobwebbed by dreams. For the proper abode of monsters is darkness and shadows, which is why no medium suits them better than the movies—unless it be the dream. And here too is a happy congruence, for monster movies have much in common with our most troubling dreams. Like the power of the dream while we are in it, the power of the movie while we are in it does not lie in its narrative—its coherence, its linearity, its superficial or even profoundly mythic storyline. It lies in its moments, its images and gaps—in what is fugitive and ambiguous, unarticulated and incoherent, dense and resonant with inexplicable feeling and meaning. To borrow a metaphor from music, to which film is so closely allied, the compelling power of movies lies, like the compelling power of dreams, not in their melodies, but in their chords: The echoing resonances of images dropped like stones into the deepest wells of human experience, generating ripple on ripple of feeling and meaning.

Monster movies are particularly dense with meanings, because they deal with the largest of human themes and hopes and fears: the nature of all that is unknowable and unknown. And since the unknown is so vast a dimension of human experience, implicated in all our explorations from infancy onward—all our relationships, all our attempts to account for how and why things and people work as they do, all our predictions and plans, hopes and fears for the future—any given set of images and moments in monster movies may evoke, simultaneously, shadowy cosmological meanings, spiritual or religious meanings, psychological meanings, political meanings, sexual meanings, social and interpersonal meanings. They also resonate with the echoes of dimly recollected notions and feelings from far back in childhood, before we learned to slice up and reorganize our experience in the tidy but inadequate categories of speech. That is one sense in which I call the themes of monster movies "primal."

The unknown has, of course, two dimensions to it: a bright and a dark. On the bright side, the unknown is the source of all our hopes: that beyond the inexplicable disorder of our lives, of events, of the world as we experience it, beyond this moment in time, with all its puzzlements and griefs and pain, there lies a greater order, a coherent meaning we do not yet see, a luminous and harmonious hidden universe that is ultimately good, ultimately on the side of life, ultimately benign. On the dark side, the unknown is the source of all our deepest suspicions and fears: that outside the tiny and fragile edifice of human knowledge, order, and light there is—nothing. Disorder. Meaninglessness. Chaos. Entropy. Nonbeing. Evil. A universe coldly indifferent, or worse, implacably hostile to us, to order, to life.

Monster movies, of course, deal with the dark side of the unknown. As a genre, they are characterized by three interwoven themes, around which most of their images center. Because I will not have time here to illustrate these in any detail, I ask you hold in mind for your own reference such movies as *Aliens* (1986) and *Alien* (1979), *Jaws* (1975), *The Thing* (1982), *Invasion of the Body Snatchers* (1978), the TV movie *V* (1983) and the host of older or lesser movies that treat of such things as werewolves, vampires, mummies and the like.

The first major theme of monster movies—perhaps the central theme—is that appearances are deceiving: that beyond the familiar and often inviting surfaces of things—the known—there is something other: something dark, unpredictable, not-like-us; something alien. Surfaces of all kinds are, of course, all that we can know through our senses. What lies under or inside them is always a matter of conjecture, and therefore a matter of uncertainty, a matter of doubt. Monster movies play heavily on our doubts about what lies beneath the appearances of things: beneath the sparkling surface of the sea (as in *Jaws*), or the serene surface of a lake (*Creature from the Black Lagoon*, 1954), or the bright glitter of snow and ice (*The Thing*), or the sands of the desert (*The Mummy*), or the surface of a planet (*Aliens*), or, most troubling of all, beneath the surface of the human body.

The ultimate unknowability from within of others who look like ourselves is, of course, a central note in the "appearances are deceiving" chord struck by monster movies: In *Invasion of the Body Snatchers*, *V*, *The Thing*, *It Came from Outer Space*, and in a large measure in *Alien*, the question whether others who look human are indeed fully human or are something else—machines, robots, alien life forms—provides the central source of tension, and often the major images of shock and horror center on the sudden revelation that what looked human is not. I might add in passing that this theme, and the larger question of what animates things, including machines and the human or human-like body, is evoked in dozens of images in monster movies and accounts, in particular, for the recurring appearance in such movies of the doll as a figure of menacing ambiguity.

Alien, for example, plays heavily on questions of human and non-human animation, giving us not only dolls but human-looking creatures animated by complex computer robotics, humans animated at least in part by alien life-forms, and machines of all kinds animated by humans—as in the many images of Sigourney Weaver climbing into one or another machine and bringing it to life. With regard to the latter set of images, it might be said that whereas in older forms of drama, the plot was often resolved by *deus ex machina*, in contemporary films it is more often resolved by *deus in machina*, or, to play on Koestler's title, a human Geist in a machine.

A second theme of monster movies—the theme that in fact distinguishes them from "bright side" fantasies of encounters with the unknown, such as *E.T.* (1982)—is the theme that the darkness and disorder of the unknown is always waiting to *break into* or *erupt from within* the apparently stable, orderly, predictable world we know, or think we do, from the appearances of things. That is, the unknown is a perpetual threat to everything humans hold dear: an enemy that, unopposed, will *take us over*, destroying all forms of biological, psychological, social, and moral order—destroying reason, sanity, goodness, democracy, meaning—destroying life itself. It follows from this that the otherworld (incarnate, of course, in the form of the monster) cannot be accommodated or assimilated into this world, into the known. It must be battled and destroyed, or if not destroyed, driven out and kept at bay by continuous vigilance and the relentless policing of every border and boundary of the known world. For borders and boundaries are the places where the otherworld, the unknown, is encountered. And they are also the places where it *gets in*.

This is, in fact, the third central theme of monster movies: that the death-dealing, order-destroying, unknown otherworld gets into the world of the familiar through boundaries and borders of every kind. Monster movies are themselves set at the boundaries of the known, at dividing lines that demark the familiar from the unexplored: the edge of space, the edge of the sea, the edge of the desert, the jungle, the lagoon, the north or south pole. The abode of the monster usually lies behind or beneath barriers to sensory perception, particularly sight: it is behind the closed door, in the dark closet, under the bed or the lid of a coffin or tomb, behind the trap door to the attic or cellar, inside the walls of the cave, the house, the mine, inside the skin, the skull, the mind—waiting to break out, or to break in.

The *time* of the monster, too, is boundary time, threshold time: between the dark and the daylight, at the edge of night. And, of course, at the edge of sleep, for sleep too is a dividing line, between consciousness and unconsciousness, knowing and the unknown, the order of daytime experience and the chaos of dreams. Sleep is the psychic dividing line, as many poets and philosophers have remarked, between what we know of life and all we can know of death. It is also the moment when we are least vigilant, when our boundaries and borders and thresholds are least defended. So sleep is always perilous in monster movies; it is an invitation to the otherworld to take over, to break in.

Children know this, of course, which is why they so often resist sleep. They also know or sense more vividly than we the otherworld—the great unknown that lies behind and within and beneath the world of surfaces, of their sensory experience. Sometimes, for children, that world is bright: It provides wonderful surprises, joyful discoveries, unpredicted pleasures. But just as often, it is dark and menacing: Exploring fingers and mouths, prying hands and teeth frequently get nasty shocks, and adults are full of warnings about the dangers of touching, opening, tasting, moving beyond established boundaries. Adults themselves, for that matter, are a source of continuous surprise to the very young, and much of the surprise is painful—as are a fair share of the toddler's encounters with other animate objects, including machines that move, animals and other children. The plain fact is that much of the world is unknown and unpredictable to very young children, and they have ample experience of its dark side to sense its menace where it lies unseen—in the closet, under the bed, down the dark hall, inside the boiler, beneath the familiar appearance and scent and touch of mommy and daddy's skin.

I talk of children here because their experience, and ours when we were very young, is part of what I mean in calling the themes of monster movies "primal": They do not only echo the recurring themes in the myths of the world's cultures—the division of the world into sacred and profane, the deceptive nature of appearances, the endless struggle of light against darkness, order against chaos, being against nothing, reason against madness, mythos against logos, self against stranger, ego against id, good against evil, life against death. They also echo our own experiences and feelings and wordless theories, from the shadowy time of our own pre-verbal childhood. And among the meanings their images evoke are nothing so clear as "memories," but resonances of inarticulate childhood notions about the world, seen and unseen, and what makes it work.

One such childhood notion or set of notions deals with what I called earlier the problem of animation—with what is inside things that move and make sounds and are responsive to our own behavior toward them—things like certain kinds of responsive machines, and dogs and cats and guinea pigs, and other people. At the earliest exploratory stages of childhood, the problem of animation is entirely focused on things and others in the external world—because that is the world young children are most affected by and therefore need most urgently to predict. At a later stage, when internalized language has begun to make the child aware of an internal landscape—of a self that corresponds to the grammatical "I"—the problem is directed inward. The question of animation is transformed from "What moves *them*?" to "What moves *me*?"

Now, young children's theories of things, like our own, are largely based on metaphor—the use of concrete sensory experience to predict what the unseen, the unknown, is like. And children's explorations of the world of objects teaches them early on that the sounds and movements of objects like rattles and pop-up toys and hand puppets come from something inside. Thus an early notion of animation is that things that move are moved by something else that moves inside: a smaller mover, so to speak, within the larger. The image in *Alien* of Sigourney Weaver climbing into the clanking robotic work machine to animate it is a near-perfect visualization of this primal—and persistent—conceptualization of the self.

But it is not the only one. As children become increasingly aware, between the ages of 4 and 8 or so, of their own internal soundscape—their wishes, desires, thoughts, and the competing claims and dictates of various internalized others, as in what we call "the voice of conscience"—as they become, in a word, self-reflective—they also construct vague theories of what directs their own decisions and behavior. Clearly, there is something or someone in them, someone who speaks in the mind, whispers prompts, makes decisions in times of difficult choice. But what is it, or who, and where did the voice of conscience come from, and how did it get in? The idea that something "got in" or got "put in" is not only based on children's explorations of how physical objects work, but is also reinforced by such repeated adult questions as, "What got into you?" and "What put that idea into your head?"

And again, children's concrete experiences provide a ready notion of how the whispery voices that guide their internal debates and conflicts and decisions got in. They got in as most things in a child's experience get into her or him: through the openings of the body. They got in as food does: through the mouth. This is, of course, one of the most primal and persistent conceptions of the origins of one's self, one's thoughts, one's ideas in the history of the world's cultures: that the internalized others who guide our thinking and decisions and behavior—the disembodied ghosts who animate the human body-machine—got in by being eaten, being ingested: that you are not only what but who you eat.

This idea is given expression not only in ritual cannibalism—which is, so to say, the highest form of flattery—but also in food taboos around the world. It is codified and perpetuated in dozens of rites, including, of course, the Christian rite of communion, in which one takes into oneself the spirit of God by eating his flesh and drinking his blood. It is reflected in our daily use of language to talk about ideas and how they get into us: a new idea is "food for thought," "something to chew on" or "get your teeth into"; but it shouldn't be "swallowed whole." We "devour" the contents of books and magazines, but take our time "digesting" them, perhaps because we fear being "fed a line." The idea that others get into and control us via eating is implicated in the often titanic struggles of will between parent and child at dinnertime: "You will sit there until you eat what I have prepared for you"; "I will starve before I eat that." It underlies the common locutions for oral sex, as well as the practices. And it is an idea whose echoes and resonances are evoked by dozens of images in monster movies—most powerfully, perhaps, in *Alien*, among films of recent note, where the monsters drive always at the victim's face, tentacles writhing furiously to reach the mouth and so gain entry to the innermost core of the self by forced ingestion. The theme of the takeover by ingestion is further underscored, in the same movie, by the eruption of the mature monster through the stomach of the human host, and is reinforced, in a least one gruesome scene, by the setting of this event at the breakfast table.

Primal images, primal themes. I do not say that these notions are what monster movies are "really" about; only that echoes of our own early childhood experiences, feelings, and conceptions—of the world and of others and of the self—are among the many meanings evoked by the dense and fleeting images of a film, and that it is the mythos of childhood that gives monster movies, in particular, their haunting familiarity, their near-universal appeal, and their compelling power.

But I have talked us, I see, from darkness into dawn, and by now you must be getting hungry for breakfast. Eat hearty—but be careful what you eat.

PART II
MEDIA ECOLOGY

From Symbol to Medium

(n.d.) course notes

Some Characteristics of Media

(1) Communications media differ in their *form*. Form includes *symbolic* form and *physical* form. *Symbolic form* refers to the characteristics of the code in which a medium presents information (e.g. analogic vs. digital symbols) and the structures in which symbols are combined (e.g. propositional vs. presentational structures). *Physical form* refers to the characteristics of the technology that "carries" the code and the physical requirements for encoding, transmitting, storing, retrieving, decoding, and distributing information.

(2) Because of differences in their form, media differ in the *accessibility* of the information they provide. The key questions here are:

   a. To whom does this medium make information accessible or available?
   b. Under what conditions is the information accessible or available?

(3) Because of differences in their form, media differ in the *speed* at which they disseminate information.

(4) Because of differences in their form, media differ in the *quantity or volume* of information they make available.
(5) Because of differences in their form, media differ in the *directions* in which they allow information to flow.

Some Generalizations about the Biases of Media

(1) Because of the different *symbolic forms* in which they encode information, different media have different *intellectual* and *emotional* biases.
(2) Because the different *physical forms* in which they encode, store, and transmit information, different media have different *temporal, spatial,* and *sensory* biases.
(3) Because of the *accessibility* of the symbolic forms in which they encode information, different media have different *political* biases.
(4) Because their physical form dictates differences in *conditions of attendance*, different media have different *social* biases.
(5) Because of the ways in which they organize *time and space*, different media have different *metaphysical* biases.
(6) Because of their differences in *physical and symbolic form*, different media have different *content* biases.
(7) Because of their differences in physical and symbolic form, and the resulting differences in their *intellectual, emotional, temporal, spatial, political, social, metaphysical,* and *content* biases, different media have different *epistemological* biases.

So there.

Nystrom's Laws of Media Change

(1) Changes in media/symbol systems/communication processes are responses to problems or inadequacies in the existing ways of acquiring, coding, storing, transmitting, and disseminating information.
(2) The more widespread and pressing the problems or inadequacies, the more quickly and widely the change in communication will spread, and the greater its consequences for the culture/species.
(3) Since humans are fallible and limited, and since the world keeps changing, every attempt to solve problems of information is itself inadequate

in some ways, and the inadequacies are sources of further problems that generate additional communication change.
(4) Changes in the ways information is acquired, coded, stored, transmitted, and disseminated introduce change into cognitive, social, and environmental systems, as well as changes in the state of our information, and these changes create new problems of information which fuel the engine of continuing communications change.

These laws suggest several useful questions to ask when considering communication and cognitive/cultural changes:

(1) What *problems* were the impetus for this change in communication? Whose problems were they? How widespread were they?
(2) What were/are the inadequacies of the new means of communication? What problems of information do the new means of communicating generate?
(3) What changes did/does the new means of communication introduce into cognitive, social, and environmental systems? What new problems of information did/do these changes produce? How did/does the new means of communication *change the state of our information*? What new problems of information does this change generate?

Some New Generalizations

(1) Every medium of communication *leaves something out* of the totality of human experience. Corollary: Cultures will develop other ways (media, institutions, activities) to try to restore what has been left out by its predominant media.
(2) Every new medium of communication takes an older medium out of its original context (*decontextualizes it*) then provides it with a new context in the new medium (*recontextualizes it*). This process *changes the meaning* of the older context.
(3) Whenever changes in media *democratize access* to information, institutions and procedures will arise to *restrict access* and maintain the status quo of power relations and control of meaning.
(4) Every new medium of communication has an "incunabula" (or cradle period), during which it primarily reproduces an older medium, but somewhat better. During that period, the revolutionary consequences of

the new medium are not usually visible. But after that period, the new medium begins to "discover" its unique form and functions. This is when consequences begin to become visible—usually too late for anyone to do anything about it.
(5) Every medium of communication that increases the amount of information available must also generate structures for reducing information to manageable proportions.
(6) When a new medium of communication does better what an older medium did, it "frees" the older medium to take on new functions.
(7) The rules for combining symbols in a particular medium, and the cognitive and social processes required to "decode" those symbols and make meaning through that medium, are specific to that medium. They are *not* "the way things are" in all of human experience.

People who are deeply immersed in a particular medium inevitably forget this, and confuse the symbol system with all life. This gives rise to weird psychological and intellectual aberrations that often sweep through a culture—for example, the "semiotic psychosis" of our times, in which it is alleged that all events are signs and all experiences are "texts." They aren't.

Media Environments

Immediate Man: The Symbolic Environment of Fanaticism

(1977, March). *ETC, 34* (1). 19–34; reprinted (2002, Summer), *59*(2). 175–191. Reprinted by permission of the Institute of General Semantics.

Fanaticism is the triumph of reflex over reflection. It differs from the more primitive reflexes in that it is conditioned—contingent on symbols rather than sensory stimuli—but it is reflex nonetheless: an absolute fixed, undifferentiated, *immediate* response of the organism to a set of self-selected signals. As a variety of reflex, fanaticism is deeply rooted in human behavior; reflection, on the other hand, is as yet only tenuously established—for we were first reacting organisms, and only lately, reason-able men. To be human, however, *means* to reflect: to delay, critique, analyze, modify our responses to sensory and symbolic reality. For it is through this process that we gain that measure of control—not so much over environment, but over *self*—which distinguishes us from the beasts. The human enterprise flourishes, then, to the extent that our reflexes—including such symbolic reflexes as fanaticism—are brought within our control through the development of our capacity to reflect. And the human enterprise is threatened when the roots of reflection—the rational process—are for one or another reason allowed to atrophy or, worse, come under subtle or direct attack. It is with some alarm, therefore, that I note what seem to me to be warning signals that we have entered now, in the West, into an environment hostile to rational thought.

Just about a year ago, at a national conference of educators in San Diego, I sat in a large meeting hall and watched two hundred teachers learn to make "psychic energy balls." The purpose of the exercise, according to the workshop leader, was to demonstrate a method for developing our students' "other" powers of consciousness and communication. The trouble with schools, we were told, is that they have spent too much time on the so-called "left brain" ways of knowing: the linear, logical, analytic, *critical* modes of thought. And these ways of thinking, it was implied, have produced disappointing returns.

So the time has come to dedicate our classrooms to the "right brain" ways of knowing—to develop our students' wordless, gestalt, intuitive, *psychic* powers of mind. As a first step in this direction, we should teach wordless meditation. Then we may move to the classroom production of "psychic energy balls." And from there, it is but a short step to "energy circles." From one such "energy circle," a San Diego panelist reported, her seventh-grade class directs "healing waves," several times a week, to sick cats, distraught teachers and ailing friends. Another panelist described, with disarming scientific tentativeness, the benefits to society which may accrue from this latest revolution in teaching: Across her city, incipient tumors and glaucoma have begun to disappear and astonished physicians (recognizing at once the handiwork of the English class) call to express their gratitude. Their gratitude, incidentally, seemed to be shared by the workshop audience, which responded to the panelists with a standing ovation.

Perhaps you do not find this episode alarming. After all, the setting was Southern California, and the sun in those climes has produced more peculiar effects on better minds. Still, we should not be too smug. At a national meeting, here in New York City, of the Association for Humanistic Psychology, a major speaker was astounded recently when half his audience stalked out, scarcely five minutes into his speech. His topic—the cultivation of sanity through the careful monitoring of one's talk—hardly seemed to call for such an expression of outrage. But the bewildered speaker learned the reason for the protest soon enough. In a workshop devoted to his topic, a young man (one of the conference organizers) arose in great anger to denounce the speaker and his views. He had not heard the speech "personally," he said, but he gathered from the tenor of the workshop that the speaker still ascribed to the same old rationalist-intellectual claptrap that had blocked the human race from achieving its full potential for the past thousand years. Conference attendees, he counseled the workshop audience, would find their time better spent if they followed his example and chose another of the workshops offered—which included, that afternoon, the educational uses of transcendental meditation, biofeedback, Rolfing, and spinal realignment.

It would be comforting to dismiss these two incidents as events of small consequence, mere ripples in an otherwise smooth-flowing mainstream of intellectual thought. But they are not so easily wished away. The people making energy balls in San Diego were not some group of wild-eyed radicals; they represent the most serious and committed of education professionals. Nor was their workshop leader the guru of some lunatic cult. He was James Moffet, whose work in the teaching of creative thinking has earned him no small reputation as a thoughtful and serious educator. As for the New York conference, it was large and important enough to draw such reputable thinkers as Carl Rogers, among others, as speakers. In short, we must grant that these are serious people, earnestly devoted to the improvement of American education. Given the peculiarity of the educational practices they were exploring, we have every reason to ask with some urgency, just what the devil is going on here?

The Evolution of Immediate Man

What is going on here is, in my judgment, symptomatic of a most disturbing development in American culture. The incidents I have described are, to be sure, ripples in the mainstream of educated thought. But they are the kind of ripples that warn of an ominous shift in the bedrock below the stream. What I am talking about is a shift in the social and, more important, the intellectual character of Western man. Different social critics have called attention to different aspects of this shift, and have labeled it according to their points of view. Philip Rieff (1966), for example, calls it "the triumph of the therapeutic" and names the emerging persona of our era "Psychological Man." By this he means that we have moved away, in this century, from a social order based on an acceptance of repression of some individual impulses in the interest of achieving communal goals, to a situation where the needs and impulses of the individual triumph over and against culture. (I use the term "situation" for the latter state of affairs because there is some question whether "social order" or "civilization" can be maintained in such conditions.) Daniel Griffiths (1975) has called attention to the social and political consequences of this shift in our national character by calling it "The Collapse of Consensus." For reasons I hope to make clear in this article, I prefer to talk, perhaps more pessimistically than either Rieff or Griffiths, about the eclipse of rationality in American culture, and the evolution of Immediate Man.

I choose the phrase, "the evolution of Immediate Man," first to call attention to what I see as the critical characteristic of the persona of our age: a fixation on the *present*, the here-and-now. We do not need to look very far for the symptoms of that fixation. It is clear enough in the proliferation and enormous popularity of "instant" food chains and "instant" weight-loss programs, "instant" success and "instant" beauty books, "instant" therapies and yes, even "instant" religions. *NOW* is the byword of our age, and the present its only tense. This is as true for our construction of problems as it is for our demands on their solutions. In the metaphysics of Immediate Man, the past is so much deadwood—at best an irrelevant curiosity, at worst a deceiving chimera that obstructs our clear vision of the here-and-now. Small wonder that our departments of history and philosophy are dying! Problems that history is powerless to inform, philosophy is powerless to solve. And both halves of that proposition are axiomatic in the metaphysics of immediacy.

I choose the term "Immediate Man" for the emerging persona of our age, then, first because immersion in the present is his dominant characteristic. Out of it, and the rejection of past and future, grow his contempt for history, his Manichean construct of the origins of problems, his intolerance for complex and long-term solutions, his mystical faith in the solving and *saving* powers of technique and technology, and his deep mistrust of reason. In short, out of his immediacy grows the fundamental *irrationality* of modern man.

But I choose the name "Immediate Man" for another reason, as well: to call attention to the role of modern communications technology in his emergence. Immediate Man is not only immersed in the present. He is also immersed in media, and in media of a totally different character from those which attended the birth and shaped the development of Rational Man. In fact, I want to argue here that the social and intellectual character of Immediate Man is very much a product of the media environments in which we find ourselves today. That argument rests on a series of propositions which I have set forth below, as economically as I can.

Culture, Character, and Information

Man does not live in a physical environment alone. He also lives—in fact, it is his distinguishing characteristic that he lives—in a complex set of symbolic environments. These symbolic environments or, more precisely, information systems, are what we mean by culture; and it is the particular way in which such information systems are organized and integrated that differentiates one culture from another.

Now, the social and intellectual character of man is largely shaped by culture—by the particular characteristics and organization of information systems predominant in his time. Unlike physical systems, information systems are subject, under certain conditions, to rapid and radical change. And our modes of perceiving, thinking, behaving, and organizing—all grounded, themselves, in symbolic rather than physical functions—are relatively quick to adapt. Consequently, when the information systems that comprise culture *change*—in particular, when they change in radical ways—they produce evolutionary changes in the social and intellectual character of man. At present, we are undergoing just such an evolutionary change. To explain it, and to account for its direction, requires a somewhat fuller understanding of the concepts of "information" and "information system."

Information, it seems to me, is best conceived of as a form of energy, somewhat on the order of light or gravity. Like them, it is not observable in itself, but only in its effects. We "see light" only because it lights things up; and we "see things" only because they are lighted.

Light, one might say, is that form of energy through which objects are rendered visible and, conversely, that form of energy rendered observable by objects. Similarly, one might say, *information is that form of energy which makes human organization and change possible and, conversely, that form of energy made observable in human organization and change.*

As a form of energy, information has five properties of overriding significance, under which are subsumed a wide variety of characteristics. These five properties are its form, its magnitude (quantity or volume), its velocity, its direction, and its accessibility. In general, these properties are not independent of one another, but stand in such relation that a change in one produces a change in all the others. And so we arrive at the concept of an information system. *An information system is that form of human organization made possible by a certain combination of characteristics in the form, magnitude, velocity, direction, and accessibility of information.*

According to this definition, the family is an information system. So are such social environments as the classroom, the courtroom, the business office, the church, the encounter group. So, too, are such media environments as television, radio, film, LP record, and the like.

They differ from each other because the characteristics of information are patterned differently in each case. One might point out that such systems also differ in their scope and boundaries, their functions, their content, their role structures, the way they distribute power, and their effects on the perceptions, values, and behavior of their participants. Of course they do. But the proposition advanced here is that such characteristics of social and media environments are products of their information characteristics.

Role structure, for example, is largely a product of the direction of information within a system. The distribution of power (however defined) is largely a product of information accessibility. The scope and boundaries of a system are determined largely by the magnitude, velocity, and accessibility of information. And the content and functions of a system are largely shaped by the characteristic forms in which information is codified, organized, and transmitted. I say "largely determined" in each case here because, as noted earlier, the properties of information are so related that one cannot properly isolate one from the others. The direction of information in a system, for example, is in part determined by its accessibility. Accessibility is in part a function of magnitude and velocity. And the magnitude and velocity of information are dependent on its form.

Form and Response in Media

What I have tried to do in the preceding paragraphs is sketch out, in its barest form, the framework in which it is possible to address the questions which are the primary focus of this article—namely, What are the major characteristics of the media environments dominant in American culture today? Why do these characteristics promote the evolution of Immediate Man? How should we assess this shift in the intellectual character of our time? And what, if anything, can we as educators do about it?

Because space and (I assume) your patience with these inquiries are not infinite, I want to center my answers to the first two questions around one information system—television—and one of its properties: form. I choose television because it is in many ways the most powerful and pervasive of our media environments, and because its characteristics illuminate, by comparison, those of many other electronic media. And I choose *form* because, of all the properties of information, it is the most central and complex. This is not the place to present the complete taxonomy of information forms. But some rudimentary distinctions are required.

To begin with, information has three formal levels or types: semiotic (or signific) form, structural (or grammatical) form, and physical form. *Semiotic form* refers, generally, to the way in which information abstracts from, codifies, and represents experience; *structural form*, to the ways in which semiotic elements are combined in larger units of meaning; and physical form to the material (including the senses) in or through which information is encoded, stored, retrieved, transmitted, and received. Like the properties of information, these characteristics of form are interdependent. In general, though, it is the semiotic and structural characteristics of form that most directly affect the content of information and our cognitive and emotional response. To understand the effects of television on our intellectual character, then, we do well to begin with some observations on its semiotic and structural form. And we may as well begin with the most obvious.

Television: The Non-discursive Bias

Television is primarily a *visual* medium. As political candidates learned in the Nixon-Kennedy debates (and the successful ones have not forgotten since), people do not listen to television. They *watch* it. And the basic semiotic element in television is the picture, not the word. And that is a difference that makes all the difference.

I do not know what it means to say that a picture is "worth" a thousand words. But I do know that it is not the *equivalent* of a thousand words, or ten thousand, or a million. Pictures and words are two different orders of representation, two different types of experience, and they evoke two very different types of response. In Susanne Langer's terms (1951), language (in both its spoken and written forms) is discursive; pictures (i.e., mimetic or presentational codifications of visual experience) are non-discursive.

Now, discursive and non-discursive forms of information differ in several important ways. Language, for example, presents its meaning-elements sequentially; in fact, meaning in language is a function of the sequence in which sounds and words are presented. The difference between /tap/ (top) and /pat/ (pot), for example, is a difference in the order of sounds; the difference between "The dog chased the cat" and "The cat chased the dog" is a difference in the order of words. A picture, on the other hand, presents its elements, not in sequence, but at once, in a gestalt. This is not to say that the elements of pictures (dots, lines, shades, etc.) cannot be articulated—that is, combined in different ways to produce different meanings. But the constituents of pictures are so myriad and minute, and their relations so complex, that they cannot be isolated and their individual significances pinned down. It is impossible to find the basic unit—the smallest significant symbol—in a non-discursive representation, and to recognize it again in a different context.

Pictures, in short, are not composed of the equivalents of words; they have no "vocabulary." As Langer points out, this means that in pictorial representation (and other non-discursive modes) there are no equivalents of *definitions*. Consequently, non-discursive symbols are neither translatable one into another nor paraphrase-able. There is no equivalent, in non-discursive representation, for the phrase, "In other words…." This means, among other things, that the *experience* of a picture (or for that matter, of music, sculpture, dance) cannot be communicated to one who was not there. I can tell you, if you missed a lecture, what the speaker said. But I cannot tell you what you missed if you did not see "Aristotle Contemplating the Bust of Homer." You had to be there.

At the semiotic level, then, the pictorial experience is non-sequential and non-analytic, gestalt,, and ineffable. It is, in a word, "presentational"; it is "immediate."

There is another characteristic of non-discursive representation that is most important to us here—namely, that it is *denotative* and *non-generalizable*. Discursive symbols (e.g., words), by their nature, stand for concepts—that is, for abstract categories of things. The word "chalk," for example, does not represent any particular piece of chalk nor, indeed, any specific property of chalk. But non-discursive symbols, and particularly those which are mimetic of experience (e.g., pictures), must always represent particular things. I cannot draw or photograph "chalk" in the abstract, or the concept "triangle." I cannot paint "landscape." What I am compelled to do is photograph a specific piece of chalk—one that is a certain shade of white or of a particular shape. I must draw a particular triangle; its sides will either be equal or they will not, and they will have a specific length. And I must paint a particular landscape—one with a tree or one without.

Because of this difference in the generalizability of words and pictures, the two have different content and functions. Language is about experience and, in particular, about ideas about experience. Pictures are experience. If they are "about" anything, they are, as Langer says, about our *feelings* of experience. Put another way, language is reflection on experience, constructed in propositional form. Pictures are immersion in experience, reconstructed in such a way as to evoke certain feelings.

Television: The Affective Response

What all this suggests about television is that, as an information system whose semiotic form is primarily non-discursive, it evokes responses that are gestalt, non-analytic, immediate, present-oriented, non-reflective, and emotional. Television is not, in short, a medium suited for the communication of abstract ideas in logical arrangements. It is a medium which focuses attention primarily on the interpersonal and affective dimensions of the experiences it represents.

This conclusion is supported, in my own experience at least, by the fact that I have almost never heard discussed (and rarely discuss myself) the *conceptual* content of a television program, no matter the quality of the show. Even in such "intellectually oriented" productions as the "Ascent of Man" series or the National Geographic documentaries on studies in ethology, the focus is on the interpersonal and affective dimensions of content. One talks about how charming, articulate, and wise Bronowski is, or how thrilling was the slow-motion sequence of the infant pulling himself triumphantly to a full stand, or how human the chimpanzees seem in their relations with the ethologist, or how difficult it must be to spend ten years in the African bush with no one but a great ape for a friend. We cannot blame television producers for this emphasis on the interpersonal and affective; cannot dismiss it as "bad television." Just the opposite: this is *good* television, for the potential of the medium is in *visual* representation. And the full exploitation of that potential must bias the medium toward the interpersonal and affective. To ask for something else would be to ask for a different medium altogether—radio perhaps. But good radio is not good television.

I want to anticipate a reasonable objection here—namely, that if what I have said is true of television, then it should also be true of such face-to-face communication environments as the classroom. After all, students also watch teachers—that is, receive non-discursive information.

Certainly. Television and teaching are both composite forms: Both mix discursive and non-discursive modes. But there is an important difference between them. As a principle, when discursive and non-discursive information is presented simultaneously, attention will focus primarily on that mode in which change is most constant and obvious. This means that, if the visual stimulus is held relatively constant, attention will focus on speech; conversely, if the discursive stimulus is held relatively constant, attention will focus on the non-discursive. In teaching, we make many efforts to hold non-discursive elements as constant as possible. Usually, for example, we have the same teacher meet with students week after week; we fix the chairs to the classroom floor so that, by shifting about, students will not keep altering their visual perspective; the teacher (traditionally, at least) maintains a relatively stable position in classroom space; even today, in most classrooms, implicit or explicit dress codes constrain the variety in appearance which students and teacher may present. These rules, it is true, are coming to be less and less observed. One of the consequences of their disappearance, and of increasing attention on the part of teachers to their non-verbal performance, is that students are majoring more in teacher personalities—the interpersonal dynamics of their courses—than in ideas.

If teaching is characterized (or was) by control of the visual stimulus and constant variation in speech, television is just the opposite. There, the visual stimulus is constantly changing, not just through the introduction of new faces, but through the unceasing manipulation of camera distance, angle, and focus; and rapid changes in costumes, sets, lighting, and now, color. Compared to the pace and variety of change in such visual elements, change in the speech elements of television is relatively small. Anyone who believes that Johnny Carson or even the CBS evening news is a *talk* show just hasn't been *watching*.

Television: Structure and Metaphysics

When we talk about the pace and variety of change in television, we are talking, not about its semiotic form, but about its *structural* form—about its rules for organizing semiotic elements into larger units. And there is one very striking structural characteristic of television I want to mention briefly here. Because of its physical characteristics—its capacity for recording experience from a variety of camera positions at once, and its capacity for storing such recordings for cutting and recombination—television is primarily *disjunctive* in structure. That is, it combines, in rapid sequence, experiences that would in real life require multiple shifts in the spatial and temporal placement of the viewer. The result is an extraordinary *compression* of experience in both space and time. A trip from New York to London that would in real life take a day is accomplished, on television, literally in the blink of an eye. Such compression of experience has, I think, far-reaching consequences for what we may call the *metaphysics* of television. It means, among other things, that the most complex of human problems can be presented, developed, and solved in extraordinarily short periods of time. In the commercial, for example, such a sequence of events is accomplished in thirty seconds or less. In dramatic programs, murders are committed and solved, justice is confounded and triumphs, and wars are threatened and averted, in thirty minutes to an hour. The concept of "delayed gratification" has no place in such a metaphysics.

Nor do the rules of conventional *logic* apply in a medium whose form is structurally disjunctive. Logic, and the forms of rational thought on which it is based, requires the articulation in sequence of the relationship between one idea and the next. It is the spelling out of the steps, so to speak, by which one moves from proposition *A* to proposition *G* and eventually to *Z*. In a disjunctive medium, meaning is communicated, not through ideas in linear sequence, but through experiences in apposition. In short, television does not promote logic or reason as a mode of representing or responding to reality.

It does, however, promote elevated levels of excitement. And this, too, is a consequence of its disjunctive structure. Disjunctive structures lead, I have said, to the compression of experience in space and time. And "excitement" may be defined as our subjective response to the number of events experienced per unit of time. The more compressed experience is, the greater the excitement it produces. And television is a super-compressed medium.

It may at first seem difficult to reconcile the observation that television is highly exciting with the observation that it is intellectually passive. And yet both statements are true. Excitement is a function of the rate or density of experience. Passivity, on the other hand, is a function of our *control* over that rate, and over other structural characteristics of a medium. Because of the physical form of television, viewers have virtually *no* control over the *sequence* in which they will experience representations, over the *pace* at which they will experience them, or over the selection of *angles* from which to view them. Given a book or a letter, I may choose to read from the end, if I like, or start from the middle and work backwards or forwards. Given a lecturer present in the flesh, I may ask for repetition or a different pace of delivery. Given an object literally before me, I may change its position—or my own—to see it in a different light. Not so with television. There, we are the manipulated, not the manipulators. And so, for all its excitement, tele-viewing is intellectually passive.

Television and Habits of Thought

We may draw, then, the following profile of television and the modes of response it evokes: They are gestalt, nonanalytic, inarticulate, immediate, present-oriented, nonreflective, and emotional. Television focuses on the interpersonal and the affective, compresses experience and stresses instantaneity. It promotes appositive rather than logical thinking, a high level of excitement, and an intellectually passive response. It promotes, in short, those habits of perception and response I have identified as characteristic of Immediate Man.

I have not argued here, nor would I, that television is *the* cause of our intellectual evolution from Rational to Immediate Man. We live in a diversity of symbolic environments, complexly intertwined, and television is but one. Still, we cannot overlook its pervasiveness and power. According to the national inventory reported in the Surgeon General's Report (LoSciuto, 1972), average viewing time for the individual American is three hours and twenty minutes a day. More important are the viewing times reported for children:

> Most children do watch at least some television every day. Most watch for at least two hours; many watch considerably longer. In the study [shown], over one-quarter of the sixth graders and only a slightly smaller proportion of the tenth graders watch at least five and one-half hours on a given school day.... Well over one-third of the first graders watched for four hours or more.... Television watching, together with sleep and school, is one of the major activities of the vast majority of children. Over a week-long period, the first graders spent the equivalent of one full day watching television; sixth and tenth graders exceed that level (Lyle & Hoffman, 1972).

As Schramm, Lyle, and Parker (1961) remarked, in reference to the *lower* figures they reported 15 years ago, "They are spectacular. They mean that throughout the years of school, a child spends within five percent as much time on television as on school. From ages 3 through 16, he spends more total time on television than on school. In these years, he devotes about one-sixth of his waking hours to television. In fact, he is likely to devote more time to television than to any other activity except sleep and perhaps play, depending on how play is defined!" (30). Given the fact that television time as a percentage of total time *peaks* for the child by the sixth grade (1972)—that is, that he spends the greatest time on television during his most formative years—one cannot but conclude that television plays a powerful role in shaping habits of thought.

Perhaps even more important, the habits of thought and response promoted by television are, in general, reinforced by most of the electronic media. Like television, radio, movies, and the LP record are primarily non-discursive media. Their semiotic, structural, and physical forms bias response in much the same direction as television. And children spend 91% of their media time in second grade, 82% of their time in sixth grade, and 85% of their time in twelfth grade immersed in these media environments (Schramm et al., 1961).

What I am saying here is that our culture has undergone a massive shift, in its symbolic environments, from discursive (rational, analytic, logical, reflective) to non-discursive (gestalt, appositional, emotional, presentational) forms of information and response. The symptoms of this shift are to be seen everywhere, and not the least in our own classrooms. Like others of my colleagues, I have been made anxious by the increasing inability of my students—particularly the younger ones—to read and write. But I am more appalled by their seeming inability to talk—to articulate in an organized way either their ideas or their feelings. For it is talk, more directly than reading and writing, that symbolizes our processes of mind.

For all it may seem otherwise, I am not attacking non-discursive modes of perception and communication here. They are equally as valuable in the full development of human potential as the modes of rational thought, and they have been ignored too long in American culture.

But now the balance has shifted, with devastating force. And I am concerned that too early and too total an immersion in the non-discursive may eclipse our capacity to reason at all. It is not the non-discursive mode, but the near-total preoccupation with that mode that is reshaping the intellectual character of our time and promoting the evolution of Immediate Man.

Immediate Man: Evolution or Regression?

What stance are we to take on this evolution in our intellectual character? How should we assess the immersion in the present, the contempt for history, the Manichean metaphysics, the intolerance for complex and long-term solutions, the technological bias, the mistrust of reason—the irrationality of Immediate Man? What should be our response to his emergence?

My own response, to be quite frank, approaches terror. Perhaps that response arises out of nothing more than love for my own species, and an inability to understand or cope with the new. Perhaps it is merely the response of the backward ape, clinging to its tree and gibbering in fear of its neighbor, who now walks upright on the ground. If so, my fear may be ignoble but, for all that, not without foundation. After all, the man-apes came soon enough against their cousins, armed with clubs. The image calls to mind the scene in Stanley Kubrick's *2001* where the old and the new breed confront each other over a waterhole at the dawn of time. We all know, of course, who won. And we would not have it otherwise.

But there is another, more powerful image from *2001* which may be more relevant here. The last thing Kubrick shows us—his metaphor for the next step in the evolution of man—is a child, triumphant. And the child is, I think, an appropriate symbol for Immediate Man. Nowhere, except in the world of childhood, do we find the same immersion in the present, the same mystical construction of reality, the same immediacy. And so the emergence of Immediate Man may be, after all, not so much an evolution as a regression.

Some people have, of course, argued the return to childhood as a positive goal. It seems to be a popular view, and not confined to movie-makers. Understandable, perhaps, since childhood has much to recommend it. There are spontaneity and creativity there, and innocence, trust, love. But as the flower children of the Sixties learned too late, there are also less benevolent impulses. Aggression. Rage. Fear. And if flowers come easily to hand for the expression of love, so too, in this age, do guns and motorcycle chains come easily to hand to express the rage, and drugs to allay the fear. Those who extol the virtues of childhood and urge us to set it as our goal would do well to read Arthur Clarke's version of the end of *2001*. His "Star Child" plays, for toys, with nuclear-armed satellites (1968, p. 221).

The point is that, if we return to childhood, we do not return as we left it. We return with an awesome technology, with the capacity to shatter the globe. And such instruments cannot be trusted to children, or sanely managed by Immediate Men.

The Conservation of Rational Man

Jacob Bronowski (1973) wrote, near the end of his life,

> I am infinitely saddened to find myself surrounded in the west by a sense of a terrible loss of nerve, a retreat from knowledge into—into what? Into Zen Buddhism; into falsely profound questions about, Are we not really just animals at bottom; into extra-sensory perception and mystery. They do not lie along the line of what we are now able to know if we devote ourselves to it: an understanding of man himself. We are nature's unique experiment to make the rational intelligence prove itself sounder than the reflex. Knowledge is our destiny (p. 437).

If we agree, what can we do, as educators, to assure the conservation of rational thought, to restore the balance between reason and experience? The key word here,

I think, is balance. Symbolic environments and the social institutions in which they are given concrete form are, like natural environments, complex ecosystems. In a natural environment, there is nothing inherently evil about deer or wolves or even potato bugs. Each serves a vital function in the life of the whole—so long as the relations among them are balanced. When those relations become unbalanced, when the deer grow disproportionate to the wolves or vice versa, the entire system becomes disordered, unhealthy, with grave consequences for all its members. So it is with symbolic environments. There is nothing inherently evil about television, radio, film, or the LP record, nor about the intellectual biases they promote, so long as those biases are counterbalanced in other symbolic environments. From this perspective, the perspective of social or media ecology, it becomes possible to assess the functions of social institutions and prescribe directions for change.

What I am proposing here is a variation on what David Riesman (1958) called the "counter-cyclical" approach to schooling: the concept that the school, as one of the major information systems in our culture, ought to serve as a counter-environment to the environments created by electronic technology. This means organizing all its efforts and energies to support "nature's unique experiment": the development of rational intelligence. From this point of view, we must adamantly reject such efforts at curriculum reform as those described at the outset of this article. We will not promote rational intelligence—the critical, reflective, analytical, logical, *discursive* modes of thought—by engaging our students in spinal realignment, transcendental meditation, and the making of psychic energy balls. And we will not achieve that goal, either, by turning our classrooms into psychotherapeutic "encounter" groups modeled after EST, as some southern California schools have done. Nor will it help to model our kindergartens after *Sesame Street*. There are institutions enough in our culture, including the mass media, to serve such functions. As Henry Perkinson (1968) has pointed out in *The Imperfect Panacea*, the schools cannot do everything, nor should they. When they try, they accomplish nothing.

I am not arguing for something as simple-minded as the "back to the basics" movement which some professional groups have adopted in response to Immediate Man. We need to reassess what is basic for the schools, in relation to other media environments. This requires scrutinizing with great care our present ways of organizing information in the schools, and identifying the intellectual biases promoted by the characteristic forms, magnitude, velocity, directions, and accessibility of information we find there. We may find some surprises. The conventional application of Skinnerian theory and the uninformed use of audiovisual aids and technologies like the computer, for example, do much to reinforce the metaphysics of immediacy. So does the overemphasis on symbolic rather than sensory experience, in the early grades. So, too, the rush into reading and writing, before speech is adequately developed as the primary discursive mode.

Once the task of reassessment is underway, we can begin to redesign the school as an information system, calling on all we know and can learn to bias it toward the rational response. This will be no easy task. It will require every ounce of intelligence, reason, logic, tolerance for ambiguity, and delayed gratification we can muster. But that should be a welcome challenge—to Rational Man.

References

Bronowski, J. (1973). *The ascent of man*. Boston, MA: Little, Brown and Company.
Clarke, A.C. (1968). *2001: A space odyssey*. New York, NY: New American Library.
Griffiths, D. (1975, Fall). "The collapse of consensus." *New York University Education Quarterly*.
Langer, S.K. (1951). *Philosophy in a new key: A study in the symbolism of reason, rite, and art*. Cambridge, MA: Harvard University Press.
LoSciuto, L.A. (1972). "A national inventory of television viewing behavior." *Television and Social Behavior* (Reports and Papers, Vol. IV). Washington, DC: U.S. Department of Health, Education, and Welfare.
Lyle, J. & Hoffman, H.R. (1972). "Children's use of television and other media." *Television and Social Behavior* (Reports and Papers, Vol. IV). Washington, DC: U.S. Department of Health, Education, and Welfare, 1972, p. 131.
Perkinson, H.J. (1968). *The imperfect panacea: American faith in education, 1865–1965*. New York, NY: Random House.
Rieff, P. (1966). *The triumph of the therapeutic: Uses of faith after Freud*. New York, NY: Harper & Row.
Riesman, D. (1958). *Constraint and variety in American education*. Lincoln, NE: University of Nebraska Press.
Schramm, W., Lyle, J. & Parker, E.B. (1961). *Television in the lives of our children*. Stanford, CA: Stanford University Press.

Television and Truth

(1979). *The Structurist*, *19/20*. 96–101. Reprinted by permission.

As an instrument for thought, the English language is a subtle and wondrous thing. Consider, for example, the homely conjunction. Through the device of a little *and* we may link together any two nouns, and thus suggest to the mind a connection between them. Sometimes, a fortuitously placed *and* triggers great leaps of thought—as in Newton's "apples *and* planets," or Einstein's "space *and* time."

Sometimes, it fuels a generation, or a century, of scholarship and debate: "free will *and* determinism," "wave *and* particle," "mind *and* body." Sometimes, it generates metaphors that endure forever in poetry or art. Burns' "my luv" *and* "a rose," Shakespeare's "the world" *and* "a stage." Sometimes. But not always. There are, alas, conjunctions that function only to deceive—to suggest a connection which no leap of the imagination, and no effort of serious thought, can uncover. So it is with the *and* that stands between "television" and "truth" at the top of this page. Try as I may, I can nowhere find the connection it alleges. Save that both begin with "t," truth and television have nothing in common.

Why this should be so is no great mystery. It has to do, again, with language—with the ways in which we may properly use the truth and with the kind of "language" television, in its various formats, speaks. My argument here, quite simply, is that there is no conventional meaning of "truth" relevant to the conventional formats of television. Not to advertising, not to drama, not even to news. (Note that I am referring here and throughout this article to television as it is produced in the United States. Perhaps television elsewhere is significantly different. But I doubt it.)

By a "conventional" meaning of truth, I mean, of course, some use of the word dignified by history and philosophy, by the intellectual traditions of the past 2,500 years. Whether television has created a new meaning of truth is another question, well worth considering. But it shall have to wait its turn. For now, let me focus on these. What do we mean when we say that something is true, and where, if at all, do these meanings touch on television?

In its narrowest and most rigorous sense, the word "true" (like its opposite, "false") applies only to a very small segment of our symbolic productions—namely, to those which make explicit assertions about events and experiences, in language which has publicly shared and relatively precise meanings. To give them the name by which they are most often called, such productions are *propositions*. And there are several important things to note about them. First, propositions are not experiences or events, but statements about experiences, events, and the relationships among them. Pain is not a proposition. Nor is a tree, a river, a chair. Of themselves, they are neither true nor false; they simply *are*. Second, propositions are statements of a certain form; that is, they are expressed in digital symbols such as words or mathematical symbols—that is, symbols that have specific denotations, publicly agreed-upon definitions, and rules for combination into structures that also have agreed-upon meanings.

In a word, propositions are *linguistic*. But not all language is propositional. For propositions have a third characteristic that distinguishes them from other forms of expression: they purport to *describe* events in the world, or to report them, or to explain them. An expression of feeling—"Ouch!"—is not a proposition. Neither is a command such as "Thou shalt not kill," nor a wish, like "Have a good day!" Wishes and commands do not purport to describe how things are in reality; they indicate, instead, how things *ought* to be. And while we may say any number of things about such statements as "Thou shalt not kill" and "Have a good day!"—that they are just or unjust, good or bad, right or wrong, noble or trite—we may not say of them that they are true or false.

Why we may not involves a fourth characteristic of propositions—namely, that they must be verifiable and, in theory at least, refutable through certain operations, principally centered on observations of non-linguistic reality. In other words, propositions admit of evidence. "Human beings do not kill other human beings" is a proposition—verifiable or, in this case, all too sadly refutable, through any number of observations of human behavior. But where would we look for evidence that humans *should* not kill? There can be none, for "should" makes no claim to describe objective reality; it permits, therefore, neither of verification nor refutation. And it cannot be said to be true or false.

In short, the words *true* and *false* apply, in the strict sense, only to the relationship between certain linguistic statements and observable characteristics of the nonlinguistic reality to which they refer. In this sense, how or to what does "truth" apply in television? To begin with the obvious, truth in the narrow sense has no application to the greatest portion of television offerings: those weekly productions their creators are pleased to call "comedy" or "dramatic" series. With the exception of some sadly confused soap opera fans—those who are reported to send letters of condolence and flowers to characters whose world has turned tragic—most of us understand that these formats do not pretend to present real persons engaged in real events, but fiction. (I say this with greater assurance than I feel. There is some evidence that more of us are confused about what is real and what is not than I like to admit. Some years ago, for example, the American Medical Association featured Marcus Welby—excuse me, Robert Young—as a keynote speaker at their national meeting. And why would Firestone feature Jimmy Stewart as their spokesman, or Alpo Pet Foods, Lorne Greene, except in the expectation that we will attribute to such real-life personages characteristics and competencies they have merely *portrayed* in their fictional roles?)

Perhaps it is worth noting, in this connection, that the question "Is it real?" is different from the question "Is it true?"—and that the former must be answered before the latter. By "Is it real?" I take it we mean, in relation to television presentations, "is this event happening now, or did it happen in historical time, to these people I am seeing? Does the sequence of events I am watching continue out of range of the camera? Is that actual blood coming out of that girl's arm, and will it continue to flow when the show is over?" If our answer to these questions is "no," then we place the events we see in the realm of fiction or, at least, of dramatic performance. And by so doing, we declare to ourselves that the question of objective truth is irrelevant here. For the function of drama is not to present refutable propositions about the nature of events and relations in reality, and we would be foolish to confuse one universe of discourse with another. We may, then, quickly set aside comedy and drama in our search for objective truth in television. They are not real. Their content is therefore not propositional. And they are in this sense neither true nor false.

The television commercial presents a different problem altogether. Commercials come in a variety of formats, and it is exceedingly difficult to determine, in many cases, in what universe of discourse they belong. Many of them are mini-dramas, like the long-running Palmolive commercial starring Madge the Manicurist, or the toothpaste and deodorant commercials in which some rejected swain is saved from despair by his roommate's Colgate or Scope, or the detergent commercial in which a young couple is rescued from marital disaster and social ridicule when Wisk puts the axe to Ring Around the Collar. For the most part, these commercials make no explicit assertions, advance no propositions. Madge the Manicurist never says that Palmolive dish detergent heals abraded hands or promotes rapid growth in fingernails. Scope doesn't claim to destroy germs, only to "fight bad breath" (a vague metaphor, not susceptible to verification or refutation). If we, in our innocence, choose to convert the imagistic story we see to some such set of linguistic propositions, why then *our* statements may be said to be true or false. But mini-dramas themselves are neither. As I mean to suggest by the label I have given them, these commercials fall clearly in the realm of dramatic fiction—or possibly, as my colleague Neil Postman has suggested, religious parable. In either case, "truth" in the objective sense has no bearing on them.

In recent years, as television producers have come to discover the true structure and function of their medium, the mini-drama has declined in popularity as a commercial format. Its major successor seems to be the commercial which consists merely of a series of visually and psychologically appealing images, often accompanied by music, followed by a tag line which identifies the product. I hope I do not have to labor the point here that the images in such commercials do not advance any propositions. Like a painting of a bowl of flowers or a photograph of a tree, they present certain aspects of experience, reconstructed in analogic symbols, but they do not make any refutable assertions about what they present. There is no way to refute an image of a child playing with a pup or laughing over a hamburger. The image may be enchanting or boring, pleasing or distasteful, appealing or not. But it is neither true nor false. The same may be said of the language (usually sung) which accompanies such ads. In most of these cases, this consists either of wishes ("Have a Pepsi Day!" "Let it be Lowenbrau!") or comments ("Fly the Friendly Skies of United!" "Don't be Sad. Be Glad!!" "Double Your Pleasure, Double Your Fun…!"). These are, of course, neither verifiable nor refutable. Nor are the occasional statements which take the structure of propositions but which, on closer scrutiny, have no clear meanings—as in the McDonald's tag, "At McDonald's we do it all for you!" Just who does what for whom, here, is something of a mystery. And in the face of such mysteries, truth must leave the arena altogether.

There is a third commercial format, however, which is not so easily dealt with—a strange hybrid that, quite frankly, I find impossible to categorize. A frequently aired example of this type begins with the shrill sound of a whistle. The camera quickly pulls back to show us a pert, energetic blonde of indeterminate age, wearing a sweatshirt labeled "COACH," with a whistle in her hand. As the shot widens, we see the setting is a "breakfast room," complete with husband (of indeterminate age) and two children (ditto). (According to television, there are only three ages in America: infancy, a perpetually young middle age that lasts from about 11 to 65, and senile old age.) As she dances about the table, the blonde announces to her adoring brood, and to us, that "We're in training. We're making sure that we eat balanced meals, watch our calories *and* our cholesterol." An important part of their training program, she goes on to say, is X-brand margarine, which is made from pure something-or-other, adds no cholesterol to the diet, and "tastes good too!" The commercial ends with some admonishment to the effect that, if we know what's good for us, we'll use X-brand margarine, too.

Now, here's what's puzzling. Clearly, the "frame" of this event places the whole thing in the realm of fantasy. Only an idiot would believe that the pert blonde is a real person, that she lives in that house, that those are her children, or that she starts her mornings with a whistle in her mouth. In other words, we are to understand that what she says is not literally true. Her family is not really in training, they're not really watching their calories and cholesterol, they don't really use X-brand margarine. And we must conclude the same thing about her statements about the margarine: They are no more literally true than the others. I do not mean that they are false—only that they have no reference to the world of events outside the frame of the fantasy. Surely nothing could be clearer than this. It is the same principle that governs our response to the statements of characters in the legitimate theatre. We would think it bizarre if the members of an audience raced out to close their car windows because one character remarked to another that the rain was falling in sheets. That response is not what we mean by "the suspension of disbelief." And the event would probably make headlines. Yet we do not find it remarkable that the television commercial expects us to make just the same confusion of dramatic statement with propositional truth. And, apparently, enough of us confuse the two often enough to make the production of such commercials profitable to advertisers and their products.

My point here is that the context, the "frame" of an event, tells us in what universe of discourse it belongs and, consequently, what criteria we are to use in evaluating and responding to it. The dramatic frame places events (and statements about those events) in the realm of literature—of imagination or subjective reality, not of objective reality. We may, of course, make judgments of events within that realm—say that characters and their statements are consistent or inconsistent, that a particular line of dialogue, or an image, is effective or ineffective in constructing character, advancing the plot, marshalling our emotional responses to the situation depicted. But to confuse dramatic consistency or effectiveness with objective truth, and to respond to one as though it were the other, blurs the distinction between reality and non-reality, with sad and dangerous consequences for thought and feeling. Yet this is precisely what television leads us to do. In the case of the hybrid commercial, statements purporting to have some connection with objective reality (for surely that is how the advertiser intends us to "read" the lines about margarine) are framed in a format that just as clearly signals "dramatic fiction." This presents us with the kind of paradox some psychologists have called a "double bind"—a situation so arranged that any choice one makes is wrong. If we treat the events depicted as propositions about objective reality, we're wrong. And if we treat them as nothing more than dramatic fiction, we're wrong, too. Our only escape is to place the entire event in a kind of half-world, where neither the criteria for evaluating propositions nor those for evaluating drama apply. In effect, we throw out of our repertoire of critical responses both the question "Is it true?" *and* the question "Is it good drama?" And what have we left is only that pale and amorphous question the advertiser had in mind to begin with: Does it *appeal?*

Very much the same problem, and the same process, applies to those television productions that program listings call "the news." In what universe of discourse are we to place the disconnected images and statements that confront us every evening between 11 p.m. and 11:30? By what criteria are we to evaluate what we see and hear? What responses are we to make?

As in the case of the hybrid commercial, the "frame" of television "news" is paradoxical. Consider, for example, the labels used to identify the context. Usually, what someone *calls* an event serves as a guide to how we are to respond. But in the case of TV news, even the labels are ambiguous. The term "news," like the terms "correspondent" and "reporter," tells us that we are dealing here with the realm of objective truth—of *reports* about events and relations in the real world. On the other hand, what we see is called a "show" (a term associated with entertainment and, on TV, with comedy or drama), and the items of which the "show" is composed are called "stories." This would be a trivial point, if not for the fact that countless other details support the interpretation of "the news" as fiction, not reality. Every such "show" I have seen, for example, begins and ends with music—a traditional device widely used in theatre, film, and television serials to indicate "dramatic performance." The people who recount the day's "stories" may be called "correspondents," but they are clearly actors, not reporters—at least, they are made up like actors, perform on a set like actors, speak their lines like actors, even *look* like actors. Have you ever seen an ugly newsreader on TV? Or a fat one? Or an old one? Like the characters who populate commercials, newsreaders are all of indeterminate age, indeterminate ethnic and regional origin, indeterminate religious affiliation. They all have the regular features, the clear skin, the perfectly aligned white teeth, the glossy, well-groomed hair of the sanitized television hero or heroine. Even their names have about them the ring of the stage: Gil Noble, Jim Jensen, Ed Bradley, Frank Reynolds, Peter Jennings. Is there anyone who believes that these are real "reporters"? That they have spent the day covering beats, racing to the site of disasters, standing in mud and wind and rain to ferret out the details of the human tragedies they tell us about? Surely not. Everything about them signals that they are actors, characters in a play called "the news."

This interpretation of "the news" is reinforced by another cue in the format of such shows. Over the years, TV news has shifted from what might be called a "first person" form of address to a "third person" form. That is, the newsreader no longer speaks directly to us, the viewers, but tells his "story" (or at least begins telling it) to another character—one of his fellow newsreaders. In other words, the form in which we are introduced to events is not the form of direct report, but of dialogue. "What's new in the Bronx today, Jim?" "Well, Dan, we had a terrific five-alarm fire in a warehouse next to the Expressway, and it slowed traffic to a crawl for thirty miles…" "That's some story, Jim. Thanks!" The point is that this form of transaction—where the audience plays no part in the exchange but is merely a silent and unseen observer of the interactions of others—is the traditional form of fiction. This is how things are when we read a novel or a play, see a film, attend the theatre, watch a TV comedy or commercial. It is a form that tells us we are not to ask whether the statements of characters are literally true or false, but what they reveal of the personality of the characters, and of their relation to each other, and of *their* situation, not ours. And this message of the dialogue form carries over into TV "news" and our responses to it.

But as I have said, the "frame" of TV news is ambiguous. Sometimes, the characters do break the dramatic frame and address themselves directly to us. When this happens in theatre, as in Thorton Wilder's *Our Town*, we "read" the event as still within the realm of drama—but a form of drama in which the audience becomes, in effect, another "character" in the play. Just what kind of character we are to be—how we are to feel and respond—is communicated to us by the way in which the "on stage" characters behave. From their tone of voice, their nonverbal demeanor, their reactions to events, we know what is expected of us. From this perspective, what can we say of our role in the nightly drama of "the news"? Clearly, we are to play the part of characters who believe the reports of the other characters to be true. This is apparent from the fact that none of the characters "on stage" ever questions the veracity of another's reports. But how we are to feel about what they tell us is less clear.

The tone of voice and facial expressions the "stage" characters assume suggest that we are to be serious, even grim, about certain things they tell us—for example, about mass starvation, earthquakes, and the death of children in fires. Yet we must be ready to revert to affability and breezy good humor within seconds. In no circumstances is our character to feel genuine horror or distress. Cued by the reactions of the "on stage" characters, we may respond to the line "A Brooklyn mother baked her newborn infant in her oven today to 'drive out demons'" with a shake of the head and a cluck of the tongue. But we are not to cry out, or weep, or give any other sign of serious disturbance. Above all, our character is to be mercurial—grim for twenty seconds, playful for ten, sad for forty, amused for nine, thoughtful for eleven, worried for nineteen … and so on. Not an easy role to play, one might think. But most of us have learned to manage it with ease, enacting our parts without so much as a pause in drinking our coffee and preparing for bed.

Is "the news" real? The frame in which it is presented says "No." It is a play. Not a very good one, for good plays, particularly when their theme is human tragedy, have some more than passing effect on us. We leave the theatre shaken, or thoughtful, or renewed. But no one ponders "the news," or feels it, or for that matter much remembers it once the play is over. Is "the news" true? The question is not even relevant.

But suppose it were? Suppose we ignore the message of the frame and treat the statements and images we see as representations of objective reality. What can we say then of their "truth"? Much of "the news" on television comes to us in pictures. Presumably, that is why we watch. But pictures do not advance propositions about reality; they merely present it, or some "slice" of it. A picture of Jimmy Carter and Ted Kennedy shaking hands on the Capitol steps makes no explicit assertions about the event. Strictly speaking, therefore, we should not ask of such an image whether it is true or false. What we may ask is whether the picture is authentic—meaning, did the event represented take place in the time, space, and visual context depicted, or is the image constructed of pictures taken at different times, in different places, and superimposed on a different background? Pictures that present abstractions of reality are authentic; pictures that present reconstructions of reality are not.

In evaluating the images present on TV news, then, we are concerned with authenticity, not truth. But how can the viewer determine whether what he sees is authentic? Having no way to check the pictures he sees (or, for that matter, the statements he hears) against personally experienced, non-mediated reality, he must settle for *consistency* as the criterion of authenticity. If a picture is consistent with the pictures (and statements about the pictures) that precede and follow it, and if several different sources produce the same pictures and statements, why, then, we assume that what we have seen and heard is authentic. But in many cases, the test of consistency (already shaky) fails us.

Television news "stories" rarely provide us with enough context to establish internal consistency, and no two "shows" ever give us quite the same pictures and statements. Besides, if you're watching one, you can scarcely check it against another at the same time. So consistency must give way, as the test for authenticity, to *credibility*. And the credibility of a report, as countless studies in communication have demonstrated, is less a function of its content than of the perceived character of the person delivering it. This is why the "tryouts" of prospective TV newsreaders before test audiences focus almost entirely on such questions as "Does he seem honest? Reliable? Mature? Serious? Reassuring? *Believable?*" And it is also why political leaders in difficulty refer to their problem, not as a "truth gap," but as a "credibility gap." They understand that the truth of their statements is not within the personal power of their viewers to assess; but their *credibility* is. And how do we know whether someone or something is credible? By judging, of course, whether he or it is *effective* in moving an audience toward behavior consonant with the aims of the speaker. And in television, as in politics, there is but one test of "effectiveness": *popularity*. And somewhere in the alchemical chain between authenticity, consistency, credibility, and popularity, the question of truth in television has quite vanished.

It may be objected that, in dwelling at such length here on the problem of television and objective truth, I have quite missed the point. Television, some might argue, is primarily an art form. What we ought to ask of it, therefore, is whether it is "true" in the sense that art is "true." That is, does it present us either with "subjective truth" or with that kind of truth we call, in great literature or painting, "eternal verity"? I have skirted these issues for a variety of reasons. By the question "is television subjectively true?" for example, I take it we mean, "Is there some correspondence between the situations, characters, and feelings presented in this imaginary world and the situations, relationships, and feelings I have experienced in my own life or the lives of those I know?" That is a question each viewer must answer for himself—and it reveals more about him than about the object of his inquiry.

For myself, I find little on television that I recognize. Charlie's Angels might be creatures from some other planet (perhaps that is what their name signifies) for all their resemblance to the people and problems and events that populate my world. And I regard Mork and Mindy, Laverne and Shirley, the Hulk, Madge the Manicurist, Mother the Coach, and the Eyewitness "news team" with just the same sense of disbelief. But perhaps it is I who am odd. Judging from the Nielsen ratings, most of my countrymen are passionately devoted to such characters and their lives. I assume, therefore, that they find something in them of themselves. But this is a question only they can answer.

As for the question, "Does television present 'eternal verities'?" meaning, "Does it present problems, motives, and relationships somehow basic to the human condition?"—that is perhaps best answered by psychologists, historians, and philosophers. The psychologists who direct the efforts of Madison Avenue tell us that the commercials they produce do reflect many of the eternal truths of our human condition: our need for affiliation, our fear of loneliness, our longing for love and esteem. To this I would respond only that any human problem resolvable in thirty seconds by a can of spray deodorant can scarcely be called "eternal." "True" art functions, I think we would agree, to dignify, or exalt, or celebrate the human condition. The "art" we see on television—in the commercials, the weekly serials, the nightly drama of "the news"—serves only to trivialize it. And if we accept Aristotle's criterion for "truth" in art—that its effect on us is cathartic—well, I leave it to you. For myself, the closest I have come to catharsis, after too long an evening at the set, is a mild dyspepsia.

If I have given the question of artistic truth in television short shrift here, it is because I do not accept the interpretation of television as art. What I have tried to demonstrate is that television is neither drama nor life but a strange hybrid—a confusing jumble of images, statements, and tunes "framed" now as fiction, now as objective reality, but mostly as something paradoxically in between. And to the extent that it has taught us to accept confusion and paradox, or worse, not to notice them or to care, it has reduced our capacity to make the distinctions that underlie all sensibility, underlie even *sense*.

Last night I stopped for a cup of coffee at a neighborhood diner. "Good morning," said the waitress, handing me the menu. "'Good morning?!" I said, thinking she meant to joke, "But it's nine at night!" A dour shrug. "What matter?" What matter, indeed. We have already learned to call fiction truth and truth, fiction; drama reality and reality, drama; life art and art, life. What matter, then, if we call the night the day and the day, night?

But this is great matter. I said at the outset of this essay that language is a subtle and wondrous instrument for thought. And so it can be if we keep it sharp, honed fine through precise and delicate use. But if we come to use "eternal truth," "subjective truth," and "objective truth" as synonyms, let "truth" slide into "authenticity," "authenticity" into "consistency," "consistency" into "credibility," "credibility" into "effectiveness," "effectiveness" into "popularity"—or worse, bury them all under an amorphous jelly called "entertainment" and "appeal"—we shall have battered our language to the bluntness of a shovel. And such an instrument can serve only to blunt our sensibilities and responses—to life *and* to art.

What Television Teaches about Sex

(1983, March). *Educational Leadership, 40*(6). 20–24. © 1983 by ASCD. Reprinted with permission. All rights reserved.
In an odd little article that led off the May 22, 1982, *TV Guide,* Stephen Birmingham took on the Reverend Donald Wildmon and the Coalition for Better Television. In particular, he charged, their complaint that television promotes sex and "scorn for Christian values" is, at the least, misplaced. There is no sex on network television, said Birmingham. Oh, there may be some "very oblique talk" of sexual matters, and sultry looks, double entendres, and "a good deal of off-camera adultery going on," but there is no "actual sex" anywhere in view. Moreover, whatever illicit carryings-on we nastily infer from those sultry looks are approached by the networks in "a tone of high moral indignation."

On *Dallas,* Birmingham noted, "J.R. has not only slept with the departed Kristin, but also with a secretary, Lucy's sister-in-law Afton, his P. R. consultant Leslie Stewart, and a widow, Marilee Stone. His wife, or ex-wife, Sue Ellen, gets even by sleeping (or something) with Cliff... and, for good measure, with Dusty the rodeo rider." (Amazing what one can learn from sultry looks and some "very oblique" remarks.)

But do their sexual cavortings make J.R. and Sue Ellen happy? "Not at all!" said Birmingham. And so the moral is just what any good Christian or Hindu or Moslem would wish: "Adultery is wrong, wrong, wrong." If Rev. Wildmon is really concerned about sex on television, said Birmingham, he will have to look to local news coverage, for example, where "he can find all the offensive material he wants … right there in his hometown of Tupelo, Mississippi."

Either Birmingham was joking with us, in some subtle way I was unable to detect, or we have directed our efforts at sex education to the wrong age group. To say there is no sex on prime-time television because we have so far been spared full-color close-ups of on-camera intercourse is just plain silly. It is the equivalent of saying, as one network representative did, that the amputation scene in *Roots* was not "graphic violence" since all we actually saw was one shot of an axe swinging down, then another shot of a severed leg.

The point is, of course, that the present concern about sex (and violence) on television does not center on questions about the number of scenes of "actual" intercourse, of shots of exposed female breasts and male behinds, of open-handed slaps, closed-fist punches and gunshot wounds. These are trivial questions and they lead, ultimately, to trivial conclusions about the role of television in American life. While I dislike the righteousness of the self-appointed "moral majority" and disagree with both their political philosophy and some of their interpretations of contemporary culture, I believe their question to be significant. That question, as I understand it, is this: What attitudes toward sex and sexuality are promoted by commercial television, and how do those attitudes shape the values, expectations, and lifestyles of the young? And, for that matter, of the rest of us?

I believe this question can be addressed intelligently in two ways. The first, and perhaps the safer, is to examine the content of television—the images, plots, characterizations, and themes it presents, not only in programming but also in commercials. (After all, the average American viewer—young and old—sees something like 1,000 commercials each week.) The second requires us to probe deeper, beyond the particular content of this or that program, this or that commercial, to the more subtle layer of unintentional messages television communicates through its structure.

Sex on TV

To be frank, there is not much new to say about the content of television and the sexual attitudes and values it promotes. Perhaps, however, there are a few points worth repeating. One of the most intriguing is that there is, as far as I can tell, no *good* sex on television. I mean the term "good sex," of course, not in the modem sense of a technically superb performance, but in the old-fashioned sense; that is, sex as a happy and healthy part of a psychologically intimate and caring—dare I say, loving?—relationship.

Sexual encounters on television have a variety of purposes, but the expression of love or even just plain, uncomplicated, joyful lust is not among them (save, perhaps, on such PBS offerings as *Brideshead Revisited* and some episodes of *Hill Street Blues*). Instead, sex is used either as an instrument for profit (watch almost any television commercial) or as a weapon—for self-aggrandizement, punishment, or revenge. (See, if you can bear it, almost any of the critical episodes on *Dallas, Flamingo Road, Falcon Crest, Dynast,y* or *Knot's Landing*.)

I thought these distorted uses of sex were supposed to be a result of unhealthy sexual repression and that, as our culture moved toward the full and open acceptance of human sexuality in all its variations, the darker purposes for which sex has historically been used would inevitably decline. On television, alas, this does not seem to be the case. In fact, as our culture has become more open about sexuality and more liberal in its attitudes, television characters have become more, not less, preoccupied with sex—and with forms of sexual behavior farther and farther removed from those an older generation would have thought healthy and "culturally acceptable." I am not referring here only to the milder distortions of sex as an instrument of power, profit, and punishment, but also to the increasing link, on television, between sex and violence (especially against women and children) and the current fascination with such themes as incest, pre-adolescent prostitution, child molestation, and child pornography.

In the past year, I have seen on prime-time commercial television only three scenes in which an adult male and female made love in an apparently caring way. In the same period, I have seen more programs than I can count that took as their theme the rape or threatened rape of young boys, adult males, and adolescent girls; the seduction into prostitution or pornography of female and male children and adolescents; the sexual-mutilation murder of priests and nuns; and several varieties of incest in the nuclear family.

I have seen dozens of commercials in which adolescent girls and children of both sexes either allude to or enact what looks like sexual frenzy, to which they are apparently driven by the tightness of their jeans, and even more in which males demonstrate their achievement of success and power by walking (or driving away) with women who serve as sexual door-prizes. Commercial-free cable television, incidentally, fails to bring much relief. A glance through the current *TV Guide* reveals that about 80 percent of the cable offerings are marked "Sexual situations; violence."

Such content messages about sex are deeply disturbing, to be sure. But they are not nearly so revolutionary as the philosophy of impulse codified in the very structure of television. That philosophy strikes at the foundations of our sexual values and behavior, and it is all the more potent because it is largely hidden from view.

Teaching Impulse Control

The history of civilization is the history of the control of impulse. As even Freud, the great explorer of impulse, concluded, a certain amount of uncomfortable repression and frustration is necessary. It is the price we must pay to live with some modicum of safety and dignity among strangers. This view does not require us to regard our base needs and desires as inherently wicked and nasty; only to disapprove their uncontrolled and untransformed expression. In our own culture, as in many others, we teach impulse control largely by carving up the natural flow of time and space into symbolically distinct and "special" times and spaces, and by surrounding the gratification of needs with ritual language and behavior—most of which serve to defer gratification. Thus, the infant is taught that not all time is eating time; the toddler, that elimination should take place only in certain spaces and at times that require notice and planning; the child, that food is not to be grabbed and gobbled but placed on a plate, managed with special instruments arranged in particular ways, surrounded by decorations of a certain kind, and accompanied by talk and behavior of a particular sort—all of which we call "table manners."

As the child learns that different times and spaces have different meanings for behavior, she also comes to learn that certain things may be said and done within the family, others among friends, others in the presence of strangers. All of this learning, which we generally term "socialization," is a process in which the child comes to regulate the expression of impulse and delay the satisfaction of needs according to cultural distinctions between different kinds of places, times, and persons. And almost all of it—this enormously complex process of becoming civilized—is learned informally, through observation and modeling, the enjoyment of rewards, and the suffering of adult disapproval for lapses in impulse control, internalized as the feeling of shame.

Because the learning of impulse control is informal and conducted at an age when the child is not competent to process rational explanations (even if adults could offer them), issues having to do with basic needs and their gratification come to be felt by the child (and later, the adult) as *moral* rather than pragmatic or technical. That is, the loss of control or the inappropriate expression of biological and emotional impulse is felt to be not just "bad for you" but bad *of* you: shameful, indecent, *wrong*. Unfortunately, because it is difficult for the young to distinguish between disapproval directed at the inappropriate *expression* of an impulse and the disapproval of the impulse itself, shame frequently comes to be attached incorrectly to the body, or to its products and functions, or to the feelings of rage or pleasure the child experiences. This kind of shame is clearly disabling to the individual and disruptive of healthy adult relationships. Perhaps that is why the word "shame" has fallen into disfavor in recent years. But it is a mistake to confuse the two meanings of shame in regard to impulse control, or we shall lose whatever remaining hold we have on the process of civilization.

I do not mean to imply, in this overview of impulse, socialization, and civilization, that a particular set of cultural rules for the management of impulse is necessarily good or healthy, or even humane. Moreover, I would argue that when a society presents the young with conflicting messages about the management of impulse; erodes the traditional distinctions between the kinds of places, times, and relationships in which different needs may be safely gratified; reconceptualizes problems in impulse control as technical rather than moral issues; and abandons the concept of shame, serious problems in sexuality and violence are bound to result. This, I believe, is precisely the state of affairs we have arrived at in our own culture. And we have reached it, not wholly of course, but in significant part, through the medium of television.

I Need It Now

Like any complex learning environment, television teaches in two ways: through its explicit and implicit content messages—what it says about the world and what it shows of human relationships—and through the kinds of responses the medium itself permits and encourages. At both these instructional levels, television presents a philosophy of impulse that is, in our culture at least, revolutionary. In a sentence, this philosophy asserts that whatever people want they deserve to have, and they deserve to have it *now*.

The clearest formulation of this principle appears in that most ubiquitous of television genres, the commercial. "Aren't you hungry for Burger King *now*?" one teases, at every hour of the day and night. "Here are your car keys!" "You *deserve* a break today," says another, "so get up and get away!" "You *need* this car," an ad for Datsun intones, and a sultry blonde in the front seat whispers, "I really *need* it'" (linking the car to a clearly implied need of a different kind).

In the symbolic world of the commercial, those who wait between the experience of a need or want and its satisfaction are fools or boors. This point is communicated by the split screen and the elapsed time indicator. In one ad, for example, the modern equivalent of the foolish son frets and sighs over his empty plate, cooking his sausage the old-fashioned way, while his technologically enlightened neighbor on the screen (the wise son of the parable) satisfies his hunger in seconds with precooked sausages. To drive home the point that impulse *deserves* immediate gratification, the commercial ends with the foolish son snatching the sausage from the other's plate—a solution to frustration that meets with the apparent approval of all.

The glorification of impulse and instant gratification is reiterated more subtly in the very structure of the television commercial. More often than not, this takes the form of a mini-drama in which the protagonist experiences a want or need (girl wants to be kissed by date), encounters frustration (date turns away), is technologically enlightened (roommate gives her Scope), and achieves satisfaction (girl and date fly off to Hawaii)—all in the space of 10 to 20 seconds.

Embedded in these modern morality plays are a variety of lessons that, taken together, constitute a revolutionary epistemology—or theology. One of its fundamental premises, of course, is that the ungratified need is the major source of human suffering and is, therefore, evil. Another is that the source of evil, our "original sin," so to speak, is ignorance of the techniques or technologies that permit the immediate gratification of our needs. And a third is that redemption may be achieved, instantly, through the acquisition and application of the appropriate technology. A significant corollary to these principles is that there is no unpleasant consequence of impulse that technology cannot eliminate. Therefore, there is no reason to exercise restraint. Eat too much? Try Alka-Seltzer. Too much alcohol give you a headache? Take Anacin. Too much fun in the sun give you a sun burn? Tired eyes? Wrinkled skin? Dried out hair? Use Solarcaine, Visine, Oil of Olay, Clairol Instant Conditioner. And so on.

This philosophy of impulse is by no means confined to television; although it seems to find its most emphatic expression there and in television-related literature. One cannot leaf through *TV Guide*, for example, without coming across a dozen announcements of "technological breakthroughs" that permit one to achieve instant weight loss, instant muscle tone, instant beauty and health without the least sacrifice of one's pleasures. Now you can "eat whatever you like," one current ad promises, "pancakes, pastry or pizza, natural food or junk food … pasta and ice cream … as *much* as you like," and still lose weight. "With all that [cigarette] puffing," another warns, "your Vitamin C could be going up in smoke." The solution? Take these specially formulated multivitamins.

The philosophy of impulse codified in television and television-related media does not arise, as some seem to suggest, from some devil-inspired conspiracy to corrupt traditional values. Nor is it an accidental by-product of the content of particular programs. Television presents this set of values because, more than any other mass medium, it is an integral part of the web of economic relationships that constitute the consumer society. Put simply, the high standard of living Americans have come to expect requires the constant stimulation of mass production. And mass production requires mass consumption, not only of existing products, but of an ever-increasing variety of new products. To maintain the required level of consumption, people must be persuaded that they need the goods produced, and need them *now*.

Advertising creates precisely the worldview I have described. And commercial television delivers that worldview, 24 hours a day, seven days a week, 52 weeks a year, because its survival depends on advertising.

TV's Economic Realities

The economics of commercial television help to explain why, even at the structural level, the medium places impulse and its satisfaction at the apex of human priorities. Quite simply, no network can afford to risk the loss of its audience's attention, even for a moment. If some need of viewers—for visual stimulation, action, excitement, titillation, novelty—is not instantly met, a simple flick of the wrist may send them (and the revenue they represent) to another station.

The economic realities of television also help to explain, in part, how the medium erodes cultural distinctions between kinds of places, times, and relationships—a key factor in the learning of impulse control. One of the consequences of television's mandate to engage and hold attention is its relentless pursuit of novelty. In a medium that operates around the clock, conventional content is soon exhausted. To satisfy the demand for something new and different, television pushes deeper and deeper into realms of human experience once considered, if not taboo, at least intensely private. On the news, on talk shows and interview programs, in docudramas, soap operas, and commercials, no topic is too intimate for exposure to public view. How do the President and his wife handle their sleeping arrangements? How does it feel to be raped? How do disabled persons obtain sexual gratification? How do women cope with menstrual problems, and men with hemorrhoids? As more and more of what used to be regarded as private goes public, the notion that *anything* is private begins to disappear. Social space becomes homogeneous, and as it does the idea that some language and behavior is appropriate for some places and not others loses its meaning.

So does the idea that different times have different meanings for social behavior. Incest is presented alongside beauty hints on morning talk shows, and the difficulties of menopause alongside the stock market report at dinnertime. Except for some early morning programming, the Sabbath is indistinguishable from any other day of the week. Were it not for sports, summer could be winter, and fall, spring. With the addition of cable and television recording technology, everything is accessible to everybody, at any time.

As it homogenizes time and space, television homogenizes personal relationships as well. Traditionally, we distinguish among strangers, acquaintances, and intimates according to the kinds of spaces, times, and information we share with them. But television is no respecter of such distinctions. Strangers reveal the most intimate details of their lives to millions of other strangers, at any hour of the day or night, in bedrooms, kitchens, even bathrooms, without the least regard for the sex, age, or background of their viewers.

As the Nielsen ratings of recent years indicate, there is very little difference in the program preference of adults and children; they are exposed to the same commercials with the same themes; increasingly, they watch at the same times. (According to recent figures, some two million children watch television between midnight and 2 a.m., every night of the year.) In this context, the notion that some things ought to be said only among adults or done only among intimates seems quaintly absurd.

The New Worldview

My point is that, through its content and structure, television communicates potent messages about the management of impulse that are diametrically opposed to those that have provided the framework for socialization in Western culture for at least the past 500 years. It is this worldview and this set of values, I believe, that so distresses the "moral majority"—and many others of us less certain about our own righteousness and numbers. And we are right to be distressed. How can young people help but be confused about sexual impulses and their expression when the messages they receive through the traditional situations of society are so thoroughly contradicted by the messages they receive through a medium as engrossing and compelling as television? How can we help but be confused ourselves? Haven't many of us already internalized the view that since impulses are natural they must be good, and their repression evil? That shame, like sin, is an archaic and unhealthy concept? That the major reason for the control of impulse—indeed, the rationale for sex education in the first place—is the avoidance of unpleasant consequences like venereal disease and unwanted pregnancy? Haven't we come to believe that the withholding of information from the young and the maintenance of adult secrets are unhealthy, and that a reluctance to discuss certain topics in public is a sign of a disordered personality? Have we not already accepted the view that children have the right to be treated as adults, and all adults as equals?

But if so, what is our reason for regarding sexual relations between children, or between adults and children, or between consenting strangers, as somehow wrong? Why hedge about sexuality—as natural and healthy an impulse as eating—with special warnings and constraints? If our sole concern is fear of consequences, what answer shall we give to the argument that consequences can always be prevented or eliminated through technology—contraception, abortion, penicillin, and the like?

I do not know the answers to questions like these. I am certain only that they will be asked with increasing frequency and urgency in the years ahead, as the teachings of the television curriculum work themselves ever more deeply into the fabric of social values, attitudes, and behavior. At least, I devoutly *hope* such questions will trouble us. Like the restraint of impulse, confusion can be painful, but it is also a prerequisite to intellectual growth. At the least, it indicates an awareness of cultural contradictions and change. Far more frightening than our present distress is the possibility that we will learn the lessons of television so subtly, so painlessly, and so well that we shall one day soon stare at the teacher all unseeing, and wonder what all the fuss is about.

Literacy as Deviance

(Summer 1987). *ETC, 44* (2). 111–15. Reprinted by permission of the Institute of General Semantics.

In this short paper, I want to take a very long perspective on literacy. And I will argue that from the point of view history affords, if I read it aright, our culture's belated and somewhat hysterical efforts to rescue literacy are at best misguided, and in any case doomed.

So that you will know from the outset my personal views on the matter, I must tell you that I do not present my argument and conclusions with any satisfaction in literacy's demise. I am not one of those whose hearts are filled with romantic yearning for the imagined blessings of a recovered orality. Like you, I am myself a highly successful product of 500 years of print. My habits of mind, even the shape of my utterances, conform to the structures and cadences of inscribed thought. My profession and all my strategies in conducting my art as a teacher assume a culture of documents, and a high level of skill in reading them. Though my political biases and a humane respect for non-literate cultures urge me to deny it, my very conceptions of intelligence, of reason itself, are tied up with the conditions and institutions of literacy. And so—though you may also deny it—are yours. The plain fact is that we have never known an alternative to literate habits of thought, and we are hard pressed, after naming Socrates, to imagine how we might conduct ourselves in a radically different state of affairs. And so I tell you what I have to say with deep regret for the passing of an era that was my own, and with a terrible anxiety in the face of the unknown. My fondest wish is that you will tell me, when I have done, how I am wrong.

My argument rests on the assumption, which I will not elaborate here, that the history of human invention is best read as a history of problem-solving in response to change. I do not mean that problem-solving is the *source* of all inventiveness. Much of our creativity arises, of course, out of what Suzanne Langer would call pure symbolific play. What I mean is that those inventions that have a large-scale cultural impact do so because they solve some pressing problems encountered by people trying to cope with change.

Writing, in my view, is just such an invention. The history of its origins and spread is everywhere tied to cultures whose complexity of social and economic organization gave rise to two problems that the spoken word could not address: one was the need for a means of transmitting large amounts of information accurately across distance and time; and the second was a need to control access to information—to protect it from those for whom it was not intended. I will not review here the long stages of development through which writing systems passed, and the variety of deficiencies from which each suffered, until we arrived at the ideal solution, some 3,000 years ago, in the alphabet.

Suffice it to say that, given the technological limitations of the time, the alphabet was the ideal solution to the cultural problems I have described. As Eric Havelock points out in *The Origins of Western Literacy* (1976), its small number of symbols and their simple shapes made for relative ease in teaching and learning the code, yet permitted full coverage of the significant sounds of a language. Better yet, because it worked on a phonetic principle, the code was useless to those who did not understand the spoken language to which the code was the key. Thus access to information codified in alphabetic script could be controlled through systems of acculturation and, more importantly, schooling. That is the key, of course, to the great flexibility of the alphabet as an instrument of political ideology. It can be used to hoard secrets and power in the hands of a few, or to democratize information and power, by deciding who goes to school. But that is a bit aside my main theme, for the moment at least.

For something peculiar happened in the evolution of writing systems. What began as a set of mnemonic devices tied to visual experience shifted at mid-point to a set of mnemonic devices tied to auditory experience, and ended up, when the Greeks had done, as a system of marks that has *no reference to sensory experience at all*. And here I must pause to charge Marshall McLuhan, Harold Innis, Walter Ong, and others who have echoed them with a very great error.

McLuhan said it first: that writing is the extension of the eye. Nothing could be farther from the truth. Writing is not the extension of the eye. It is not the extension of the ear. Nor of the hand, or the skin, or of any other organ of sensory perception and experience. Writing is through and through an extension of another part of us altogether—of the abstracted, conceptual, digital, deductive mind. What the alphabet did was separate thought from sensation, knowledge from experience, utterance from context, speech from speaker, and truth from presence, space, and time. Along with the idea of zero and place notation in numbering systems—themselves dependent on forms of writing for their elaboration—alphabetic reading and writing constructed a new meaning of thought and knowledge, a new epistemology, so different from the epistemology of the senses and of sense-based speech that we have only just begun to penetrate how it works.

If I seem to belabor the point, it is because our habits of thinking and talking about writing have suffered so monumentally from misdirected analogy. We say that writing is merely a "secondary code for speech," obscuring the fact that it is a different sort of code altogether. We say that it is "disembodied voice," as though disembodied voice can exist in nature and is not something totally new under the sun. We say that written words stand for spoken words, and that spoken words stand for things—neither of which is true, or at best, true only in such a complex and mysterious way that we haven't the least idea what "stand for" means.

But let me collect myself and assume you grant my point. Here is what it means: I am saying that writing and reading were radical departures from the ways of knowing for which we are biologically suited and in every waking moment of our lives rely on still. One hundred million years of evolution lie behind our ability to apprehend the world through our organs of sight and hearing. At least 20 million years of evolution lie behind our ability to augment and correct seeing and hearing through co-present speech. All that lies behind literacy—this sense-less, timeless, placeless world of abstracted thought—is a driving set of cultural needs for communicating across distance and time, and a primitive technology for doing it.

I said earlier that the alphabet was the ideal answer to those needs—for its time. But it was a woefully deficient technology all the same, because it could not transmit visual, auditory, and other sensory information across time and space along with abstracted thought. Ironically, it is this very inadequacy in writing as a technology—its sense-lessness—that drove mind to a different plane altogether and led to all those constructions—logic, deduction, critical reasoning, science—that we now identify with rational thought.

I am arguing, you see, that literacy is a form of deviance, a lunge of mind in a direction at right angles, so to speak, from where we would seem to have been headed by virtue of our cognitive history and biological organization. I say "at right angles" because the modalities and conclusions of literate, digital reasoning do not so much complement the logic of the senses as contradict it. The two modes are so different that their conjunction leads us, time and again, not merely to puzzlement but to paradox. And the ultimate irony, perhaps, is this: that we stand now at a point where the literate, digitalizing mind presents us with knowledge of the universe that our senses cannot fathom. We know more than we can understand.

Now, I do not believe that biology is destiny—or that history is destiny, either. But I would argue that some departures from our organic makeup and cognitive past are so extreme that only desperate need and the full resources of culture can preserve them. Even then, their survival is precarious. So it had been with literacy. Wherever a culture does not depend on it for survival, or had diverted its attention elsewhere, the senses have rushed in to re-assert their priority and the abstracted word had died. Whatever its religious significance may be, I take the story of Moses and his tribe as a parable on this point.

Moses came out of the mountain with the command that the Jews must put aside their senses, and worship only the disembodied Word. And the second command was this: that they must make no images, no carvings, no statues, lest they fall again to idolatry and be forever prisoners of the sensuous world. And the people swore, and they swore again, to keep those commands. But every time Moses went for a nap, he came back to find them raising another golden calf. In the Christian extension of the parable, even God, in his infinite mercy, finally bows to human biology, and for the salvation of a sensory species that cannot follow the Word alone, embodies the Word for a time in flesh. But even that is not enough. After the crucifixion the risen Christ encounters his disciples on the road to Emmaus. "I have lived and talked and eaten with you," He says. "With your own eyes you saw me die, and with your own hands you wrapped my body and buried me. With your own eyes you see me now before you again, and you hear me speak. Now will you believe?" And Thomas answers, speaking for us all, "Not unless I *touch.*"

The wonder of literacy is not that it flourished so briefly, but that it flourished at all, with all of the senses warring against it. The reason it did, I say again, is that cultures needed telecommunication in order to survive. But their primitive technology could only transmit that part of the human package that is the abstract, digital mind. Writing was all there was, and we seized upon it, and transformed our own minds to its shape.

For years I have struggled to answer the question: Why do people watch TV, when all the world of books, with all its incomparable riches, lies open to easy reach? Why don't they *read*? But I asked from the bias of literacy that has come to disdain the senses and delight in the pure play of mind. So I could not find any answer, until I turned the question around. Not, Why *don't* people read, but Why did they *ever* read? And the answer is so simple that you will think I say it in jest: We read because we couldn't invent TV. But our senses never gave up their clamor, and as soon as the literate mind could do it, we remedied the deficiencies in writing that gave birth to the literate mind. We restored human appearance, if not presence, to the word, and reinvested it with color and movement and sound.

If you will forgive an almost blasphemous analogy, we followed God's example, 2,000 years ago, in making the Word flesh. And for much the same reason: because the human, sensory creature cannot comprehend the word alone. The struggle is too great. And so we created a technology for experience at a distance that a child can comprehend by virtue of biology and the natural development of speech—a technology more consonant with the peculiar package that is human than writing could ever be. That is why it has swept away books and all else before it and holds all who see it in thrall. Thus the literate mind itself put an end to the peculiar conditions that required and nourished it, and eradicated its own reason to be.

The literate era was an anomaly, an accident, a wrinkle in time. It was generated out of need and an incomplete technology, with an unforeseeable consequence for the development of human mind. But the kind of mind that grew out of books, as it happens, is too great for the flesh to bear—too strange and divergent for the senses to grasp and comprehend. But neither will leave the other in peace. So we have invented two great new technologies, one for each: television to restore some measure of the senses; the computer to house the disembodied mind. What state of affairs this will lead to, none of us can see.

Nor can I see what *our* role is, who stand between one era and the next. We are anomalies ourselves, transitional creatures, neither here nor there—cartoon figures trapped on a frail limb far from the main trunk of cultural evolution with the saw in our hands, looking back in the moment of realization that we have just hacked it through, before the limb falls. It has happened before in the long story of the emergence of human culture and mind. If you will accept an even more egregious insult, our nearest relation in the story is Neanderthal, standing at a fork in history, his brain too big for his body, looking in puzzled wonder at the others who have come. Well, we were the others then, so no one grieves for Neanderthal. But I think the tables have been turned, and at least part of our fear for the young who will not read is fear *of* them, and grief for our line's passing away.

But I do not wish to end on such a somber note, so let me strive for optimism and a more flattering view. We literates are, after all, the ultimate extension of a peculiar line of development—the outcome of a noble, if short, experiment: the housing in sensory flesh of a powerful digital mind. We stand at a moment in history where the two seem likely to diverge, each to work out its destiny in a different way. Perhaps our task will be to mediate between them—between the excesses of restored sensation and the blindness of sense-less mind. Our stand, I assume, is with the human kind, and so our business is with the young. But how do we prepare them, and for what?

Five hundred years of literacy have estranged us from the past, and even if we could recover it, it would not be the same. Television will not restore orality, because it does not restore presence. It has its own peculiarities—disembodied *bodies*, to name the strangest—and will require new and different compensations, pose new problems, chart new directions for the sensate human mind. And so will the computer, as we try to make adjustments to what it cannot provide. We cannot hide in monasteries, and prepare for the day when orality, or literacy, will return. This time, we have not forgotten but outgrown them, and no pleas for time or campaigns for literacy will squeeze human minds and culture back into their worn-out shapes. We have an urgent problem before us, and an awesome responsibility, and I will close by putting it to you as forcefully as I may: How are we to prepare the young, whom we already scarcely know, for a future we cannot imagine, from a past that has been swept away?

The Crisis of Narrative

(1989). *Translation Review*, 29(1). 2–4. Reprinted with permission.

Confession, they say, is good for the soul, and in that hope I offer you mine. I am not going to offer you any practical guidance in your daily affairs as translation professionals. I am no expert in that field, and besides there is a more urgent matter on my mind. I believe that American and world culture are facing a communication problem of the gravest kind—a problem that has not just a scholarly but a *moral* claim on every communication professional. And I am here, quite frankly, to recruit your help, as people particularly qualified to give it, in searching for a solution.

The problem I am talking about is not the well-documented crisis in literacy, although that plays a part. It is a problem larger and more serious even than that. Our species survived for countless ages, and in many places functions still, without the ability to read and write. But from the dawn of speech itself, no family, group, or nation, no human alone or in tribes, has survived without integrating experience into a coherent and life-sustaining tale. Without an adequate narrative to guide and direct us, we humans cannot survive. And narrative is the name of the crisis of our age, the problem that *we* may not survive. That is why I have come to recruit you today: because my reading of history and of our time tells me that we are in desperate narrative straits. But I cannot expect you to take my word for it, or my diagnosis of our problem, on faith. So let me take a few moments here to show you how I come to it, and why.

I work in a field called media ecology—a branch of environmental studies especially concerned with the human species and how we use information to adjust our physical and social environment, and ourselves to them, in order to survive. I am a student, in other words, of ecologies of information and their consequences for human affairs. In the course of my studies, I have come across two facts about information and life so incontrovertible, so universally observed, that I will call them laws. The first is that no species can survive with inadequate information about its world. And the second is that no species can survive with too much information about its world. The first law is by now a commonplace, and I need not pause to elaborate it here. But the second may come as a surprise, especially in an age when we have accustomed ourselves to think that information is always a good thing. I must assure you that it is not. A surfeit of data, pouring in on every channel, so to speak, can swamp a living cell, a creature, a species and destroy it as surely as no information at all. That is why wherever we look in nature we see structures that limit the amount and type of information any living thing can receive.

Have you ever wondered why the reproductive molecule in a biological cell should take the now-famous double helix shape, or for that matter, any shape at all? It is because the shape itself prevents the accretion of too much information, too much diversity, of the wrong kind. And that is why biology provides every creature and species with "filters" for sensory data, thresholds and barriers to sensation and perception, structures that direct and limit what can be seen, felt, heard, and attended to. Without such structures, which function as biological commands to "Ignore Information," sensory creatures would be inundated by detail and difference, overwhelmed by choice, paralyzed by change.

As creatures of biology, we humans are protected, like others, from excesses of biochemical and sensory information by millions of neurological structures that limit what we can sense and perceive. But unlike any other species, we humans are also creatures of the word. And words are a non-biological way of coding information and storing it and passing it on. But words are also a way of creating new distinctions and re-combinations, of generating new ideas in mind and then introducing them into the physical and social world to enlarge and transform it. Through words we have acquired the capacity to invent—not only new technologies, but new techniques, new ways of social living and doing, and these in turn continually expand and complexify our world. But that is not the end of it, for the enlargements of our physical and social experience must in turn somehow be coded and transmitted and stored, and so on. Language, in short, engages our species in a perpetual struggle to find ways of managing a mass of information that every advance in coding and storing inexorably expands. And there are no *biological* regulators to protect us from the quantity and diversity of information we ourselves produce, no genetic structures to slow the process down.

And yet we have managed, our peculiar word-expanding, world-expanding species, to survive in this perpetual struggle for some 70,000 years since language, at a conservative estimate, began. We have done so by developing, of necessity, a set of non-biologic structures for regulating the ecology of language, thought, and social experience—for regulating the ecology of human life and information. And the central device in these non-biologic structures, the name that sums them up, is *narrative*.

A narrative, whether a history, or a scientific theory, or a religious myth, or one's personal tale, is a non-biologic way of organizing information, of selecting what is relevant to survival and ignoring what is not. Without tales as organizing frameworks, our ancestors would have been swamped by the volume of experience language permitted them to enlarge and encode. Too much information, taken in the raw, so to speak, would have been just as deadly to the species as too little. A narrative functions as a kind of information sieve, retaining only those chunks of information that fit the pattern of the tale and allowing the rest to fall away unheeded. Thus, by ignoring, in effect *destroying* some information, a tale makes experience manageable. Tales also provide the framework through which we assess our present position and define our problems. Thus they tell us what more we need to know and direct our efforts to acquire further information.

Narratives, in short, play the central role in *regulating* the ecology of information. And that is why, psychologically, we experience life without a coherent narrative as overwhelming, paralyzing, meaningless. Without a tale we cannot connect ourselves to others or our future to our past. We would be overwhelmed by data, experiencing nothing, moment to moment, but change. A tale is a way of constructing continuities, of explaining oneself to oneself. Every waking moment, indeed, even in your sleep, you are weaving your experience into a story in which you are the central character and, one hopes, the hero or heroine.

This need arises out of language and consciousness as inevitably as the need to breathe arises out of biology. That is why children ask, as soon as their language is fully formed, "Where did I come from?" and shortly after, "What will happen when I die?" They require a story to give meaning to their existence. Without air, the body dies. Without a tale, the self dies. That is what a catatonic is: A human body in which the self has died because it could not make a coherent tale.

Tribes and nations, as well as individual people, require tales, and may die for lack of a believable one. In America, for 200 years, we have told ourselves that our experiment in government is part of God's own plan. In the Soviet Union, they have told themselves that *their* experiment in government is *history's* plan. Perhaps neither nation believes these tales now—and woe unto us all if they do not find some other, large enough to accommodate both, for we are living now in a world that technology has made too small for tribal tales.

But that is where our problem lies. In the past 200 years, science and technology have unloosed a veritable deluge of information upon the world. At the same time, they have attacked at its roots the vital regulator that we require to organize, manage, and make it meaningful. For in solving the problem of acquiring information, science took apart our Master Narrative, by making the prevailing tale of origins and endings, the great tale of Genesis in all its thousand cultural forms, insupportable. In its place it gave us Darwin's tale—the tale of evolution. And hard on its heels, the tale of technological progress, with paradise to be restored, not in some misty hereafter, but here on earth, through the wonders of technology. But those tales have proven woefully inadequate. To the question, "Where did we come from?" science answers, "An accident." To the question, "How will it end?" technology answers, "Probably by accident." To the question, "How should we live between accidents?" capitalism answers, "Amuse yourselves. Consume." And to the question, "To what end?" Technopoly—my term for the triumph of technological totalitarianism—answers, "To divert yourselves from noticing that life in Technopoly has no other end."

But people are beginning to notice anyway, and more and more are finding the accidental life not worth living. The technology tale is losing its power to organize human life and activity in any meaningful way, at least in the West. It has led in the end only to cynicism and hopelessness. If you doubt this, you might run a survey of the slogans most widely used on tee shirts and bumper stickers in America today. I have done that, and here is what the three most popular say "Whoever dies with the most toys wins." "Life's a bitch, then you die." And "Beam me up, Scotty. There's no intelligent life down here." These are worth reflecting on as narratives for directing the conduct of one's life.

If "whoever dies with the most toys wins," then how you *get* your toys doesn't really matter. The point is to get them as quickly as possible, through the most direct means. I asked a young student in one of my classes what kind of career she looked forward to. "I'm not sure," she said. "Something where I can get in easy, get a lot of money, and get out quick." Not much different from the goal of a bank robber, is it? It comes down to the same thing: a program of barbarism. "Life's a bitch, then you die," and "Beam me up, Scotty," tell an even sadder tale, in which the only solution to meaninglessness is escape. And how else should we interpret the rising suicide rates among the young, and the wholesale flight of people of all ages and classes into drugs and alcohol, except as attempts to escape? Catatonia, I said before, is the extermination of the self because it cannot construct a coherent narrative. Drugs, alcohol, and suicide serve the same end, and for the same reason.

Like the Sorcerer's Apprentice, we are awash in a flood of information. And all the sorcerer has left us is a broom. From millions of sources all over the globe and beyond, through every possible channel and medium—light waves, air waves, telephone wires, ticker tapes, computer banks, televisions, printing presses—information pours in a mounting tide. And behind it, in every imaginable form of storage—on paper, in books and libraries, on video and audio tapes and disks, on film and silicon chips—is an even greater volume of information waiting for our questions. And more is being added every hour, every minute, every second. We are swamped by information, drowning in it. And we don't know how to reduce it to manageable proportions, or organize it coherently, or sort the relevant from the irrelevant, or even what we want to ask from all that is available to us.

Our problem lies, in short, with narrative. In our personal lives, our lives as workers, students and scholars, our lives as citizens of nations, members of cultures, humans on a fragile planet spinning somewhere in the void, people are suffering from a breakdown in meaningful narratives, of organizing and life-sustaining tales. And this means that it is the need for narrative that is driving the engine of change. I take it as confirmation of this point that many people who once abandoned religion as untenable or dangerously tribal are returning to it—because some tale, no matter how flawed, is better than none. That is also why George Bush's campaign had some appeal, among the remnant who care anymore, and Dukakis' did not. Evocations of a vanished America make an achingly poignant, if deceitful, tale. The federal deficit does not.

Somewhere, our age must find a truer, larger tale, a narrative sweeping enough, and hopeful enough, to restore dignity and purpose to all of human life. We need a tale that goes beyond chanting of here and now and tribal triumphs and despairs, a tale that sings of the future of our species and ennobles the long and painful journey from the savannas of our past. It is in the hope of finding such a song, a species song, a *universe* tale, that I come to you.

You have worked among the world's cultures all your lives, and you have encountered thousands of tales. Your calling is to help people speak to each other across cultures and tongues and times. You have a special gift, and a special way of listening, that makes you invaluable allies in the crisis of our times. What old tales have you found that might help us, that contain the seeds of a new? What tales does each culture tell, that might be enlarged to sing of us all?

People will have narratives. They must have them to survive. If they cannot construct new and better ones, they will search for meaning elsewhere—in the misty images of a vanished past or in darker, uglier tribal tales. And I do not need to speak of where such "solutions" can lead. The problem and the challenge before us are clear, and our choices for good or ill. And I will leave you with this: Either our age will be called, in the future, the Age of Narrative, or it will need no name. For there will be no one looking back to tell our tale.

Lance Strate
General Editor

This series is devoted to scholarship relating to media ecology, a field of inquiry defined as the study of media as environments. Within this field, the term "medium" can be defined broadly to refer to any human technology or technique, code or symbol system, invention or innovation, system or environment. Media ecology scholarship typically focuses on how technology, media, and symbolic form relate to communication, consciousness, and culture, past, present and future. This series is looking to publish research that furthers the formal development of media ecology as a field; that brings a media ecology approach to bear on specific topics of interest, including research and theoretical or philosophical investigations concerning the nature and effects of media or a specific medium; that includes studies of new and emerging technologies and the contemporary media environment as well as historical studies of media, technology, and modes and codes of communication; scholarship regarding technique and the technological society; scholarship on specific types of media and culture (e.g., oral and literate cultures, image, etc.), or of specific aspects of culture such as religion, politics, education, journalism, etc.; critical analyses of art and popular culture; and studies of how physical and symbolic environments function as media.

For additional information about this series or for the submission of manuscripts, please contact:
    Lance Strate, Series Editor | strate@fordham.edu

To order other books in this series, please contact our Customer Service Department:
    peterlang@presswarehouse.com (within the U.S.)
    orders@peterlang.com (outside the U.S.)

Or browse online by series:
    www.peterlang.com

CPSIA information can be obtained
at www.ICGtesting.com
Printed in the USA
BVHW040607100621
609166BV00001B/79